OXFORD STUDIES IN
MODERN EUROPEAN HISTORY

General Editors
SIMON DIXON, MARK MAZOWER,
and
JAMES RETALLACK

All This is Your World

Soviet Tourism at Home and Abroad after Stalin

ANNE E. GORSUCH

OXFORD
UNIVERSITY PRESS

*This book has been printed digitally and produced in a standard specification
in order to ensure its continuing availability*

OXFORD
UNIVERSITY PRESS

Great Clarendon Street, Oxford OX2 6DP
United Kingdom

Oxford University Press is a department of the University of Oxford.
It furthers the University's objective of excellence in research, scholarship,
and education by publishing worldwide.

Oxford is a registered trade mark of Oxford University Press in the UK
and in certain other countries

British Library Cataloguing in Publication Data
Data available

Library of Congress Cataloging in Publication Data
Data available

ISBN 978-0-19-960994-9

For Hal, Ellie, and Hannah, as always.

Acknowledgments

I am very grateful for the company of so many colleagues, friends, and family members on the journey of researching and writing this book. Like all trips, this one has been greatly enriched by my traveling companions. I could not have done it without you.

In Russia, I offer my appreciation to library and archival staff, especially to Galina Mikhailovna Tokareva of the Komsomol Archive (RGASPI) for her professionalism, endless cups of tea, and willingness to tell me about her own experiences as a traveler. So too to Valeria Emmanuilovna Kunina who showed me photos and told me stories of her early trips abroad. Andrei Golubov generously shared transcripts from his own research on Soviet tourists to Finland. Elena Malysheva has been a close and supportive friend for over twenty years, beginning when I was a graduate student living at MGU and continuing now through two books about the history of her homeland. In Estonia, Andres Kurg and Eva Näripea took me around Tallinn and shared their knowledge and curiosity about Estonia in the 1950s and 1960s. Their interests in architecture and film greatly influenced my own thinking about these topics. The Estonian Film Archive (Eesti Filmiarhiiv) kindly provided permission to reproduce photos from their collection.

Colleagues and friends in England provided a first home away from home for this project during an early sabbatical and many have continued to be among my strongest bulwarks of intellectual support ever since. I am very grateful to Bob Allen, Wendy Bracewell, Mary Buckley, Simon Dixon, Juliane Fürst, Julian Graffey, Barbara Heldt, Polly Jones, Catriona Kelly, Stephen Lovell, Hilary Pilkington, Gerry Smith, and especially, Susan Reid. Harold Shukman and Gerry Smith kindly allowed me to interview them about their experiences guiding groups of Soviet tourists around England. Barbara Folscher has been an inspiring example of writerly commitment and a generous friend.

Closer to home, I am grateful for the warm support of Susan Solomon (be in it North American cities or Paris), and the enthusiasm of Bob Edelman. My work life in Vancouver has been greatly enriched by my thoughtful and intellectually generous colleagues at the University of British Columbia. Two who have played a particular part in this intellectual journey are Bill French and Tina Loo. Thank you too to Alexei Kojevnikov for tracking down Soviet films. Caroline Grover, Nina Kreiger, and Victor Zatsepine provided invaluable research assistance. Jocelyn Smith cheerfully and professionally provided great assistance with the bibliography. Canada's Social Science and Humanities Research Council provided financial support. I acknowledge the kind permission of the Larry Zim

World's Fair Collection, Archives Center, National Museum of American History, Smithsonian Institution for the images they provided.

My friends Kathryn Gretsinger, Deb Hollett, Susan Rome, and Liz Scully warmly celebrated my book writing efforts in the midst of our wide-ranging discussions about novels, non-fiction, and life. Carolyn Heller, Alan Albert, and Melanie and Pietro Abela have been curious about and very supportive of my project in the midst of their own book writing and other creative efforts. My parents, Bev and Jack Gorsuch, and my sister Meg Hopkins, have been a very important part of this journey.

Of all people, apart from my family, the one to whom I owe the greatest debt of gratitude is Diane Koenker. Diane has been fellow traveler extraordinaire, sharing enthusiasm as well as archival materials. Diane has been willing to endlessly discuss questions of tourism (of both import and minutia) via e-mail, via skype, and in person over coffee and good food in cafes and restaurants across the globe. I am deeply grateful for her companionship.

I am most thankful to the three people to whom I dedicate this book. My husband, Hal, and our daughters, Hannah and Ellie, have warmly encouraged my efforts and gamely spent dinners thinking of book titles. Best of all, they have involved me in their own rewarding, full, and joyful lives and made my life so much the better as a result.

Contents

List of illustrations

Introduction: Crossing Borders

In August 1955, *Pravda* proudly displayed on its front page a picture of smiling Leningrad tourists, suitcases in hand, leaving for the first Soviet tourist trip abroad, to Poland.[1] It was not only *Pravda* that paid attention. "Tourism is apparently beginning to be a two-way business at last for Soviet citizens," marveled *The Times* of London.[2] The ability to travel signaled a shift away from the ideological rigidity and unalloyed fear of the other under Stalin toward the comparative openness of the Khrushchev era. Stalin had promoted a defensive and largely static notion of Soviet identity, a construction requiring constant vigilance through propaganda, violence, and closed borders. Soviet vacationers were told that it was only within the boundaries of the Soviet Union that they could be confident of a warm welcome. Beginning in the Khrushchev era, Soviet citizens were newly encouraged to imagine themselves exploring the medieval towers of Tallinn's Old Town, relaxing on the Romanian Black Sea coast, even climbing the Eiffel Tower. By the mid-1960s, hundreds of thousands of Soviet citizens traveled abroad as tourists each year. "Dance and then leap into your saddles," Victor encouraged his younger brother Dimka in Vasilii Aksenov's 1961 novel, *A Ticket to the Stars*: "Dive into the depths of the sea, climb mountains, fear nothing, all this is your world."[3] *All This is Your World: Soviet Tourism at Home and Abroad after Stalin* explores the meaning and experience of travel and encounter in late socialism. It examines the gradual integration of the Soviet Union into global processes of cultural exchange in which the Soviet Union increasingly, if anxiously, participated in the national and transnational circulation of people, as well as of ideas and items.

Tourist travel by Soviet citizens was part of a larger, well-documented, opening to the wider world in the Khrushchev era. The Moscow International Youth Festival, the Brussels World's Fair, and the American National Exhibition in Moscow are the best-known examples of an unprecedented exchange of art,

---

[1] "Sovietskie turisty vyekhali v Pol'shu," *Pravda* (August 13, 1955), 1; The National Archives, London, Foreign Office, FO 371 116783 (Report from the British Embassy, Moscow, 1955).
[2] "Russian Tourists Again: First Party Leaves for Poland," *The Times* (17 August 1955): 7.
[3] Vasilii Aksenov, *A Ticket to the Stars* (New York, 1963), 18.

music, material items, and people.[4] Foreign tourists were welcomed to the Soviet Union in record numbers, roughly one million foreigners visiting the Soviet Union between 1957 and 1965.[5] Khrushchev, who according to his biographer "loved to travel," was the Soviet Union's most famous international traveler and advocate for embodied nationalism.[6] His first trip abroad was to Poland with the Red Army in 1939, but reflecting the importance of the West, he later described Geneva, followed by Britain in 1956, as his "first official trip[s] abroad."[7] His voyages included, among others, trips to China, Indonesia, and Burma, to Afghanistan and India, to Britain, France and Switzerland, and, most famously, to the United States in 1959. Khrushchev traveled for political purpose as the head of the Soviet Union, but also as tourist, drinking champagne in France, eating hot dogs in the United States, and taking in the sights everywhere. Khrushchev sometimes traveled with his wife and children, whose itineraries were even more touristic than his: in France they visited Fontainebleau and went shopping at the Galeries Lafayette. So too in the United States, where Khrushchev's daughters told their American hosts that what they would most like to do while in New York would be "to see a big store."[8] "Can we use the letter "T" to describe all of the leaders of the Soviet Union?" one Soviet joke asked in the mid-1950s. "We can: Lenin –Titan, Stalin – Tyrant, Khrushchev and Bulganin – Two Tourists."[9]

All This is Your World is situated at the intersection of a number of topics: the history of a post-Stalin Soviet Union; the history of tourism and mobility; the

[4] David Caute, *The Dancer Defects: The Struggle for Cultural Supremacy during the Cold War* (Oxford, 2003); Walter L. Hixson, *Parting the Curtain: Propaganda, Culture, and the Cold War, 1945–1961* (New York, 1997); Yale Richmond, *Cultural Exchange and the Cold War: Raising the Iron Curtain* (University Park, 2003); Vladislav Zubok, *Zhivago's Children: The Last Russian Intelligentsia* (Cambridge, 2009); "'Loose Girls' on the Loose: Sex, Propaganda, and the 1957 Youth Festival" in *Women in the Khrushchev Era,* ed. Melanie Ilic, Susan E. Reid, and Lynne Attwood (New York, 2004); Pia Koivunen, "The 1957 Moscow Youth Festival: Propagating a New, Peaceful Image of the Soviet Union," in *Soviet State and Society under Nikita Khrushchev,* ed. Melanie Ilic and Jeremy Smith (London, 2009); Susan E. Reid, "Who Will Beat Whom? Soviet Popular Reception of the American National Exhibition in Moscow, 1959," *Kritika* 9, no. 4 (Fall 2008): 855–904; Eleonory Gilburd, "Picasso in Thaw Culture," *Cahiers du Monde Russe* 47, no. 1–2 (January–June 2006): 65–108.

[5] Shawn Salmon, "Marketing Socialism: Inturist in the Late 1950s and Early 1960s" in *Turizm: The Russian and East European Tourist under Capitalism and Socialism,* ed. Anne E. Gorsuch and Diane P. Koenker (Ithaca, 2006), 190.

[6] William Taubman, *Khrushchev: The Man and his Era* (New York: Norton, 2003), 408.

[7] Taubman, *Khrushchev,* 355.

[8] Henry Cabot Lodge, confidential memorandum about Khrushchev's trip to the US, 1959, Office of Soviet Union Affairs, National Archives and Records Administration (hereafter NARA), RG 59, Box 4, File 3.4; Mrs. Llewellyn D. Thompson's confidential memorandum about Khrushchev's trip to the US, 1959, Office of Soviet Union Affairs, NARA, RG 59, Box 4, File 3.4; "M. 'K.' recevra treize caisses de champagne," *Le Monde* 4723 (29 March 1960), 2; "Massée devant et à l'intérieur des Galeries Lafayette," *Le Monde* 4721 (26 March 1960), 4; "Mme de Gaulle a fait visiter Fontainebleau," *Le Monde* 4728 (3–4 April 1960), 2.

[9] With thanks to personal correspondence from Amandine Ragamey, the author of *Prolétaires de tous pays, excusez-moi! Dérision et politique dans le monde soviétique* (Paris, 2007).

cultural history of international relations, specifically the Cold War. Although rooted in Soviet history, the project is transnational, offering an enriched perspective on our view of the continent as a whole by exploring the Soviet Union's relationship with both Eastern and Western Europe through, in this case, the experience of Soviet tourists. The book begins with a domestic tour of the Soviet Union in late Stalinism, moving outwards in concentric circles to explore travel to the inner abroad of Estonia, to the near-abroad of Eastern Europe, and to the capitalist West. It returns home again with a discussion of Soviet films about foreign travel. I focus on the Khrushchev era as the key period of post-Stalinist transition to what Andrei Yurchak has called "late socialism."[10] Because most travel, by its very nature, crosses boundaries, tourism is an excellent vantage point from which to examine Soviet understandings and anxieties about what it meant to be Soviet after Stalin. Because tourism is by nature a fantasy-generating process, it is also a good entry into state-sponsored utopianism and its limitations.[11] A history of Soviet tourism in the 1950s and 1960s enables us to explore questions and contradictions fundamental to our understanding of late socialism. Could de-Stalinization be instituted without challenging the very legitimacy of socialism? What experiences or expressions of "difference" were now permitted, and which were regulated or forbidden? What was the significance of new opportunities for cultural exchange and transnational encounter on Soviet identity both individual and national? What, in sum, did it mean to be "Soviet" in a country no longer defined as Stalinist?

Khrushchev's de-Stalinizing Soviet Union has long been described as a period of "Thaw," a term taken from Ilya Ehrenberg's 1954 novella of that name and used as a metaphor to describe Khrushchev-era challenges to Stalinist authority, greater tolerance of diversity and difference, and cultural internationalism. Ehrenberg himself was more ambiguous about the concept of Thaw. For Ehrenberg, Nancy Condee has argued, the idea of a Thaw implied "the notion of instability, and impermanence, incompleteness, of temperature fluctuations in nature, when it is hard to foresee what turn the weather will take," a conception that Khrushchev, not surprisingly, objected to.[12] Recent work on the Khrushchev era has tended to emphasize this aspect of the Thaw, some focusing on the limits of Khrushchev-era reforms, some emphasizing the continuing, even expanding, intervention of the state into private affairs, and some questioning the uniqueness of the era's liberalizing tendencies, situating the roots of reform in late Stalinism and/or extending them well past Khrushchev's ouster into the

---

[10] Andrei Yurchak, *Everything Was Forever Until It Was No More: The Last Soviet Generation* (Princeton, 2006).

[11] On vacationing as "an arena in which fantasy has become an important social practice" see Orvar Löfgren, *On Holiday: A History of Vacationing* (Berkeley, 1999, 2002), 7.

[12] Nancy Condee, "Cultural Codes of the Thaw," in *Nikita Khrushchev*, ed. William Taubman, Sergei Khrushchev, and Abbott Gleason (New Haven, 2000), 69.

Brezhnev period.[13] A history of international encounter allows for possibilities sympathetic to the notion of the Thaw both as optimistic opening and as anxiously authoritarian. Soviet citizens were newly treated, if unevenly and within definite limits, as responsible and reliable, as individuals confident in their Soviet identity and trustworthy to send abroad. These very changes permitted, however, behaviors and beliefs which threatened to outrun a sometimes apprehensive regime.[14]

A history of Soviet tourism also helps us consider the place of the 1950s and 1960s in the longer sweep of Soviet history, and in comparison to other national and international projects of modernization, consumption, and empire building. Socialist *turizm* as a tool of self-improvement and socialist state-building did not begin with the Khrushchev era. Domestic tourism as a Soviet project for building knowledge, strengthening the body, and encouraging patriotism began in the 1920s. Even international tourism was not a product of de-Stalinization alone. The Soviet international tourist agency, Intourist, was founded in 1929, and the possibility of permitting limited Soviet tourist travel abroad was openly discussed in the press in the late 1920s, if firmly rejected.[15] If this book looks backwards to the connections between the period of the New Economic Policy and the Khrushchev era, however, it also looks forward, seeking to understand how the 1950s and early 1960s helped establish the nature of the Soviet state and its relationship to Soviet society in late socialism. Travel abroad did not end with Khrushchev's ouster in 1964; the number of Soviet citizens traveling

---

[13] For some examples of work which address these and other questions related to the Thaw, see Priscilla Johnson and Leopold Labedz, ed. *Khrushchev and the Arts: The Politics of Soviet Culture, 1962–1964* (Cambridge, 1965); Elena Zubkova, *Russia after the War: Hopes, Illusions, and Disappointments, 1945–1957*, trans. Hugh Ragsdale (Armonk, 1998); Julie Hessler, "A Postwar Perestroika? Towards a History of Private Enterprise in the USSR," *Slavic Review* 57, no. 3 (Fall 1998): 516–42; Robert D. English, *Russian and the Idea of the West: Gorbachev, Intellectuals, and the End of the Cold War* (New York, 2000); Ted Hopf, *Social Construction of International Politics: Identities and Foreign Policies, Moscow, 1955 & 1999* (Ithaca, 2002); Susan E. Reid, "Cold War in the Kitchen: Gender and the De-Stalinization of Consumer Taste in the Soviet Union under Khrushchev," *Slavic Review* 61, no. 2 (2002): 211–52; Iurii Aksiutin, *Khrushchevskaia 'ottepel' i obshchestvennye nastroeniia v SSSR v 1953–1964 gg* (Moscow: ROSSPEN, 2004); Polly Jones, ed. *The Dilemmas of De-Stalinization. Negotiating Cultural and Social Change in the Khrushchev Era* (London and New York, 2006); *Repenser le Dégel: versions du socialism, influences internationales et société soviétique*, a special issue of *Cahiers du Monde Russe* 47, no. 1–2 (January–June 2006); Juliane Fürst, ed. *Late Stalinist Russia: Society between reconstruction and reinvention* (London, 2006); Stephen V. Bittner, *The Many Lives of Khrushchev's Thaw: Experience and Memory in Moscow's Arbat* (Ithaca, 2008); Ilic and Smith, ed. *Soviet State and Society*; Zubok, *Zhivago's Children*; Miriam Dobson, *Khrushchev's Cold Summer: Gulag Returnees, Crime and the Fate of Reform after Stalin* (Ithaca, 2009); Juliane Fürst, *Stalin's Last Generation: Soviet Post-War Youth and the Emergence of Mature Socialism* (Oxford, 2010).

[14] Khrushchev's was not the first Russian Thaw to enable travel abroad. Alexander II's reforms 100 years earlier included easing foreign travel restrictions put in place by Nicolas I. Susan Layton, "The Divisive Modern Russian Tourist Abroad: Representations of Self and Other in the Early Reform Era," *Slavic Review* 68, no. 4 (Winter 2009), 855.

[15] With thanks to Diane P. Koenker, "The Proletarian Tourist in the 1930s: with the masses or away from them?" unpublished paper.

internationally continued to increase annually. In 1970, more than 1.8 million Soviet citizens traveled abroad. In 1985, this figure had risen to 4.5 million.[16]

The significant growth of international tourism (echoed by an even more impressive rise in domestic travel[17]) resembles the meteoric increase in tourism throughout much of the world in the postwar period. A recuperating economy encouraged people, middle-class but also increasingly working-class, to travel via bus tour from Northern Europe to sunny beaches on the Adriatic, on double-decker train cars with panorama windows throughout the United States, and on Pan Am's new eight-hour transatlantic flights between New York and Paris.[18] Pan Am's 1960 annual report proudly concluded that, with its new worldwide routes to Europe and Africa, South America, Australia, and the Middle East, "the free world has become a neighborhood."[19] As this suggests, tourism was closely tied to a rising commitment to cultural internationalism.[20] Travel was "fundamental to the internationalism of the postwar years," Richard Ivan Jobs has argued. "[R]econstruction projects, exchange programs, and hostel networks were organized in Western Europe to facilitate travel by the young for the purpose of promoting international understanding and cooperation among populations who had been engaged in brutal and repeated warfare." Europeans, Jobs argues, "were now encouraged to travel abroad, to visit other nations and meet and interact with other nationalities."[21] This book adds the communist world to this equation. *All This is Your World* integrates and compares tourist experiences under socialism and capitalism, considering both the similarities—a commitment to modernity, mobility, internationalism, state building, and consumption—and the fundamental differences.[22]

---

[16] The exact numbers vary according to source, but are roughly commensurate. Randolph M. Siverson, Alexander J. Groth, and Marc Blumberg, "Soviet Tourism and Détente," *Studies in Comparative Communism* 13, no. 4 (Winter 1980): 364; *Turist*, no. 10 (1975): 29; V.I. Azar, *Otdykh trudiashchikhsia SSSR* (Moscow, 1972), 41; G.P. Dolzhenko, *Istoriia turizma v dorevoliutsionnoi Rossii i SSSR* (Rostov, 1988), 154.

[17] See Diane P. Koenker, "Whose Right to Rest? Contesting the Family Vacation in the Postwar Soviet Union," *Comparative Studies in Society and History* 51 (2009): 409–11.

[18] Orvar Löfgren, *On Holiday: A History of Vacationing* (Berkeley, 1999, 2002), 41, 170–71; George E. Burns, "The Jet Age Arrives," www.panam.org/default1.asp.

[19] Burns, "The Jet Age Arrives."

[20] For a history of cultural internationalism, see Akira Iriye, *Cultural Internationalism and World Order* (Baltimore, 1997) and *Global Community: The Role of International Organizations in the Making of the Contemporary World* (Berkeley, 2002).

[21] Richard Ivan Jobs, "Youth Movements: Travel, Protest, and Europe in 1968," *American Historical Review* 114, no. 2 (April 2009): 376–404. A first influential book on tourism and politics was Colin Michael Hall, *Tourism and Politics: Policy, Power and Place* (Chichester, 1994).

[22] On socialist tourism in Russia and the USSR, see Anne E. Gorsuch and Diane P. Koenker, ed. *Turizm: The Russian and East European Tourist under Capitalism and Socialism* (Ithaca, 2006); Diane P. Koenker, "Travel to Work, Travel to Play: On Russian Tourism, Travel, and Leisure." *Slavic Review* 62.4 (2003): 657–65; Koenker, "Whose Right to Rest?;" On the history of Intourist see Shawn Connelly Salmon, "To the Land of the Future: A History of Intourist and Travel to the Soviet Union 1929–1991," (PhD dissertation, University of California, Berkeley, 2008) and V.E. Bardasarian et al, *Sovetskoe zazerkal'e: Inostannyi turizm v SSSR v 1930–1980 gg* (Moscow, 2007).

DOMESTIC *TURIZM*

For American tourists traveling by cruiseship to Alaska, or British tourists enjoying the sun in Spain, tourism is a leisure activity involving travel away from home and work for the sake of pleasure, relaxation, education, and consumption.[23] The Russian term *turizm* has a different flavor, emphasizing the purposeful and the physical, and often referring to walking, hiking, biking, and camping. A set of four forty-kopeck stamps issued in 1959 showed young men (and one young woman) canoeing, rock climbing, cross-country skiing, and reading a map. A second series of stamps showed places of natural beauty, including mountains, lakes, and seasides.[24] *Turizm* was self-improving and socially constructive: building knowledge, restoring and strengthening the body, encouraging patriotism. "The Soviet vacation did not provide an escape from the mobilization of citizens toward a common goal," Diane Koenker has argued. "From its beginning it was a continuation of that mobilization using an alternate setting."[25] An emphasis on the purposefully civic rather than the idly pleasurable, was not exclusively Soviet. In mid-nineteenth century Russia, Susan Layton demonstrates, writers and journalists across the political spectrum agreed that Russian travel to Western Europe should yield educative, moral, and civic benefits, a belief that distinguished them from their compatriots among the English traveling elite, for example.[26] In the USSR, this was held to be true of

---

On tourism in socialist China, see Pál Nyíri, *Scenic Spots: Chinese Tourism, the State, and Cultural Authority* (Seattle, 1996); Suggestively, Yugoslavia, with its unique place between east and west, is the subject of much of the recent work on socialist tourism. See *Yugoslavia's Sunny Side: A History of Tourism in Socialism (1950s–1980s)*, ed. Hannes Grandits and Karin Taylor (Budapest, 2010); Wendy Bracewell, "Adventures in the in Marketplace: Yugoslav Travel Writing and Tourism in the 1950s–1960s," in Gorsuch and Koenker, *Turizm*; Patrick Hyder Patterson, "Dangerous Liaisons: Soviet-Bloc Tourists and the Yugoslav Good Life in the 1960s & 1970s," in *The Business of Tourism: Place, Faith and History*, ed. Philip Scranton and Janet F. Davidson, (Philadelphia, 2006), 186–212; Igor Tchoukarine, "Politiques et représentations d'une mise en tourisme: le tourism international en Yougoslavie de 1945 à la fin des années 1960" (PhD dissertation, École des hautes études en sciences sociales, June 2010).

[23] Amongst scholars, tourism has rarely been so simply defined and there is a large literature exploring distinctions (or not) between tourism, travel, and most recently, vacationing. On the distinction sometimes made between the "mass" tourist and the "sophisticated" and superior traveler, see James Buzard, *The Beaten Track: European Tourism, Literature, and the Ways to Culture, 1800–1918* (Oxford, 1993). Jean-Didier Urbain introduced the question of tourism's relationship to the "vacation." Jean-Didier Urbain, *Sur la plage: Moeurs et coutumes balnéaires* (Paris, 1994). See also Löfgren, *On Holiday*.

[24] H.E. Harris, ed. *Statesman Deluxe Stamp Album*, 1968 (no publisher, no page number).

[25] Koenker, "Whose Right to Rest?," 1.

[26] Layton, "The Divisive Modern Russian," 870. On tourism in Imperial Russia also see Louise McReynolds, "The Prerevolutionary Russian Tourist: Commercialization in the Nineteenth Century," and Susan Layton, "Russian Military Tourism: The Crisis of the Crimean War period," both in Gorsuch and Koenker, *Turizm*; Sara Dickenson, *Breaking Ground: Travel and National Culture in Russia from Peter I to the Era of Pushkin* (Amsterdam, 2006); Christopher Ely,

Figure 1 Enjoying the outdoors. With permission from the Estonian Film Archive.

domestic and international travel, and it was made an official project. Some tourist excursions were nature-based, such as the day hike of sixty young people to a picnic site on the Moscow River in 1952, but others were explicitly ideological.[27] In the early 1950s, travelers earned the badge of "USSR Tourist" for traveling to Gori, Baku, and Tbilisi in a touristic re-renactment of the childhood and early revolutionary life of Stalin.[28] Often, the two were combined—the student group that enjoyed the "picturesque" beauty of the Moscow River also stopped in the pouring rain to listen "with attention" to a lecture relating to nearby Borodino.[29] Tourists were also supposed to be of assistance to local people along the way. This same group took a break from their hike to help peasants with their mowing. *Turizm* was a form of mass action through *doing*, similar to other forms of active mass participation such as "collectivizing the

"The Origins of Russian Scenery: Volga River Tourism and Russian Landscape Aesthetics," *Slavic Review* 62, no. 4 (Winter 2003): 666–82.

[27] Gosudarstvennyi arkhiv Rossiiskoi Federatsii (hereafter GARF), f. 9520, op. 1, d. 252, ll. 2–4 (Tourist journals, 1952).

[28] *Trud* (29 February 1952), 4/*Current Digest of the Soviet Press* (hereafter *CDSP*) 4:9 (12 April 1952).

[29] GARF, f. 9520, op. 1, d. 252, ll. 2–3

countryside and industrializing the periphery, doing mass calisthenics, [and] writing poetry in workers' clubs."[30]

The purposeful physicality of proletarian tourism distinguished it from a vacation for the purposes of healing "rest" (*otdykh*). Soviet citizens in need of healing or relaxation traveled to a health spa (*kurort*) or rest home (*dom otdykha).* The visitor to a *kurort* enjoyed a three- to four-week stay for treatment and relaxation. Health professionals were available to design diet, exercise, and mineral water regimes specific to the needs of a particular client such as "milk days" for those with cardiovascular problems, and "apple days" for colitis and dysentery.[31] Rest homes were vacation rest houses, often in natural settings, that provided meals and simple lodging. They were condemned by at least one observer as places of slothful indulgence in which a "young, healthy man whose organism craves physical activity... falls into the hothouse environment of a *dom otdykha* where he spends idiotic... numbing hours of fattening and obesity, putting on weight."[32] Other recreational opportunities included sports and sunbathing, as well as cultural entertainment in the evening—amateur concerts, film, dancing. Despite the supposed difference between *turizm* and *otdykh,* however, the boundary between the two was porous, increasingly so by the 1960s and 1970s. Trips to health spas, and certainly to rest homes, were often closer to what we might consider a vacation than a hospital sojourn.[33] Although health spas were intended for those sent under doctors' orders, well-connected people sometimes managed to maneuver the system so as to enjoy a month's holiday in the relative luxury of the Black Sea.[34]

---

[30] James von Geldern, "The centre and the periphery: cultural and social geography in the mass culture of the 1930s," in *New Directions in Soviet History,* ed. Stephen White (Cambridge, 1992), 71.

[31] GARF, f. 9228, op. 1, d. 302, ll. 64–76, 106–108, 143–45 (Medical reports). In 1937 there were over 60,000 All-Union and republic health resorts of various kinds, d. 3, l. 1 (Report on expansion of *kurorti*).

[32] The supposed "hothouse" environment of the rest home (and the sanatorium) may refer to their reputation as places of illicit sexual encounter, fostered in part because husbands and wives so rarely traveled together due to the challenges of obtaining authorized passes for the same location. GARF, f. 9520, op. 1, d. 69, l. 7 (TEU meeting, 1948); Mary M. Leder, *My Life in Soviet Russia: An American Woman Looks Back* (Bloomington, 2001), 121, 132–33; Anna Rotkirch, "Traveling Maidens and Men with Parallel Lives—Journeys as Private Space During Late Socialism," in *Beyond the Limits: The Concept of Space in Russian History and Culture,* ed. Jeremy Smith, Studia Historica 62 (Helsinki, 1999); Koenker, "Whose Right to Rest?" 407.

[33] On sanatoria as vacation resorts in the late Imperial period, see Louise McReynolds, *Russia at Play: Leisure Activities at the End of the Tsarist Era* (Ithaca, 2003), 171.

[34] Ronald Hingley, *Under Soviet Skins: An Untourist's Report* (London, 1961), 45. In 1919, the new Soviet state published a decree on sanatoria and health resorts that nationalized pre-revolutionary resorts and opened them to a wider public. However, there were still special sanatoria for the cultural and political elite including members of the Academy of Sciences and the Union of Soviet Writers. In the 1970s, the "thirteenth-month" bonus Soviet elites took home was sometimes called "hospital" or "cure" money. S.V. Kurashova, L.G. Gol'dfailia, G.N. Pospelovoi, ed. *Kuroty SSSR* (Moscow, 1962), 10–11; Fitzpatrick, *Everyday Stalinism,* 101;

In contrast to vacations for rest and healing, *turizm* had a toughening quality. The diarist of one extremely rainy hike insisted that "everything went well" and that "nobody paid any attention to [the pouring rain]." Of special note was the "fortitude" of the girls: in Moscow, "all of the girls would have sheltered under newspapers or umbrellas, but here they paid no attention."[35] Goals for *turizm* reflected long-held beliefs about exposure to the elements, and travel itself, as a source of physical and ideological strengthening. In Sergei Aksakov's 1852 memoir *Years of Childhood*, he attributed his recovery from debilitating illness to "movement," "air" and the "marvelous effect of travel upon health."[36] Lenin likewise "preached the virtues of clean mountain air and long hikes in the forest."[37] In 1947, O. Arkhangel'skaia, the author of *How to organize a tourist trip*, argued that "fresh air" and movement would "strengthen the nervous system" and lead to "a healthy appetite and sleep."[38] Connections were made between the physical strengthening and know-how provided through active tourism and the "practice of communist construction." Tourism authority, V.V. Dobkovich, defined active tourism as a form of what he called "health-improving purposefulness" (*ozdorovitel'nyi napravlennost'*).[39] He argued that vigorous tourism would "strengthen the nervous system, [and] improve the working of the cardio-vascular system" thus enabling "the Soviet tourist to more successfully do his part in the active construction of a communist society."[40] Tourists venturing to the Tien Shan Mountains, to the Caucasus or to the Urals, were said to find "new strength, good spirits and health."[41] The athleticism of tourism and its association with bodily strengthening, were especially relevant (if not exclusively so) to the prewar and postwar periods, when so many people were either preparing for war or recovering from it.

Turizm was not just a form of *doing*, however. It was also a form of what James von Geldern has called mass action through *seeing*.[42] Excursions to cultural events, historical museums and collective farms demanded mental concentration rather than physical agility, but were also highly valued forms of touristic behavior. "There is a hush over the place," John Steinbeck observed about the Lenin Museum in 1947. "People speak in whispers, and the lecturers with their

---

Mervyn Matthews, *Privilege in the Soviet Union: A Study of Elite Life-Styles under Communism* (London, 1978), 36.

[35] GARF, f. 9520, op. 1, d. 252, l. 14. Others were more honest about the dampening effects of rain. GARF, f. 9520, op. 1, d. 252, l. 30.

[36] Serge Aksakoff, *Years of Childhood*, trans. J.D. Duff (London, 1916), 7–8.

[37] John McCannon, *Red Arctic: Polar Exploration and the Myth of the North in the Soviet Union, 1932–1939* (New York, 1998), 83.

[38] O. Arkhangel'skaia, *Kak organizovat' turistskoe puteshestvie* (Moscow, 1947), 4, 6; I.I. Fedenko, *Volga—velikaia russkaia reka* (Moscow-Leningrad, 1946), 35.

[39] V.V.Dobkovich, *Turizm v SSSR* (Leningrad, 1954), 10.

[40] Dobkovich, *Turizm v SSSR*, 11.

[41] *Zdorov'e* 4 (April 1956), 24.

[42] von Geldern, "The centre and the periphery," 71.

pointers talk in a curious melodic litany."[43] John Urry has drawn our attention to the fundamentally visual nature of the modern tourist experience in an analysis of the "tourist gaze."[44] Museums, postcards, photography, the very notion of sightseeing, all confirm the importance of the visual for tourism, something Soviet travel experts also acknowledged. In her guide to travel, Arkhangel'skaia wrote about the way in which the photograph might give "shape to travel." She insisted that the subject matter of the tourist photograph was to be "figured out before hand so that after the trip the photographs reflect all sides of the trip and the life of the group."[45] The importance of seeing sights only increased. By the late 1950s, sightseeing in Moscow and Leningrad, sailing around Europe on the cruiseship *Victory* [*Pobeda*], and looking at the historical monuments of Rome were all enthusiastically defined as *turizm*.[46]

Many tourist activities—helping peasants with their mowing—stretched the boundaries of what we might consider a vacation. This did not mean, however, that pleasure was entirely absent. Indeed, one of the goals of proletarian tourism, in contrast to bourgeois tourism, was to make the pleasures of the Soviet Union's natural beauty available to everyone.[47] Still, in the 1920s and 1930s, it was primarily the purposeful that was meant to give pleasure: travelers looking for pleasure could choose excursions to the Black Sea rather than energetic marches over Caucasian mountain passes, but the excursions were primarily meant to improve the tourist's intellectual and physical capacity. Increasingly, however, the Soviet vacation was about pleasures of shopping, sun, sand, and the sea, in addition to sightseeing and public service, a change to be explored in the chapters that follow.[48]

INTERNATIONAL TOURISM

In the spring of 1955, a Soviet Central Committee resolution introduced the possibility of allowing Soviet citizens to cross Soviet borders and experience foreign countries firsthand.[49] For the moment, according to the resolution,

---

[43] John Steinbeck, *A Russian Journal* (London, 1949), 37.

[44] Urry, *The Tourist Gaze*.

[45] Arkhangel'skaia, *Kak organizovat' turistskoe puteshestvie*, 32.

[46] G.A. Zelenko, "Chto takoe turizm," *Turistskie tropy* (Moscow, 1958), 8.

[47] Diane P. Koenker, "The Proletarian Tourist in the 1930s: Between Mass Excursion and Mass Escape," in Gorsuch and Koenker, *Turizm*.

[48] Koenker, "Whose Right to Rest?;" Christian Noack, "Coping with the Tourist: Planned and 'Wild' Mass Tourism on the Soviet Black Sea Coast," in Gorsuch and Koenker, *Turizm*, 281–304.

[49] Rossiiskii gosudarstvennyi arkhiv noveishei istorii (hereafter RGANI), f. 5, op. 30, d. 70, ll. 110–22 (Resolution on foreign tourism in the Soviet Union, 1954); d. 113, l. 32 (Central Committee resolution on international connections, 1955). The April 1955 version closely resembled the resolution from March 1954 about renewing tourism to the Soviet Union by foreigners, except that the 1955 version also included the possibility of Soviet citizens traveling abroad.

Figure 2 Soviet tourists on Capri, 1957. RIA Novosti.

Soviet tourists would travel only to socialist countries, but in "subsequent years" they would also be allowed to travel to capitalist countries. In actual practice, by July, Soviet authorities were already approaching the British travel agency Progressive Tours and soon after Norway, Italy, and Sweden, about developing tourism to and from the Soviet Union.[50] George Jellicoe, a high-ranking Soviet expert in the British Foreign Office, was skeptical, doubting whether they would have "two-way traffic," but change was afoot: thirty-eight Soviet tourists visited Sweden for the first time in September 1955.[51] Intourist, established as a travel agency for foreigners traveling to the Soviet Union, now took on the new responsibility (together with other groups as described in the chapters that follow) of organizing trips and regulating access for Soviet citizens wishing to travel abroad. "Some 450 Russian tourists reached Naples today . . . on the first cruise abroad by private Russian citizens since the time of the Tsars," the *The Times* marveled in June 1956. The tourists "followed the best bourgeois traditions," touring Pompeii and Amalfi by bus, eating at a well-known restaurant in Naples, and making a "traditional tourist pilgrimage" to Capri.[52]

---

[50] The National Archives, London, Foreign Office, FO 371 116783 (Report from British Embassy in Tel Aviv, 1955); "Exchange of Tourists: More Soviet Visitors Proposed," *The Times* (13 July 1955): 5.

[51] The National Archives, London, Foreign Office, FO 371 116783 (Record of meeting in Lord Jellicoe's office, 1955); "Sovetskie turisty vyekhali v shvetsiu," *Trud* (10 September 1955).

[52] "Soviet Tourists in Italy: First Cruise Abroad," *The Times* (13 June 1956): 8. *The Times* was wrong about this; the first cruise abroad, as described below, was in 1930.

Before 1955—apart from diplomats, trade officials, journalists, cultural figures, and the two sets of exemplary workers sent on cruises around Europe in
1930 and 1931—the vast majority of more ordinary Soviet citizens had to be
satisfied with reading about the rest of the world in journals and magazines such
as *Vokrug sveta* [Around the World] and *Na sushe i na more* [By Land and by
Sea].[53] In some ways, there was nothing specifically Soviet about this. Many
ordinary people in most parts of the world did not travel abroad until the
introduction of the package tour and the great explosion of cheap air travel via
jet planes in the late 1950s and 1960s. But while the ability of a Frenchman to
travel abroad for vacation in 1920 or 1960 was largely dependent on his financial
resources, the Soviet citizen had to apply to the government for permission to
leave the country for any reason, let alone for vacation travel.[54] Beginning in
1955, although the application procedure was complex and standards rigorous,
many were now newly encouraged to imagine themselves cruising on the Danube
River.

Why? The introduction of foreign tourism was closely tied to international
politics. Travel, as Shawn Salmon has argued in her history of Intourist, was an
"ideologically charged topic at the heart of internal and foreign policy discussions
throughout the Cold War."[55] In 1946, North Americans and Europeans begin
considering international standards for passport and visa processes. The USSR
under Stalin rejected any such overtures. The United States was also uncertain,
enacting hostile measures of its own by restricting travel abroad by American
communists and travel by Americans to communist countries.[56] Indeed, a
tentative conciliatory effort by Malenkov at Stalin's funeral was stonewalled by
a still-fearful United States; he retracted his position in April 1954.[57] Following
Stalin's death in March 1953, however, there was a steady effort on the part of
the new Soviet regime to reestablish and expand international contacts. In April,
an Intourist representative told a Danish tourist organization that they were eager
to make arrangements for foreign tourists to visit the USSR, reestablishing travel
connections cut off before the war.[58] An October 1953 article in *Komsomolskaia
Pravda* included an appeal for more exchanges: "Only those who want to spread
enmity and hatred among nations can object to international exchange. . . . with
all their hearts, Soviet youth and Soviet students are happy to broaden the

[53] On working class travel abroad see Koenker, "The Proletarian Tourist in the 1930s," 131. On
international travel by the Soviet governmental and cultural elite, see Michael David-Fox, "From
Illusory 'Society' to Intellectual 'Public': VOKS, International Travel and Party-Intelligentsia
Relations in the Interwar Period," *Contemporary European History* 11, no. 1 (2002): 7–32.
    [54] David-Fox, "From Illusory 'Society' to Intellectual 'Public,'"16–22; Mervyn Matthews, *The
Passport Society: Controlling Movement in Russia and the USSR* (Boulder, 1993), 22–26, 37.
    [55] Salmon, "To the Land of the Future," 171.
    [56] Salmon, "To the Land of the Future," 168–71.
    [57] Hixson, *Parting the Curtain*, 96.
    [58] The National Archives, London, Foreign Office, FO 371 106579 (Report by a representative
of the British Trade Council, 1953).

cultural and scientific ties among nations."[59] Beginning in 1954, Central Committee files include descriptions of trips by Soviet scientists, artists, and other delegates to foreign countries and instructions to increase foreign tourism from both socialist Eastern Europe and capitalist countries to the Soviet Union.[60] These efforts were novel enough that reports about the itineraries and activities of visiting artists and delegations were on occasion addressed directly to Khrushchev.[61]

The April 1955 resolution permitting Soviet citizens to travel abroad followed expressly from these and other international efforts aimed at normalizing foreign relations, first with Eastern Bloc countries and then with capitalist ones. The establishment of the Warsaw Pact, reconciliation with Yugoslavia's Tito, and the success of the Austrian State Treaty all occurred in late spring 1955. Tourism to Eastern Europe was meant to encourage friendship and mutual understanding between ordinary citizens in the Soviet Union and in Eastern Bloc countries, and to contribute to the Soviet Union's ideological and economic appropriation and integration of recently acquired territories, territories considered especially important in the Cold War battle for hearts and minds, as well as geographical spaces. Normalizing relations with Eastern Europe bolstered Soviet confidence going into the Geneva summit conference that brought together the heads of state of the Soviet Union, United States, Britain, and France in July 1955.[62] Historians have generally criticized the summit as producing few tangible results on fundamental questions such as the future of Germany.[63] But the "spirit of Geneva," with its focus on "tourism, trade, and culture,"[64] had a profound longer-term effect on international relations. Soviet leaders were emboldened by their ability at the summit to get western leaders to talk with them as equal partners. They were reassured through personal contact and informal talks that, in the words of Khrushchev, "there was not any sort of prewar situation in existence at that time, and our enemies were afraid of us in the same way as we were afraid of them."[65] Tourists to capitalist countries would, in this context, travel as envoys for peaceful coexistence between the socialist East and capitalist West, reinforcing the ideological and economic goals of newly normalized relations through personal encounter and political performance. As Khrushchev

---

[59] Ye. Burgov, "Seminar in Lund," *Komsomolskaia pravda* (7 October 1953), 3/*CDSP* 5, no. 40 (November 18, 1953): 41.

[60] RGANI, f. 5, op. 30, d. 70, ll. 110–22.

[61] RGANI, f. 5, op. 30, d. 71, ll. 48–49 (Report on visit to Moscow by a French theater troupe).

[62] On bolstering Soviet confidence, see Vladislav M. Zubok, "Soviet Policy Aims at the Geneva Conference, 1955," in *Cold War Respite: The Geneva Summit of 1955*, ed. Günter Bischof and Saki Dockrill (Baton Rouge, 2000), 61.

[63] Saki Dockrill and Günter Bischof, "Geneva: The Fleeting Opportunity for Détente," in Bischof and Dockrill, *Cold War Respite*, 3, 19.

[64] "More East-West Contacts: Tourism and Culture—Soufflé of Geneva Conference," *The Times* (17 October 1955): 9.

[65] As cited in Zubok, "Soviet Policy Aims," 73.

asserted, in a message presented to the first United Nations conference on international trade and tourism in Rome, tourism is "a vehicle of fruitful contacts between people." It "provides people with an opportunity to see with their own eyes and appreciate the way of living of other peoples as well as their economic, cultural, and social achievements."[66]

All of this suggested an expanded tolerance of international difference, something that stemmed, according to Ted Hopf, from a newly secure and consolidated sense of Soviet identity at home, a confidence that permitted minor differences as long as people were ideologically united on fundamental principles. Permitting difference at home, Hopf argues, made it less threatening to accept differences abroad.[67] As Khrushchev asserted in November 1955 with reference to peaceful coexistence: "Friendship has different meanings. There is the friendship when people live in harmony (*dusha v dushu*), but there is also such a *friendship* when people live as neighbors, but don't call on each other as guests. . . . So it is with states. Between some of them there is no real friendship, but they live on the same planet, and somehow must get along."[68]

The political use of tourists was not particular to the Soviet Union in the 1950s. American travel abroad, as described by Christopher Endy, also "represented an economic and cultural tool that could help win the Cold War."[69] (The Soviet regime understood American tourism in this vein, suggesting in 1951 that the United States was "preparing a new world war" via tourism to Western Europe.[70]) For neither the USA nor the USSR, in other words, did peaceful coexistence mean the end of competition. If, as stated in the Soviet Union's 1955 resolution, one goal of tourism was "expanding international connections," a second was "strengthening the international authority of the Soviet Union."[71] Tourism was an example of what Joseph Nye has called "soft power," the "ability to get what you want through attraction rather than through coercion."[72] David Caute has described the cultural contest between communism and capitalism in the Cold War as a "Cultural Olympics," an ideological competition fought by actors, musicians, sports heroes, and (I will argue) tourists.[73] It was a cultural contest without precedent. The Soviet Union had tried to influence international

[66] Open Society Archive, Budapest (hereafter HU OSA), Records of Radio Free Europe/Radio Liberty Research Institute (hereafter RFE/RL RI), 300-80-1 Box 1048 (Khrushchev message to tourism conference, 1963).

[67] Hopf, *Social Construction*, 92.

[68] As cited in Hopf, *Social Construction*, 95.

[69] Christopher Endy, *Cold War Holidays: American Tourism in France* (Chapel Hill, 2004), 2.

[70] Salmon, "To the Land of the Future,"137, fn. 35. Tourism was also a form of economic competition, Soviet experts noting with envy how much money western Europe gained from American tourism. GARF, f. 9520, op. 1, d. 428, l. 15 (Report on meeting of International Union of Official Travel Organizations, 1961).

[71] RGANI, f. 5, op. 30, d. 113, l. 32.

[72] Joseph S. Nye, *Soft Power: The Means to Success in World Politics* (New York, 2004), x.

[73] Caute, *The Dancer Defects*, 3.

opinion prior to the 1950s, but its efforts in the 1920s and early 1930s through the auspices of the All Union Society for Cultural Ties Abroad (VOKS) were primarily directed at individuals—communist sympathizers, the working class, and "fellow travelers"—assumed to be sympathetic with the Soviet project.[74] Beginning in the mid-1950s, Soviet efforts were newly aimed at a much wider audience of the capitalist public.[75]

If Soviet tourism in the Cold War was partially about selling, it was also about buying. Tourists were sent abroad as emissaries, but they were also instructed to "familiarize themselves with the lives of other people," with "foreign science and technology," and with history, art, and culture.[76] International travel was a source of information about foreign industrial and professional activities. Touristic consumption was not only technological or cultural, however. In a Cold War contest that was as much about which country took best care of their citizens as it was about the arms race, the pleasurable aspects of tourism were also important. In the capitalist West, "tourism signaled the 'good life' of consumerism and leisure," a commodity which, Shelley Baranowski and Ellen Furlough assert, was evidence of the West's superiority.[77] For the Khrushchev regime, Soviet tourism was a weapon in this battle over the good life. Tourism to the Baltics and to the French Riviera via airplane and cruiseship were used as evidence of Soviet technological achievement and commitment to modern, consumptive pleasures.[78] International politics aside, Soviet citizens were increasingly seen as individuals with needs and desires that the state needed to fulfill: for comfortable living conditions, for more rights in the workplace, for better clothing and food, for the possibility of a holiday abroad.[79] "The

[74] David-Fox, "From Illusory 'Society' to Intellectual 'Public'," 7–32.

[75] That these peaceful efforts were matched, at least in Eastern Europe, by more aggressive ones, and that the possibilities for tourism remained limited, is suggested by a Soviet anecdote.

"An American brags to a Russian:
— I have three cars. I travel to work in a Ford, to visit friends in a Cadillac, and around Europe in a Volvo.
— So what? – responds the Russian – I take a trolley bus to work and the Metro to see friends.
— And to Europe?
— I travel by tank to see Europe."
(With thanks to Alexey Golubev, Petrozavodsk State University.)

[76] RGANI, f. 5, op. 30, d. 161, l. 35 (Meeting of the Cheliabinsk KPSS obkom, 1956).

[77] Shelley Baranowski and Ellen Furlough, "Introduction," in *Being Elsewhere: Tourism, Consumer Culture, and Identity in Modern Europe and North America* (Ann Arbor, 2001), 17. The idea of tourism as a right for the majority was a gradual process. Before the First World War, most American middle-class and manual workers did not have and did not expect paid vacations of any sort, let alone vacations in which they might travel. Michael Berkowitz, "A 'New Deal' for Leisure: Making Mass Tourism during the Great Depression," in Baranowski and Furlough *Being Elsewhere*, 188.

[78] East Germany used tourism similarly in its competition with West Germany. Scott Moranda, "East German Nature Tourism, 1945–1961: In Search of a Common Destination," in Gorsuch and Koenker, *Turizm*.

[79] Steven E. Harris, "In Search of "Ordinary" Russia: Everyday Life in the NEP, the Thaw, and the Communal Apartment," *Kritika: Explorations in Russian and Eurasian History* 6, no. 3 (Summer

fundamental difference in the Khrushchev era," Susan Reid has argued, "was the shift toward mass consumption and democratization of provision."[80] In contrast to the Stalinist model, which focused on providing for a relatively few privileged people, under Khrushchev, "the toiler of the Thaw was acknowledged to be not just a producer but also a consumer, a consumer with tastes" and desires.[81] This book explores the consequences of allowing for consumer desire, specifically, the impact of experiencing the relative consumerist plenitudes of Eastern and Western Europe.

CLOUDY WEATHER

Even as they learned about new places and people, exposure to the foreign was supposed to help tourists become more "Soviet," the multiple, shifting definitions of which are a central problematic in this book. To that end, travel authorities, trip leaders, and guidebooks doggedly instructed tourists about the proper lessons they should learn from a trip abroad. Thus this reminder from an Intourist guidebook for Soviet tourists traveling by cruiseship to Europe: "Familiarity with life in capitalist countries, direct contact with people will help Soviet tourists to understand even better the differences between socialist and capitalist systems, to love their homeland even more strongly."[82]

Capitalist tourism has been described by scholars as an active search for authenticity;[83] as a potentially mind-opening experience with the possibility to reaffirm or alter "the traveler's sense of self in unpredictable ways;"[84] and as a "cultural laboratory where people have been able to experiment with new aspects of their identities."[85] What happened to the authoritarian tourist experience when the didactic elements were heightened and alternatives minimized? Did the tourist to the capitalist West return "from vacation as a homeless person," as Walter Benjamin famously described his own tourist experience?[86] Or was their sense of belonging to the Soviet homeland reinforced, as the state certainly hoped it would be?

2005): 583–614; Christine Varga-Harris, "Forging citizenship on the home front: reviving the socialist contract and constructing Soviet identity during the thaw," in Jones, *The Dilemmas of De-Stalinization*: 101–16; Donald Filtzer, *Soviet Workers and De-Stalinization. The consolidation of the modern system of Soviet production relations, 1953–64* (London: Macmillan, 1993); Filtzer, "From mobilized to free labour: De-Stalinization and the changing legal status of workers," in Jones, *The Dilemmas of De-Stalinization*, 154–169; Reid, "Cold War in the Kitchen," 211–52.

[80] Susan E. Reid, "Khrushchev Modern: Agency and Modernization in the Soviet home," *Cahiers du monde Russe* 47, no. 1–2 (January-June 2006), 232.
[81] Victoria Bonnell as cited in Reid, "Khrushchev Modern," 248.
[82] *Kruiznoe puteshestvie vokrug Evropy na teplokhode "Estoniia,"* (Intourist brochure, 1961), 3.
[83] Dean MacCannell, *The Tourist: A New Theory of the Leisure Class* (New York, 1976).
[84] Rudy Koshar, *German Travel Cultures* (Oxford, 2000), 8.
[85] Löfgren, *On Holiday*," 7.
[86] As cited in Koshar, *German Travel Cultures*, 8.

Even though the regime hoped that tourism would encourage loyalty, trust in the Soviet public had its limits. Some of these limits, and the concerns that spawned them, were unchanging. Beginning in 1955, and ending only with the fall of the Soviet Union, only applicants who were "politically prepared" and "stable from the perspective of morality and everyday life" were accepted to go abroad.[87] Other anxieties were episodic. Contemporaries, Steven Bittner has argued, "spoke not of one continuous thaw, but of numerous thaws and freezes, of cloudy weather, and of uncertain forecasts."[88] If in November 1962, Victor Nekrasov was allowed to publish his intimate, honest travel account of trips to Italy and the United States, a year later Soviet authorities accused him of "promoting peaceful coexistence in the field of ideology" and of "bourgeois objectivism."[89] In 1963, Khrushchev was rapidly backpedaling on almost every front. Khrushchev condemned Nekrasov along with two other famous cultural mediators, Ehrenberg and Evgenii Evtushenko, in a speech on culture which reflected a general retreat to the right after the flowering of liberal opinion and prose in 1962:

[T]here have been occasions when visits by writers to foreign countries have not only failed to be of use, but have actually proved against our country's interests. One reads the materials on the statements made by some Soviet writers abroad and wonders what they were concerned with, whether they were concerned with telling the truth about the successes of the Soviet people, or with trying by any and every means to curry favor with the bourgeois public abroad. With amazing irresponsibility, such "tourists" give interviews right and left to various bourgeois newspapers, magazines, and news agencies, including the most reactionary ones—interviews in which they disseminate fairy tales about life in their own country.[90]

Khrushchev argued against what he called the "peaceful coexistence of ideologies," describing it as a "Trojan horse," that "enemies of communism" were slipping in under the guise of peaceful exchange.[91] Opportunities for travel always remained closely tied to politics, reflecting if not the unbridled fear of the Stalinist era, then the ever-present anxieties of the Khrushchev regime. In 1957, tourist travel to Britain was curtailed because of tension between Britain

---

[87] RGANI, f. 5, op. 30, d. 161, l.

[88] Bittner, *The Many Lives*, 4. The United States Information Agency noted peaks and troughs in radio broadcasts about peaceful coexistence. The first peak followed the Twentieth Party Congress in 1956; a second peak came in the second quarter of 1957, a third peak after the launching of Sputnik I in the last quarter of 1957. "Soviet Propaganda and World Public Opinion since the Twentieth Party Congress," Confidential report, USIA Office of Research and Intelligence, 14 July 1958, NARA, RG 306, Box 15, S-10–58, 8, 12, 17.

[89] Elias Kuluknis, "Translators Forward" to Victor Nekrasov, *Both Sides of the Ocean: A Russian Travel Writer's Travels in Italy and the United States* (New York, 1964), viii.

[90] N.S. Khrushchev, "Khrushchev on Culture," as found in Johnson, *Khrushchev and the Arts*, 184.

[91] As cited in Condee, "Cultural Codes of the Thaw," 164–65.

and the Soviet Union over Hungary.[92] In 1960, at the same time as Intourist was eagerly inviting foreign tourists to visit the Soviet Union, the Soviet press anxiously warned citizens about American tourists, who were engaging in anti-Soviet behavior including spying and the importing of religious books.[93] Indeed, the United States always remained a particular point of both opportunity and anxiety. So few Soviet tourists traveled to United States—just 228 in 1961, for example[94]—that I will not be discussing their experience in any detail in this book.

Still, for all of the anxiety, the right to travel abroad was not taken away. Indeed, the number of people traveling abroad continued to increase exponentially every year. According to the president of Intourist, V. Ankudinov, 560,000 Soviet citizens traveled abroad in 1956, a figure that doubled to over a million in 1965.[95] These numbers likely include the number of Soviet citizens traveling abroad not only as tourists but as members of delegations, as participants in cultural, artistic, and sporting events, and possibly even as Soviet seamen or military personnel.[96] My own rough estimate of the number of Soviet *tourists* traveling to foreign countries from 1955 through 1964 is approximately half a million, with the numbers increasing significantly each year from a low of just 2000 tourists in 1955.[97] Calculations are made difficult by the number of agencies involved in sending people abroad, by accounting discrepancies found

[92] HU OSA, RFE/RL RI, Soviet Red Archives, 1953–1994, Old Code Subject Files, 300-80-1, Container 1048 (Does Moscow really want foreign tourists, 1960).

[93] HU OSA, RFE/RL RI, Soviet Red Archives, 1953–1994, Old Code Subject Files, 300-80-1, Container 1048 (Thousands in Soviet Union to go abroad, 1957).

[94] GARF. f. 9520, op. 1, d. 432, ll. 3, 29 (Lists of numbers and categories of tourists going abroad in 1960 and 1961). International travel by Soviet citizens was used to rebut arguments—especially American arguments—that the only Soviet citizens allowed to travel outside of the USSR were government officials or individuals involved in commercial activities. See "Memorandum: Meeting with Nicolas Kamensky, 16 April 1957," NARA, RG 43, Box 5, BEG 401. More Americans traveled as tourists to the USSR than vice versa, something Soviet authorities insisted was due to how slowly visas were issued, the cost of tourism, the absence of tours of substantive interest, and the humiliation of having to be fingerprinted. Records of an interview with Intourist representatives in "Soviet Tourism in the United States," NARA, RG 59, Box 2176; Robert F. Byrnes, *Soviet-American Academic Exchanges 1958–1975* (Bloomington, 1976), 60.

[95] 1,150,000 to be exact. V. Ankudinov, "Vazhnaia forma mezhdunarodnogo obsheniia," 96; Ankudinov, Our Hospitality," *Izvestiia* (28 October 1966), 4/*CDSP* 43 (1966): 22.

[96] On problems with data and definitions, see Jill. A. Lion, "Long Distance Passenger Travel in the Soviet Union," Paper prepared for the Research Program on Problems of International Communication and Security, MIT, October, 1967, 56; Randolph M. Siverson, Alexander J. Groth, and Marc Blumberg, "Soviet Tourism and Détente," *Studies in Comparative Communism* 13, no. 4 (Winter 1980): 359–60; HU OSA, RFE/RL RI, Background reports, 300-80-3 available at http://fa.osaarchivum.org/background-reports?col=8&id=35217; Vladislav Zubok provides a figure similar to that of Ankudinov based on Soviet archival sources, but this also likely reflects a conflation of tourists with other kinds of travelers. Zubok, *Zhivago's Children*, 90.

[97] RGANI, f. 5, op. 30, d. 225, l. 53 (On the cost of travel abroad, 1957); GARF, f. 9520, op. 1, d. 468, l. 29 (TEU meeting, 1962).

even within the same agency, and by the addition of different sets of calculations from international tourist organizations.[98] For 1960, for example, there are figures ranging from a low of 60,000 tourists, to 112,000 tourists, to double the first number at 124,000.[99] Roughly three-quarters of tourists (whatever the total) traveled to East European countries, the rest to capitalist countries and a small number to Asia, Africa, and India. In 1962, the Vice-Chairman of the Soviet travel agency Intourist, would proudly declare: "[T]here is not a single region of the Soviet Union that has not sent a Soviet tourist abroad, and no corner of the earth where Soviet people have not been."[100] This was not entirely hyperbole. In the 1960s, entire families of Siberia's native peoples were sent on holidays to Eastern Europe. As the anthropologist Piers Vitebsky recounts about his experiences in the Siberian north: "I had not expected the rugged men and women who looked as if they had never left their mountainside to tell me about their . . . conversation about Kafka in a Prague café with an intellectual from Cuba."[101] By the 1970s, over a million Soviet citizens a year traveled as tourists to Eastern Europe. What was once a revelation had, for some, become routine.[102]

---

[98] This figure is based on adding up the number of people traveling with Intourist and Sputnik via hard-currency excursions, non-hard currency exchanges, and trips for rest and healing. As the number of people traveling is not available for every year, I have made estimates based on general trends for the years that are unavailable. RGANI, f. 5, op. 30, d. 225, l. 53; Rossiiskii gosudarstvennyi arkhiv sotsial'no-politicheskoi istorii (hereafter RGASPI), f. m-5, op. 1, d. 52, l. 8 (Number of Soviet youth tourists traveling abroad, 1960); d. 161, l. 3 (Soviet tourists traveling by year with the Komsomol); d. 195, l. 9 (Report on tourism 1964). GARF, f. 9520, op. 1, d. 363, l. 1 (Sending tourists abroad, 1958); d. 391, l. 4 (TEU meeting, 1961); d. 430, ll. 172–73 (On sending Soviet tourists abroad, 1960); d. 432, ll. 1–64 (Number of tourists traveling abroad via Intourist, 1960 and 1961); d. 468, l. 29; d. 618, ll. 156–57 (On sending Soviet tourists abroad, 1962); d. 613, l. 18 (On international tourism, 1963); op. 2, d. 28, l. 11 (On sending Soviet tourists abroad); op. 2, d. 26, ll. 5, 10 (On fulfilling the plan for trips abroad, 1964); International estimates can be found in the United Nations, *Statistical Yearbook*, 1958–1979, travel data from which is reproduced in Siverson, *Soviet Tourism*, 364.

[99] GARF, f. 1, op. 9520, d. 468, l. 29; RGASPI, f. m-5, op. 1, d. 161, l. 3. The second number is from the United Nations Statistical Yearbook as cited in Siverson, "Soviet Tourism," 364, and John Bushnell, "The 'New Soviet Man' Turns Pessimist," in *The Soviet Union since Stalin*, ed. Stephen F. Cohen, Alexander Rabinowitch, and Robert Sharlet (Bloomington, 1980), 192. The highest number comes from the HU OSA, RFE/RL RI, Soviet Red Archives, 1953–1994, Old Code Subject Files, 300-80-1, Container 1049 (Tourists in the USSR and Soviet citizens abroad).

[100] GARF, f. 9520, op. 1, d. 468, l. 29.

[101] Piers Vitebsky, *Reindeer People: Living with Animals and Spirits in Siberia* (New York, 2005, 2006), 47.

[102] The process was also more routine. In 1976, of 5870 people from the Crimean region applying to travel abroad as tourists, all but 21 were accepted. Aleksei Popov, "Sovetskie turisty za rubezhom: ideologiia, kommunikatsiia, emotsii (po otchetam rukovoditelei turistskikh grupp)," *Istorichna panorama: nayk. statei*, vol 7 (Chernovci, 2009), 50.

"WE ALWAYS KNOW ABOUT THE
BEHAVIOR OF OUR TOURISTS"

The primary sources for this book include Soviet, East European, and Western archives, works of fiction, memoirs, film, visual and material culture, the popular press, and travel accounts. My reading of these sources has been informed by historical methodology, but also, when appropriate, by theories and concepts developed for tourism studies by sociologists, anthropologists, and literary and film scholars. I want to briefly consider the complexities of three of these primary sources: travel accounts, trips reports as found in archives, and memoirs. In a spirited defense of his travel account of a 1962 trip to Italy, *Both Sides of the Ocean: A Russian writer's travels in Italy and the United States,* Victor Nekrasov attacked the encyclopedic approach of the typical Soviet traveler to telling his tale: "I remember when a friend of mine came back from a trip and started telling us about it. He pulled out his notebook . . . and started off: 'So, on the first day, we arrived at such and such a place, on the second at such and such, on the third—"[103] "Boring," Nekrasov concluded. In imitation of this style, and with tongue firmly in cheek, Nekrasov briefly summarized his trip in the form of a "little report" devoted to the "pedantic reader, the devotee of absolute clarity," in which he provided dates, a list of those traveling, descriptions of meetings attended, and cities visited.[104]

As described by Nekrasov, the typical Soviet travel account was a far cry from the exuberant, deeply reflective, sometimes exhibitionist contemporary travel writing we are used to. Soviet travel accounts reflected the fact that Soviet tourism was an official project. Possibilities for travel were determined by Central Committee resolutions. Meaning too was officially prescribed in the authoritative language of Soviet newspapers, Intourist propagandists, and of Khrushchev himself. My sources of official discourses about travel include central Soviet newspapers such as *Izvestiia* and *Komsomol'skaia Pravda,* local newspapers such as *Sovietskaia Estonia,* and the popular press including, among others, the illustrated magazines *Ogonek* and *Vokrug sveta.*[105] These sources show that if in theory, travel accounts are windows on private experience, in practice, given the studied and censorious nature of the Soviet press, they are best read as authoritative texts. Many were what literary scholar Marina Balina has called "travel-missionary" accounts, in which the Soviet traveler both carried the "truth about the Country of the Soviets" abroad, and helped convince readers at home "about the

---

[103] Nekrasov, *Both Sides,* 22–23.
[104] Nekrasov, *Both Sides,* 22–23.
[105] On Soviet guidebooks see Karl D. Qualls, "'Where Each Stone Is History:' Travel Guides in Sevastopol after World War II," in Gorsuch and Koenker, *Turizm.*

advantages of the socialist system."[106] Some were group travel accounts such as the one published in *Literaturnaia gazeta* in 1949, which purports to be a description of entire delegation's "twelve days in America" and in which opinions about America are presented as if they were held without dispute by the group as a whole.[107] Likewise, the writers and journalists who accompanied Khrushchev on his 1959 trip to the United States wrote a 600-page collective account of the trip. There are no chapters identified by individual authors; the narrator of the entire book is identified as "we."[108] The author of the typical Soviet travel account was like a camera, focused outwards to bring back images for armchair tourists and authorities at home rather than inwards in a risky exploration of the personal encounter with the other. As Derek Gregory and James Duncan argue about travel accounts more generally: "[t]his space of translation is not a neutral surface and it is never innocent: it is shot through with relations of power and desire."[109] Soviet travel writers did this in especially obvious and intentional ways.

That said, in the 1950s and 1960s, some travel accounts become less heavy-handed than they had been earlier and begin to tell us more about desire and pleasure as well as about purpose. Some were closer to what we might call a "travel-explorer" account; they were aggressively positive about the travel experience—notably so in terms of tourism in the capitalist West—and some-times more personal as well. In a 1957 travel account published in *Vokrug sveta* called "A day in Geneva," Geneva is described as a place not only worth exploring, but one that the Soviet citizen might hope to visit. The essay casually walks the armchair traveler through the streets of the city as if they were traveling together: "You are growing a little hungry? Let's go to a café, after all it's already time for dinner."[110] For travel writers in the Khrushchev era, the concept of peaceful coexistence necessitated, as Eleonory Gilburd has argued about Sergei Obraztsov's admiring and optimistic travelogue of his two trips to London, "a new language for talking about capitalism" including "open comparisons and acknowledged borrowings."[111] Western Europe is not without its problems in

---

[106] Marina Balina, "The Literature of Travel," unpublished paper, 10, 12. On the development of a more "subjective" travel literature after Khrushchev see Marina Balina, "A Prescribed Journey: Russian Travel Literature from the 1960s to the 1990s," *Slavic and East European Journal* 38, no. 2 (1994): 261–70.

[107] Sergei Gerasimov, "Twelve Days in America," *Literaturnaia gazeta* (May 7, 1949), 4/*CDSP* 1:20 (June 14, 1949), 15. This is true not only of Soviet travel accounts. The official account of Captain James Cook's third voyage across the Pacific was a composite of Cook's ship's log entries and journal, the journal entries of Cook's officers, and John Douglas' revisions and editing under the direction of the Admiralty. James Duncan and Derek Gregory, ed. *Writes of Passage: Reading Travel Writing.* (London and New York, 1999), 3.

[108] *Face to Face with America* (Moscow, 1960).

[109] Duncan and Gregory, *Writes of Passage,* 5.

[110] "Den' Zhenevy," *Vokrug sveta* 3 (March 1957): 62.

[111] Eleonory Gilburd, "Books and Borders: Sergei Obratzov and Soviet Travels to London in the 1950s," in Gorsuch and Koenker, *Turizm,* 237.

these accounts—many authors still resort to the standard tropes of unemploy-
ment and decadent commercialization—but as Gilburd observes about Obratzov's *What I Saw, Learned, and Understood during Two Trips to London,* "the tone
is more restrained, while the colors are brighter."[112]

Travel writing was purposeful. It was designed to produce knowledge about
the rest of the world such that those reading the accounts could learn how to
think about other places, how to think about the Soviet Union, and how to be a
tourist themselves should the opportunity arise. Published accounts of tourism to
Eastern Europe provided smooth and reassuring accounts of travel to countries
said to be appreciative of the Soviet Union and described tourists glad of restful
adventure. Archival documents, in contrast, tell a different story about the
physicality of travel, about challenging conditions and unfriendly reception,
about the resources and planning involved in sending people abroad, and
about the multiplicity of responses to the experience of tourism itself. Although
archival documents are also official, they remind us that tourism was not only an
official project. "Leisure has its own history," Rudy Koshar insists, "neither
wholly determined by the structures and constraints of the mode of production
in which it develops, nor fully shaped by patterns of social power."[113]

I have used archival materials in Russia, Estonia, Hungary, England, and the
United States to explore the experiences of Soviet citizens as they crossed
geographic, cultural, and ideological borders for the first time. One of the best,
if not unproblematic, sources of experience are the trip reports filed by Soviet
group leaders with Intourist, the Trade Union Excursion Bureau, and the
Komsomol travel agency, Sputnik, after each trip abroad. These sources are far
from private. But the intimate, everyday details of travel, both positive and
negative, that they provide are invaluable. They depict routes taken, means of
travel, touristic sites seen, and encounters with local people. They describe
organizational difficulties; trip leaders complain about the many missed connections, challenging conditions, and poorly trained local guides. Trip leaders also
report in careful detail on the many tourists who violated accepted "norms of
behavior" for the Soviet tourist abroad. Because these reports are a key source for
this book, it is worth pausing briefly to consider the role and writings of the trip
leader.

Each trip leader had to fulfill the multiple, and sometimes untenable, roles of
cultural guide, political leader, and informant. The job of trip leader was not
simple; even before departure, leaders working for Sputnik were supposed to
learn about the economy, history, culture, and politics of the country they would
be visiting; familiarize themselves with every aspect of their charges' biographies;
"guarantee" the participation of their tourists at pre-trip informational and
educational sessions; and retrieve the necessary trip documents for every tourist

---

[112] Gilburd, "Books and Borders," 235.
[113] Koshar, *German Travel Cultures,* 5.

from the regional authorities.[114] Most trip leaders were party members and many were also party or trade union activists.[115] But their authority as trip leader was sometimes undermined by the greater authority of their privileged tourists who sometimes refused to do as told.[116] To add to this confusion, trip leaders were participants as well as leaders, an ambiguous position suggested by the fact that some trip leaders to Eastern Europe had to use vacation time, rather than work time, to lead a trip.[117] In this sense, their reports can be read as travel diaries—a window on their own experience—as well as a report on the experience of others. International tourism's sometimes uneasy blending of purpose and pleasure is evident if we compare the report of the typical tourist trip leader to that of a head of a delegation. Delegate reports were typically full of detailed information gathered about the country, factory, or educational institution visited. The lengthy 1955 report of a group of agricultural delegates who traveled to Sweden describes, in numbing detail and with numerous charts, Swedish agricultural production.[118] Tourist trip reports, in contrast, were sometimes factual in tone, at other times more literary. They varied in their composition, in their formality, in their attention to detail. Some appear to have been dashed off quickly, while others are lengthy and labored. Some reports of trips to Eastern Europe are breathtakingly enthusiastic. The trip leader him- or herself is evidently rapturous about crossing the border.

Whether traveling to a fellow socialist country or to capitalist countries, all trip leaders would have known that any possibilities for future trips, as well perhaps as possibilities for advancement at home, depended on their own behavior and that of their charges while abroad. They were a source of information for the regime, enabling authorities at home to travel virtually by gathering information about foreign countries, and about foreign countries' attitudes to the Soviet Union. But if group leaders were themselves surveyors, of both their tourists and of the countries they traveled to, they were themselves also kept under surveillance. They were a point of anxiety for tourist authorities. How to find enough experienced guides with the requisite languages for tours when so few Soviet citizens had traveled and/or were politically acceptable?[119] That everyone, including the trip leader, was considered vulnerable is suggested by the multiple layers of surveillance on international trips. Some groups were accompanied by a leader (*starosta*) from a local trade union who was of stature equal to the group

[114] RGASPI, f. 5, op. 1, d. 52, ll. 26–27 (Instructions for group leaders of Soviet youth traveling abroad).

[115] GARF, f. 9520, op. 1, d. 391, l. 94.

[116] See, for example, GARF, f. 9612, op. 1, d. 563, l. 36 (Trip report, Poland and Czechoslovakia, 1963) and GARF, f. 9520, op. 1, d. 430, ll. 105–106 (On the inadequate behavior of Soviet tourists abroad, 1960).

[117] GARF, f. 9520, op. 1, d. 468, l. 17.

[118] RGANI, f. 5, op. 30, d. 117, l. 93 (Trip report, agricultural delegation to Sweden, 1955).

[119] GARF, f. 9520, op. 1, d. 391, l. 172.

leader, and who would also report to the trade union upon his return about the behavior of the tourists.[120] KGB agents also traveled abroad with some groups for the purposes of surveillance (especially to capitalist countries), a fact widely known as suggested by the use of the colloquial term *nian'ka* (nanny) to denote such a person.[121] "We know everything," a trade union delegate from Irkutsk claimed. "We always know about the behavior of our tourists."[122]

Memoirs are a different, final source of the experiential. In contrast to the travel account or the trip report, they are openly preoccupied with the personal, the emotional, and the transformative. They are also the most likely of all of the sources to idealize the foreign, and to distance themselves from the Soviet project. This is consistent with their retrospective, post-Soviet, viewpoint. Memoirs often emphasize the authors' long-standing moral and ideological distance from Soviet socialism, a distance sometimes produced only retrospectively.[123] Nonetheless, they are extraordinarily helpful. The importance of a first trip across Soviet borders, and especially of a first trip to the capitalist West, means that these trips are described in extraordinary detail, including in some cases every accommodation, every excursion, every revelation. Art historian Mikhail German— and this is typical—devotes a paragraph to describing the process of buying a Parisian metro ticket.[124] At the same time, however, as they are grounded in specifics, memoirs of trips to Western Europe also have a fantastical quality, authors describing a feeling not dissimilar from Alice's experience of falling down the rabbit hole. "I lost any sense of reality," historian Evgeniia Gutnova writes about her trip to Italy, "I felt as if I was in some kind of fairytale dream."[125] Film director Andrei Konchalovskii also felt as if he were in a "dream," one he preferred to the nightmare of life in the Soviet Union. His dream experience "turned [his] life inside out for good."[126] These memoirs need to be used carefully, but so too for any source.

Our journey begins with an exploration of domestic tourism in late Stalinism, when Soviet citizens were encouraged to turn inwards in order to avoid dangerous border zones literal and imaginative. Chapter Two concerns the "inner abroad" of Estonia. Under Khrushchev, Estonia's combination of historic West European architecture and contemporary "European" style were newly marketed for Soviet citizens as a form of local difference now acceptable by virtue of Soviet political control. Chapter Three explores the experience of Soviet tourism to

---

[120] See, for example, GARF, f. 9520, op. 1, d. 468, l. 22.

[121] Irina H. Corten, *Vocabulary of Soviet Society and Culture: A Selected Guide to Russian Words, Idioms, and Expressions of the Post-Stalin Era, 1953–1991* (Durham and London, 1992), 90–91.

[122] GARF, f. 9520, op. 1, d. 468, l. 22.

[123] See the discussion on this point in Yurchak, *Everything was Forever*, 6–7 and Irina Paperno, "Personal Accounts of the Soviet Experience," *Kritika: Explorations in Russian and Eurasian History*, 3, no. 4 (Fall 2002): 577–610.

[124] Mikhail German, *Slozhnoe proshedshee: Passé composé* (St. Petersburg, 2000), 430.

[125] Evgeniia Vladimirovna Gutnova, *Perezhitoe* (Moscow, 2001), 323.

[126] Andrei Konchalovskii, *Nizkie istiny* (Moscow, 1998), 116.

Eastern Europe, including the challenges of applying to travel abroad as well as the pleasures of sightseeing and shopping. This chapter uses the tourist experience as a window into the relationship between Soviet center and East European periphery. In Chapter Four, I examine the performative function of Soviet tourism to Western Europe, in which the traveler was sent abroad as an envoy for cordial, if careful, relations between socialist East and capitalist West. Tourism to Western Europe in the Cold War was not only about performance, however, but also about consumption. A fifth chapter considers tourists' consumption of European culture, leisure experiences, and material items. Finally, Chapter Six focuses on Soviet films about travel, considering what portrayals of travel and tourism in Soviet feature films suggest about a mutually constitutive relationship between Western other and Soviet self.

1

"There's No Place like Home:"
Soviet Tourism in Late Stalinism

Between 1947 and 1953, Soviet citizens were encouraged to turn inwards, to avoid dangerous "border zones" both literal and imaginative. After the relative openness of the war period, the postwar years were ones of "containment" directed both at limiting the threat of the Western other and at reinforcing Soviet patriotic identity.[1] The change could be seen in the Soviet travel and exploration magazine *Vokrug sveta* [Around the World]. In 1946, which was still a period of continuing if hesitant openness, *Vokrug sveta* included articles and images of the non-Soviet world, as well as information about pre-revolutionary and Soviet-era explorers. There were stories about trips to Prague and to New Guinea, about ocean exploration at the time of Columbus, and a favorable review of Ilf and Petrov's 1936 book *One-Storied America*.[2] But in 1947, when Andrei Zhdanov's campaign against "servility before the West" was well established, the permissible world shrunk, and most of the articles were now about travel within the Soviet Union, including pieces on Moscow, on Lenin's exile (within Russia), and on Stalin's childhood in Georgia.[3] Even in a magazine devoted to world exploration, good travel was now defined as domestic.[4]

The late-Stalin regime controlled information about foreign countries in order to advance its own xenophobic interpretation of world events, in which the

---

[1] This, of course, evokes George Kennan's famous arguments in 1946 and 1947 about "containment." In addition to containing an external threat, Kennan noted that a "diplomatic victory" also depended on the United States' ability to "improve [the] self-confidence, discipline, morale, and community spirit" of its own people. George Kennan, *Memoirs, 1925–1950* (New York, 1967), 559.

[2] *Vokrug sveta* 1 (1946), 63; *Vokrug sveta* 3–4 (1946), 16, 20, inside back cover; *Vokrug sveta* 7 (1946), 48–51. On Zhdanov, see Robert D. English, *Russia and the Idea of the West: Gorbachev, Intellectuals, and the End of the Cold War* (New York, 2000), 46–47.

[3] *Vokrug sveta* 1 (1947), 2–4; *Vokrug sveta* 9 (September 1947), 2–3, 8–11. In his memoirs Khrushchev described his ignorance about the West with frustration. See for example Nikita Khrushchev, *Khrushchev Remembers*, trans. and ed. Strobe Talbot (Boston, 1970), 392–3.

[4] Later issues returned to international portrayals, but often for propaganda purposes. Articles from 1950 about Italy and about Cuba described the horrible effects of American policy on these countries. *Vokrug sveta* 4 (April 1950), 13–14; *Vokrug sveta* 7 (July 1950), 10–16.

bourgeois West was cast as the enemy.[5] Creating enemies was only part of the solution to the foreign policy and domestic challenges of the postwar period, however. The regime also demanded a heightened "Sovietness" from those still considered loyal. Domestic tourism was one response to this perceived need, intended to produce physically and ideologically healthy Soviet citizens. Moscow was a particular focus of Soviet patriotic education for the postwar tourist, but tourism also contributed to the construction of Soviet identity on the larger collective level of the Soviet Union. It aimed to create a correct understanding of the "socialist homeland" by inscribing historical sites and "exotic" spaces with Soviet significance. Last, but by no means least, tourism was a means of reassuring a weary, war-torn, population. Descriptions (even if not realized) of beautiful beaches and luxurious resorts suggested to loyal citizens that conditions would improve and their future would be comfortable and bright. In every case, travelers were reminded that it was only within the borders of the socialist homeland that the Soviet citizen could let down his or her guard and hold out his hand in confidence of a warm welcome.

Many aspects of tourist organization and experience discussed in this chapter are not particular to the late Stalin period; as described in the introduction, tourism was appropriated as a "Soviet" project in the late 1920s, and developed into a mass movement in the 1960s and 1970s.[6] The importance of tourism is suggested by the fact that even in the difficult and hungry years of late Stalinism, the Soviet state was eager to restore and rebuild tourist facilities. Soviet newspapers and magazines carried multiple articles in the postwar period about the wonderful new possibilities for domestic tourism and healing travel now available, and archives documented significant state interest. "The tourist movement must become a mass movement!" exhorted one enthusiastic journalist in 1951.[7]

---

[5] On Soviet views of America see Jeffrey Brooks, "The Press and Its Messages: Images of America in the 1920s and 1930s," in *Russia in the Era of NEP: Explorations in Soviet Society and Culture*, ed. Sheila Fitzpatrick, Alexander Rabinowitch, and Richard Stites (Bloomington, 1991) and Jeffrey Brooks, "Official Xenophobia and Popular Cosmopolitanism in Early Soviet Russia," *American Historian Review* 97:5 (December 1992):1431–448; Denise Youngblood, "Americanitis: The *Amerikanshchina* in Soviet Cinema," *Journal of Popular Film and Television* 19: 4 (Winter 1992).

[6] The Society of Proletarian Tourism (OPT) was founded under the initiative of the Komsomol in the late 1920s following the liquidation of the still functioning pre-revolutionary Russian Society of Tourists. On Soviet domestic tourism, see Diane Koenker, "The Proletarian Tourist in the 1930s: Between Mass Excursion and Mass Escape," in *Turizm: The Russian and East European Tourist under Capitalism and Socialism*, ed. Anne E. Gorsuch and Diane Koenker (Ithaca, 2006).

[7] N. Makarov, "For Mass Touring," *Trud* (27 May 1951), 4/*Current Digest of the Soviet Press* (hereafter *CDSP*) 3:21 (7 July 1951), 28.

XENOPHOBIA

Stalin promoted a defensive and largely static notion of Soviet identity, a construction requiring constant vigilance through propaganda, violence, and closed borders. In the late 1930s, almost all international exchange of ideas or people was shut down as the Soviet Union was seized by a fear of enemies both internal and external.[8] This isolationism was briefly lifted during World War II, when as a result of the wartime alliance between the Soviet Union and anti-Nazi Western countries, the USSR opened its borders to economic aid and to cultural exchange.[9] For a brief moment, Soviet journalists could still express hope that the Soviet Union might work together with "peace-loving states" in the capitalist world.[10] In 1946, local bureaus of Intourist still operated in Finland, Switzerland, Germany, and England for foreign tourists wanting to travel to the Soviet Union. By 1947, however, the Cold War was in full swing and most Intourist offices were closed.[11] Cultural interchange did not stop altogether: in December 1952, six Soviet musicians performed in a "half-full Usher Hall, Edinburgh, on a cold Monday evening."[12] But while Soviet citizens might be able to read about the new Odessa–New York "passenger line" as described in *Pravda* in 1947, very, very few were able to travel on it.[13] Published travel accounts in this period were written by journalists, only rarely by delegates, and certainly not by tourists, and they all reported being happiest when returning home. As A. Goncharov wrote in 1947 about his departure from New York on the Soviet ocean liner *Victory*: "It

---

[8] Michael David-Fox, "From Illusory 'Society' to Intellectual 'Public': VOKS, International Travel and Party-Intelligentsia Relations in the Interwar Period," *Contemporary European History* 11, no. 1 (2002): 31–32; *Sovetskoe zazerkal'e: Inostannyi turizm v SSSR v 1930–1980-e gody* (Moscow, 2007), 67–77.

[9] VOKS encouraged cultural ties and promoted war time exchanges including jazz concerts, art exhibits, film showings, and tours by chess teams. Todd Bennett, "Culture, Power, and *Mission to Moscow*: Film and Soviet-American Relations during World War II," *Journal of American History* 88 (September 2001), 515. Some sections of popular opinion remained hostile to the Allies despite the more favorable portrayals in official propaganda. Sarah Davis, "Soviet Perceptions of the Allies during the Great Patriotic War," in *Russia and the Wider World in Historical Perspective*, ed. Cathryn Brennan and Murray Frame (London and New York, 2000), 187.

[10] Jeffrey Brooks, *Thank you, Comrade Stalin! Soviet Public Culture from Revolution to Cold War* (Princeton, 2000), 207.

[11] Gosudarstvennyi arkhiv Rossiiskoi Federatsii (hereafter GARF), f. 9612, op.1, d. 174, ll. 2,14 (Intourist report on international tourism in the postwar period, 1947). Intourist even sent a representative to the London meeting of the Travel Association of Great Britain and Northern Ireland in October 1946. The situation also worsened on the American side with the enforcement of the Foreign Agents Registration Act against Soviet cultural and scientific exchange groups. Walter Hixson, *Parting the Curtain: Propaganda, Culture, and the Cold War, 1945–1961* (New York, 1997), 7.

[12] David Caute, *The Dancer Defects: The Struggle for Cultural Supremacy during the Cold War* (Oxford, 2003), 20–22, 395–96, 420.

[13] "Passazhirskaia liniia Odessa-N'iu-Iork," *Pravda* (14 March 1947): 4.

was a wonderful feeling to leave ... the summer heat, noise, and dirty soot of New York behind."[14]

The Soviet Union did not cut out all contact with the rest of the world. Western Europe was reported about more positively than the United States; in a 1948 article in *Vokrug sveta,* French workers were said to live in poverty, yet Paris was positively described as "one of those cities, the history of which is not only well-known but dear to the people of the whole world."[15] An Intourist document from October 1947 reveals that a few Soviet authorities hoped for continued contact and the economic benefits it might bring. The report described in envious terms the impressive increase in tourism in North America and Western Europe following the war, noting the amount of tourist revenue that Canada brought in, for example, from restaurants, tickets to cultural events, and sales of gasoline. The report provided prices for travel in the United States, Canada, and England including the cost of a room with a bath, breakfast, lunch, and dinner and argued that in order to prepare for international tourists, and attract their hard currency, the Soviet Union needed to build more and better hotels, improve air transportation, and educate guide and translators.[16] The author was envious not only of the efforts of capitalist countries to reap the benefits of international tourism, but of Czech and Yugoslav efforts to develop foreign tourism through their local travel bureaus, Chedok and Putnik. Both countries, the report notes, had published persuasive advertising materials about where to travel in their countries, leading to about 30,000 foreigners visiting Czechoslovakia in 1947.[17]

This report built on prewar Intourist activities, and was also consistent with postwar efforts by North American and European tourist promoters to encourage tourism both domestic and international. It ran counter, however, to the prevailing trend in the Soviet Union. Personal exchange of the kind suggested by an increase in international tourism was unlikely given the implementation of the Soviet State Secrets Act of 1946, which in the words of American Ambassador Walter Bedell Smith, made it a "grave offense to speak to a foreigner of anything which, by the most remote flight of imagination, might be considered state information."[18] All contacts with a foreigner, oral or otherwise, had to be reported to authorities.

It was not only capitalist countries that were off-limits. All ties between the Soviet Union and Yugoslavia were cut off in 1948 due to Tito's refusal to accept Soviet authority. Contact with other socialist countries was possible, but closely monitored and still unavailable to ordinary Soviet citizens. Small numbers of

[14] A. Goncharov, "Ot N'iu-Iorka do Batumi," *Vokrug sveta* no. 7 (July 1947): 38.

[15] Olga Chechetkina, "Parizh posle voiny," *Vokrug sveta* no. 1 (January 1948): 22–27.

[16] GARF, f. 9612, op.1, d. 174, ll. 1–18.

[17] GARF, f. 9612, op.1, d. 174, ll. 1–18.

[18] Walter Bedell Smith, *Moscow Mission 1946–1949* (London, 1950), 93; "V biuro prezidiuma soveta ministrov SSSR," (4 January 1952) in *Sovetskaia zhizn', 1945–1953: Dokumentov Sovetskoi historii* (Moscow, 2003), 690–93.

delegations did travel to Eastern Europe, including the young people who traveled to the 1947 International Youth Festival in Prague, a few high-ranking artists who visited Bulgaria, and the Soviet actors who traveled to Czechoslovakia on the occasion of the 34th anniversary of the October Revolution.[19] Soviet youth associated with the Anti-fascist Committee of Soviet Youth exchanged letters with "foreign youth."[20] But in the late-Stalin era, even postal exchanges between socialist countries had to be closely watched; a 1950 Party resolution condemned "the uncontrolled individual exchange of letters between Soviet and foreign [socialist bloc] youth."[21]

"THE TOURIST MOVEMENT MUST BECOME A MASS MOVEMENT"

Domestic tourism, in contrast, was warmly encouraged. In April 1945, while the Red Army was still fighting in Berlin, the Secretariat of the Central Trade Union ordered its Tourist-Excursion Bureau back to work.[22] A few of the many ambitious tasks of restoration included organizing excursions for those living in Moscow (meant to service a half a million a year), in Leningrad (to service over a quarter of a million a year), building tourist facilities in Borodino, Dombai, Kislovodsk, Sochi, and Tbilisi, providing sufficient car transport for tourists and guides, and organizing new informational materials about available tourist excursions.[23] The challenges of postwar recovery were enormous, however, and had an impact on resources available for tourism, just as they did on every other facet of Soviet life after the war. Tourist bases and sanatoria struggled with poor quality facilities, with a lack of trained workers, and with a deficiency of proper "healing foods."[24] Factory clubs, which sometimes sponsored tourist activities, found it hard to support even the simplest of excursions in the immediate postwar period.[25] A limited, often damaged transportation system made it

[19] "Na mezhdunarodnyi festival molodezhi," *Izvestiia* (23 July 1947): 3; Boris Chirkov, "Gordost' za podinu," *Ogonek* 45 (November 1951): 18.

[20] In 1950, of 19,000 letters, 18,000 were from Eastern Europe correspondents. "Zapiska sekretaria TsK VLKSM," (16 May 1950) and "Zapiska predsedatelia Vneshnepoliticheskoi komissii TsK VKP (b)," (2 August 1950) in *Sovetskaia zhizn', 1945–1953*, 361–65.

[21] "Zapiska predsedatelia," 365.

[22] GARF, f. 9520, op. 1, d. 24, l. 85 (Report on the status and expansion of tourist facilities, 1945).

[23] GARF, f. 9520, op.1, d. 24, ll. 87–89.

[24] GARF, f. 9228, op.1, d. 302, l. 56 (Medical inspection), op.2, d. 3, ll. 6–7 (Report on sanatoria). There were organizational struggles as well. See Kurashova, Gol'dfailia, Pospelovoi, ed. *Kuroty SSSR*, 12; V.V. Dvornichenko, *Razvitie turizma v SSSR (1917–1983 gg)* (Moscow, 1985), 40.

[25] "Informatsiia orginstruktorskogo otdela MGK VKP(b) G.M. Popovu—o rabote fabrichno-zavodskikh klubov," in *Moskva poslevoennaia, 1945–1947. Arkhivnye dokumenty i materialy* (Moscow, 2000), 646–47.

difficult to transport people from one place to another.[26] In 1948, tourist advocates complained that funding was still inadequate and that tourist work remained highly disorganized. Romashkov, a hydroelectric engineer who parti-cipated in Trade Union planning meetings about tourism both before and after the war, worried that "apart from in the Crimea and Caucasus, there are no [developed] tourist locations."[27] An exception was the priority sometimes given to international tourist facilities in particularly strategic locations. In 1947, the Intourist hotel in Stalingrad was repaired sufficiently to house international tourists, though its "windows looked out on acres of rubble, broken brick and concrete and pulverized plaster."[28]

In the earliest years of reconstruction and recovery many workers had a little interest in travel and little ability to pay for it.[29] There were increases in 1947 and 1948 in the number of workers participating in tourist excursions, but the numbers were still lower than in the prewar period. Only seventy percent of Tourist Bureau capacity was used.[30] This hardly seems surprising: after the war many Soviet citizens could think very little about such extravagances as tourism. "How can we continue like this?" wondered one individual in 1946, "Sacrifices and sacrifices. Understand me, if a family of three now needs 600 to 700 rubles [to buy food on ration cards], that is not all that has to be bought. The government is not giving away soap, there is no butter or lard, only substitutes, there is no kerosene. We are at the last extremity."[31] Maria Sadchikova, who was a doctor and army officer, thought little about possibilities for travel. Although she was lucky enough to move to Moscow for permanent settlement from a provincial city, she spent fifteen years living in a tiny basement room in Moscow before she could afford to move into a decent apartment. Like many Soviet holiday-makers, she visited relatives once a year (in Kuibyshev) but apart from this she could not afford any recreational travel further than the Moscow suburbs.[32] Despite the challenges of the postwar environment, however, Soviet citizens were not immune to the possibilities of a few weeks away from work. Indeed, the severe overcrowding of the postwar period in which per-capita urban living space actually decreased from what it had been in 1940, surely added to the

[26] The railroad authorities were unprepared, for example, for the enormous number of people using the trains simply to return home in 1946 and 1947. Holland Hunter, "Successful Spatial Management" in *The Impact of World War 2 on the Soviet Union*, ed. Susan Linz (New Jersey, 1985), 55–56.

[27] GARF, f. 9520, op.1, d. 69, l. 8.

[28] John Steinbeck, *A Russian Journal* (New York, 1948), 120.

[29] Dvornichenko, *Razvitie turizma v SSSR*, 44. Soviet experts admitted that not every worker could afford to pay for a trip, especially to places other than the discounted rest homes. GARF, f. 9520, op.1, d. 69, l. 29.

[30] Dvornichenko, *Razvitie turizma v SSSR*, 44.

[31] Elena Zubkova, *Russia after the War: Hopes, Illusions, and Disappointments, 1945–1957*, trans. Hugh Ragsdale (New York, 1998), 42.

[32] Interview by research assistant, Victor Zatsepine, of his Great-Aunt, June 2001.

pleasure of time away from home.[33] Tourism does appear to have increased in the early 1950s, by which point the economic situation of urban dwellers had began to improve and there were also more tourist facilities. In 1952, there were seventy-six tourist bases, as compared to just twenty-two in 1947.[34]

Who traveled? According to a Decree of the Presidium of the Central Council of Trade Unions from August 1950, "first priority" for Tourist-Excursion Bureau facilities was supposed to go to "working trade union members who are productive innovators, basic cadre workers, employed war invalids and production engineers and technicians." Deserving others included nursing mothers, mothers without support and adolescents.[35] Soviet workers were re-minded that they were fortunate to have their "right to relaxation" guaranteed by the Soviet Constitution, in contrast to bourgeois countries, where tourism was said to be a means of profit operated by independent companies and available mainly to wealthy tourists.[36] But in 1947, according to *Ogonek*, it was "the best and most respected members of the nation's coal mining industry" who rested at one well-known sanatorium on the Black Sea (although the magazine insisted that in the next ten years enough spaces would be built at sanatoria to hold 18,000 people).[37] Perks for a Soviet elite were part of what Vera Dunham has called the "Big Deal," in which a cohort loyal to the regime and eager for stabilization were rewarded by "material incentives," of which leisure was an important component.[38] It was professionals, for example, who could take advantage of official permission to travel for business and squeeze in extra vacation time in coveted locations. Under Stalin business trips were more closely monitored than they would be later and possibilities for a *tvorcheskaia komandir-ovka* (creative business trip) were limited,[39] but at least one Moscow lawyer managed to add a week on the Black Sea onto a brief work trip in a nearby area. She asked fellow travelers at the bus stop where to find a good hotel and good

[33] Sheila Fitzpatrick, "Postwar Soviet Society: The 'Return to Normalcy', 1945–1953," in Linz, *The Impact of World War 2*, 137.

[34] On postwar economic conditions see Donald Filtzer, "The Standard of Living of Soviet Industrial Workers in the Immediate Postwar Period, 1945–1948," *Europe-Asia Studies* 51 (1999): 1013–38. The number of available places to stay was still under ten thousand. Rossiiskii gosudarstvennyi arkhiv sotsial'no-politicheskoi istorii (hereafter RGASPI), f. 1, op.47, d. 412, l. 11 (TEU report, 1957).

[35] *Trud* (13 December 1951), 4/*CDSP* 2:50 (27 January 1951), 30.

[36] Dobkovich, *Turizm v SSSR*, 3–4.

[37] Aleksandr Shinskii, "Zdravnitsa ugol'shchikov," *Ogonek* 38 (September 1947), 23–24. The Komsomol also earmarked places for its members. "Vocem' tysiach putevok dlia studentov," *Izvestiia* (23 May 1946), 1.

[38] Vera S. Dunham, *In Stalin's Time: Middle-Class Values in Soviet Fiction* (Cambridge, 1976), 5, 17.

[39] The expression *tvorcheskaia komandirovka* has been in use since the 1930s, referring to writers and other members of the "creative intelligentsia" who took advantage of official permission and funding to travel to places otherwise unavailable because of cost or location. Irina H. Corten, *Vocabulary of Soviet Society and Culture. A Selected Guide to Russian Words, Idioms, and Expressions of the Post-Stalinist Era, 1953–1991* (Durham, 1992), 148.

restaurants, and boasted about her ability to use her lawyerly status to change compartments and travel [illegally] in the international car on the train trip from Moscow.[40] In contrast, families rarely traveled together. Despite the attention given postwar to strengthening the nuclear family, hard-won excursions such as a weekend pleasure-cruise near Moscow were filled almost entirely by adults, although these are just the kind of adventures that might have been full of children elsewhere.[41]

Individuals without access to desirable resorts sometimes traveled on their own in what was commonly called *dikie turizm* (wild tourism)—tourism without the usual *putevka* (voucher) to a tourist camp, rest home, or sanatorium. As Irena Corten explains in her lexicon of this term: "Because of inadequate transportation, hotel, and restaurant facilities in the Soviet Union . . . [o]ften, people ended up spending their vacation in rough conditions—hitchhiking, camping or staying in small rented rooms without basic conveniences, eating irregular meals not properly prepared, and so forth. Such circumstances validate the metaphor of living in the wild."[42] And yet, while "wild tourism" was common in the prewar period, and again in the 1960s and 1970s, it appears have been comparatively rare in the postwar period. Mary Leder, a long-term American emigrant to the Soviet Union, described her own experiences traveling "wild" to the Sukhumi in July 1950, including the ease with which she purchased plane tickets and found a room to rent in a local's cabin. But Leder writes that while the practice later "became widespread," "few venturesome souls attempted to travel in this way" in 1950.[43] Leder traveled "wild" because there were no hotels or hostels "open to the public" in Sukhumi. For others, these restrictions may have proved too intimidating. Beginning in 1940, republic capitals and many *kurorty* (health spas) and seaside resorts were regulated by stricter passport control laws than major industrial towns and areas.[44] Despite its challenges, however, the appeal of "wild travel" was clear. As Leder remarks: "We read no newspapers [and] talked

---

[40] Michel Gordy, *Visa to Moscow*, trans. Katherine Woods (London, 1953), 381. Official travelers on state business, including, in one case, an Army Colonel and Komsomol teacher, often stayed in local hotels with simple rooms, hard beds, and communal sinks in the corridor. Marie Noële Kelly, *Mirror to Russia* (London, 1952), 51.

[41] Kelly, *Mirror to Russia*, 195. On the lack of family vacations, see Diane P. Koenker, "Whose Right to Rest? Contesting the Family Vacation in the Postwar Soviet Union," *Comparative Studies in Society and History* 51 (2009).

[42] Corten, *Vocabulary of Soviet Society and Culture*, 41.

[43] Mary M. Leder, *My Life in Stalinist Russia: An American Woman Looks Back* (Bloomington, 2001), 307.

[44] Gijs Kessler, "The Passport System and State Control over Population Flows in the Soviet Union, 1932–1940," *Cahiers du Monde Russe* 42: 2/3/4 (April-December 2001), 495. Registration procedures were also selectively applied (and not always effectively) to satisfy the varying policing and purging urges of the regime in different periods. Paul M. Hagenloh, "'Socially Harmful Elements' and the Great Terror," in *Stalinism: New Directions*, ed. Sheila Fitzpatrick (London, 2000), 286–308.

no politics." Most days were spent on the beach.[45] The unscheduled nature of "wild tourism" contrasted with the official Soviet tourist experience, which often resembled an adult version of the Pioneer camp. The schedule for visitors to the Krasnodar tourist base on the Caucasus Black Sea Coast included an ocean swim after breakfast, followed by an excursion to a nearby city or collective farm, a nature walk in the afternoon, and a "cultural activity" such as dancing or watching a film after dinner.[46]

PATRIOTIC TOURISM

That tourism of any kind should be offered as an answer to postwar needs and to the anxieties of the Cold War is worth exploring, given the regime's preoccupation with controlling movement. Indeed, tourism was just one form of "travel" in the postwar period. Millions of people were "traveling," some returning home after the dislocations of war, others forcibly evacuated from border areas and newly acquired territories.[47] The regime was especially concerned about soldiers returning home from Central Europe and Germany, who often brought back personal experiences of a West different than what they had been told to expect.[48] Stalin responded to the threat generated by these "travel accounts" by arresting and imprisoning those "travelers" who seemed most dangerous, especially returning prisoners of war.[49] Posters were put up warning those at home not to believe all returning soldiers, explaining that "after all the blood and hardship that the troops had undergone, their judgments [are] lopsided, that they [are] nervous and dazed, and that some of them even [will] try to claim that the cities and villages of capitalistic countries provide everyone with a mansion filled with luxuries."[50]

Domestic tourism was a form of patriotic redress. The Komsomol Central Committee described tourism as "one of the most important forms of educational work among youth, especially patriotic education."[51] Patriotic tourism engaged the tourist in rituals of public self-admiration, in which the prestige of the Soviet Union was perpetually re-affirmed. In 1945, the Secretariat of the Central Trade Union emphasized tourism's role in teaching workers about "the

---

[45] Leder, *My Life in Stalinist Russia*, 310.

[46] GARF, f. 9520, op.1, d. 79, l. 108 (Report on Krasnodarsk tourist base, 1948).

[47] Fitzpatrick, "Postwar Soviet Society," 130–37.

[48] Some soldiers expressed amazement that "over there" was nothing like what they "had been told for so many years before the war;" they discovered that Westerners "lived more dignified, richer, and freer lives" than they did. English, *Russia and the Idea of the West*, 44. See also Zubkova, *Russia after the War*, 18, 33.

[49] Zubkova, *Russia after the War*, 105–106.

[50] Walter Bedell Smith, *Moscow Mission 1946–1949* (London, 1950), 280.

[51] As summarized by Dvornichenko, *Razvitie turizma v SSSR*, 46.

heroic spirit of the Great Patriotic War, the socialist construction of our country, the cultural growth of our people—the peoples of the USSR—[and] the economic, geographic, natural wealth of the country."[52] Some of the earliest postwar excursions were to recently erected monuments and memorials to Soviet victories. As early as 1945, a Moscow student sports group organized a twenty-three day trip "Along the path of the Great Patriotic War."[53] Indeed, war monuments were often built before cities themselves were reconstructed. The memorial obelisk in Stalingrad stood in a fenced-in site with well-tended flowers but shadowed by the battered shells of ruined buildings.[54] The number of museums to the war almost doubled from ninety in 1941 to 163 in 1952. Of all types of Soviet museums (museums of history, industry, the Russian revolution, natural history, art), "memorial" museums were one of only two types to increase in number in the postwar period, the other being, with a much less dramatic rise, the local lore and history museum.[55]

Moscow was a major focus of Soviet patriotic tourism. In published guides to local and regional tours in the Soviet Union, the capital city was Itinerary Number 1.[56] In part, the emphasis on Moscow was a practical one because of the resources, both financial and personal, that could be found more easily in the capital. But Moscow, as one lengthy lecture from 1945 on the reconstruction of Moscow reminded its listeners, was also the "heart of the socialist motherland."[57] Travel articles about other parts of the Soviet Union sometimes began and ended with Moscow, just as other kinds of articles began and ended with references to Stalin. An article from *Vokrug sveta* entitled "My country," praised Moscow as the modern capital of the Soviet Union, as the place where Stalin lived, and as an example to every other city and region.[58] An opening illustration in a 1947 children's book, *Around old and new Moscow*, was of the expanding territory of

---

[52] GARF, f. 9520, op. 1, d. 24, l. 85. Battlefields have been objects of tourism in other times and places. In 1900, Thomas Cook advertised tours to the sites of the Anglo-Boer War before the fighting had even concluded. David W. Lloyd, *Battlefield Tourism: Pilgrimage and the Commemoration of the Great War in Britain, Australia, and Canada, 1919–1939* (Oxford, 1998), 21.

[53] Dvornichenko, *Razvitie turizma v SSSR*, 41–42; Loginov and Rukhlov, *Istoriia razvitiia turistsko-ekskursionnogo dela*, 38. Patriotic trips to war memorials or even excursions that recreated, for example, the path of the Soviet army from Stalingrad to Berlin, were common in the 1950s and 1960s as well. See RGASPI, f. 1, op.47, d. 416, ll. 66–72; d. 551, ll. 9–11, 63–72 (Reports on youth tourism).

[54] Steinbeck, *A Russian Journal*, 125; Arkhangel'skaia, *Kak organizovat' turistskoe puteshestvie*, 3.

[55] This applies for the period at least through 1956. From a high point in 1941, the numbers of every other type of museum either stayed largely the same, or in some cases (industrial museums, museums of revolutionary history) decreased dramatically. Despite the increase in numbers of memorial museums, the greatest number of people visited historical and/or revolutionary history museums. *Kul'turnoe stroitel'stvo: Statisticheskii sbornik* (Moscow, 1956), 286–88.

[56] *Turistskie marshruty po SSSR* (Moscow, 1956), 280.

[57] GARF, f. 9520, op.1, d. 23, ll. 1, 5, 27–34, 35 (Information on Moscow tours and a lecture for excursion guides).

[58] N.N. Mikhailov, "Moia strana," *Vokrug sveta* 1 (January 1946), 10.

the city. Perched in the center of this growing city was the Kremlin, a reminder of how Moscow itself sat in the center of an expanding Soviet Union.[59]

The symbolic significance of Moscow postwar resembled the rhetoric of the 1930s when, as James von Geldern explains, Moscow had served "as a model for the state, where power radiated out from the centre to the periphery."[60] But during the Cold War, Moscow's preeminence was also explicitly comparative and international. In Stalin's published greetings on the occasion of Moscow's 800th anniversary in 1947, he emphasized the ways in which Moscow was "not only" the "center of Soviet democracy," but the capital of "all working people in the world;" not only the initiator of "new forms of everyday life for workers in the capital," but the world center of such efforts.[61] Some of this international superiority was military. *Around old and new Moscow* opened with an account of Moscow's repeated victories against legions of foreign invaders.[62] Postwar Gorky Park contained a war trophy display in which there were "German airplanes of all kinds, German tanks, German artillery, machine guns, weapon-carriers, tank-destroyers, specimens of the German equipment taken by the Soviet army."[63] Some of the superiority was cultural. A 1945 theater tour did its best to reinforce the notion of Moscow's continuing world prominence despite the destructions of war, reassuring tourists that Moscow was not only "the center of [Soviet] artistic life," but the home of "the best theater in the world."[64] (Contradictorily, the instructions for the guides of this tour also reminded them to behave actively and dramatically in order to make up for the fact that the tour did not include any live performances.)[65] Moscow's architecture was said to compare favorably to Paris, where Haussmann's admittedly grand boulevards "had made the housing situation in the city worse [for workers]."[66] The author of *Our Moscow* argued that both Moscow and Paris were better than the "capitalist city" of New York. In Moscow, as in Paris, "one could walk along the street and think, maybe dream." In New York, this "never" happens as "at every step something [unpleasant] lies in wait for you."[67]

If in *Our Moscow*, the Soviet capital was represented as more civilized because of its similarities with Paris, more often, Moscow's "modern" facilities were marketed for tourists in an implicit contrast to backward-looking Western countries whose monuments and churches were said to commemorate oppressive and exploitative events. In part, tours of a rebuilt, modern Moscow offered hope

---

[59] V. Sytin, *Po staroi i novoi Moskve: istoricheskie raiony, glavnye ulitsy i ploshad velikogo goroda* (Moscow-Leningrad, 1947), 7–8.

[60] von Geldern, "The centre and the periphery," 64.

[61] "Privetstvie I.V. Stalina k 800-letiiu Moskvy," in *Moskva poslevoennaia, 1945–1947*, 249–50.

[62] Sytin, *Po staroi i novoi Moskve*, 5–6.

[63] Steinbeck, *A Russian Journal*, 114.

[64] GARF, f. 9520, op.1, d. 23, l. 66 (Instructions for Moscow theater excursion leader).

[65] GARF, f. 9520, op.1, d. 23, l. 66.

[66] Anatolii Loginov, *Nasha Moskva* (Moscow, 1947), 111.

[67] Loginov, *Nasha Moskva*, 112.

Figure 3 Modern Moscow. *Moskva: istoriko-arkhitekturnyi ocherk* (1947).

that other cities in the Soviet Union would also recover from the devastation of war. But the focus on the "modern" was also one way of addressing a central dilemma for Soviet tourist advocates, namely that so much of the Soviet Union's historical legacy and too many of its monumental buildings were connected to the autocracy or to Orthodoxy. As Georgii Popov, head of an organizing committee for Moscow's anniversary celebrations complained about a book on Moscow architecture: "three quarters of the [historical monuments] shown are churches and only one quarter [of the monuments] have been built in our Soviet period."[68] If we don't watch out, he concluded, our anniversary celebrations will look like something they might dream up to celebrate Riazan, "and not Moscow."[69] It is no surprise, then, that a 1947 "historical-architectural" guidebook to Moscow included pictures of pre-revolutionary buildings and churches, but also cars speeding by new office buildings, "modern" double-decker buses, new housing that towered over older wooden buildings, and a sparkling clean Moscow metro system.[70] A 1954 historical guidebook was devoted similarly to the seven new "high-rise" buildings now dominating the Moscow skyline.[71] In

---

[68] "Iz stenogrammy soveshchaniia sekretarei RK VKP(b) i predsedatelei ispolkomov raionnykh sovetov g. Moskvy—o podgotovke k prazdnovaniiu 800-letiia Moskvy," in *Moskva poslevoennaia, 1945–1947*, 226.

[69] "Iz stenogrammy soveshchaniia," 225.

[70] Iu. Savitskii, *Moskva: Istoriko-arkhitekturnyi ocherk* (Moscow: 1947).

[71] N. Kuleshov and A. Pozdnev, *Vysotnye zdaniia Moskvy* (Moscow, 1954).

guidebooks and in excursions, Moscow was presented as larger than life—a full description of Moscow was said to require tens of volumes (or tens of excursions), not just one.[72]

THE CENTRAL CIRCULATORY SYSTEM

The privileged position of Moscow in the Stalinist tourist itinerary was gradually reversed in the Khrushchev era. Moscow might still be considered "Itinerary Number 1," but the periphery, not the center, became a place of renewal and transformation. In the 1954 movie *True Friends* [Vernye druz'ia], a Moscow-based bureaucrat is rescued from inertia and returned to communist consciousness through tourism, in this case a lengthy trip on a small raft with two childhood friends. Although he returns to Moscow at the end of the film, it is his adventures in the rough, and on the periphery, that transform him.[73] In late Stalinism, however, while tourism to areas outside Moscow was encouraged, it was still with a highly centralizing and containing goal in mind. In 1951, *Pravda* published the "story" of a Gorky auto-worker who wanted to spend his vacation on "Mother Volga" but struggled to find a guidebook that could help him properly decipher what he would see:

He wanted to have a complete picture of the great construction projects and so naturally wanted a guide[book]. His quest was met with surprise in the bookstores: "There is no such thing as a Volga guide."

In the library he was told: "Ah, so you are interested in books on [the] Volga? Well here is Olearius' "Description of Adam Olearius' Travels in Muscovy, Tartaria and Persia," and he was given a book written in the first half of the 17th century . . .

"I would like something . . . about our times," insisted the vacationist.

The traveler finally found a guide written in 1947, but even this proved unsatisfactory to the author of the account in *Pravda*:

About Nizhny, [the book] mentions the process of food products there in the seventeenth century as reported by Olearius but forgets to mention what splendid automobiles are produced in the city's automobile works. [The book] never mentions a Stakhanovite by name despite the fact that at the time when the book was written the great city was famous for other things besides its monasteries. It is famous today for its innovators and scientists, but the author seems to be exclusively interested in the past.

The *Pravda* article concluded with a plea for better guidebooks and travel accounts: Pushkin, Tolstoi, Gorky, Mayakovsky and others have written travel

---

[72] Sytin, *Po staroi i novoi Moskve*, 8.

[73] *Vernye druzia* [True Friends]. Director: M. Kalatozov. USSR, 1954. Katerina Clark traces the "reversal of the symbolic meaning of Moscow" in post-Stalin fiction in *The Soviet Novel: History as Ritual* 3rd Edition (Bloomington, 1981, 2000), 227–29.

books and considered this a very important literary genre because it develops love for the motherland and helps people to get to know it better.[74]

As this suggests, tourism was also a means of imaginatively and experientially integrating the Soviet body at the larger, collective level. "Travel in our country is great and purposeful; it is as beneficial as blood circulation," N. Moskvin argued in an article entitled "The Hospitality of Cities."[75] The 30th anniversary of the October Revolution was celebrated by an almost 6,000-kilometer motorcycle and automobile race around the Soviet Union. The race began and ended in Moscow, which was both the literal and figurative "heart" of the collective communist body. The thirty participants raced down to the Crimea, up through the Baltics, over to Leningrad, and back "home" to Moscow.[76] Tourism was a way in which the more "exotic" parts of the USSR were made part of the central circulatory system of the Soviet Union.

The happy cohesiveness of the Soviet Union was compared to the divisiveness of United States, which was said to be torn apart by class, race, and region. In Ilya Ehrenberg's published travel account of his trip to the United States in 1946, he emphasized ethnic and regional differences and hierarchies. A significant portion of Ehrenberg's report focused on his travels in Mississippi and Alabama and the racism he saw there.[77] Soviet citizens were reassured that such was not the case in the Soviet Union. According to *Ogonek*, although thousands of kilometers separated Kaliningrad in the far west and Vladivostok in the far east, the people of these cities lived "in a single Soviet atmosphere:" "The people of Kaliningrad and those of Vladivostok greet [the anniversary of the October Revolution] with the same happiness."[78] An article about the trip of artist N. M. Romanov to Lake Issyk-Kul' in Kirgizia's Tien Shan Mountains, explained similarly that "no matter where [Romanov] went, he was at home; everywhere was part of his Soviet homeland."[79] The "socialist homeland" even extended to Soviet ships, which provided a safe haven for those traveling to or from Western Europe or the United States. Woodworker Khemaiak Kazandzhian left the United States to "return home" as part of the "Return to the Homeland" project. As he described it to the readers of *Ogonek*, "genuine democracy was evident" from the moment he received his new Soviet citizenship on board a Soviet ship while still docked in

[74] A. Yerokhin, "Guide through Antiquity," *Pravda* (23 September 1951, 3)/*CDSP* 3:38 (November 3, 1951), 33–34.

[75] N. Moskvin, "The Hospitality of Cities," *Literaturnaia gazeta* (5 July 1951), 2/*CDSP* 3:28 (25 August 1951), 17. Moskvin became the editor in chief of *Turist* in 1966, continuing at this post until well into the 1980s.

[76] G. Shirshov, "Pervyi vsesoiuznyi motoprobeg," *Izvestiia* (15 October 1947), 2.

[77] Ilya Ehrenburg, "Ilya Ehrenberg's America," *Harper's Magazine* (December 1946), 568. The portions of Ehrenberg's travel account devoted to race relations were reprinted, and accompanied by photos from *Ebony*, in Ilya Erenburg, "Bel'ye i chernye," *Vokrug sveta* 1 (1947), 22–27.

[78] S. Gerasimov, "Na beregu Tikhogo okeana," *Ogonek* 43 (October 1947), 24.

[79] "Rodnaia sovetskaia zemlia . . ." *Ogonek* 43 (October 1947), 28.

New York.[80] "Everywhere else is good, but there is no place like home," "Peoples' Artist" Nikolai Golovanov reassured the readers of *Ogonek*.[81]

Tourism helped inscribe and integrate far-flung and/or new territories (the Baltics, parts of the Far East, Western Ukraine) with Soviet significance. Many accounts of non-Russian peoples minimized their exotic particularities. Thus Romanov was praised for describing everywhere he went "simply and naturally without being captivated by exoticism."[82] An article on the "sixteen capitals" of the Soviet Union admitted that they differed from each other geographically and culturally, but the photos chosen of each marked them as "Soviet," including images of monumental buildings in the Stalinist neo-classical style, trolleybuses, and in Baku, "a view of the city from the Kirov Park of Culture and Rest."[83] *Pravda* exclaimed similarly that Leninabad, "Tajikistan's oldest city," was no longer a "squalid feudal city" but an industrial center with streets that had been "remapped," a drama theater, Palace of Culture, and three motion-picture houses.[84] Travel accounts did sometimes describe ethnic and cultural difference, but often through photos of people in national dress.[85]

The tourist experience itself was also uniformly "Soviet" from the moment of arrival in a train station or airport. Instead of advertising regional tourist sites, local airports displayed busts of Stalin and Lenin and the same quotations from Beria or Molotov about the importance of Soviet aviation. The only difference lay in which local heroes had their photos on the walls.[86] Most cities contained a park of culture and rest, and "the benches, the long plots of flowers, the statues of Stalin and of Lenin, the commemorations in stone of the fighting that was done in this town at the time of the Revolution" varied very little.[87] Tourist bases were similarly standardized, leading one inspector after Stalin's death to complain that a Georgian tour base had nothing in it—neither pictures, dishes in the café, curtains, or carpets—of a Georgian nature.[88]

[80] Khemaiak Kazandzhian "Amerikanskaia deistvitel'nost'," *Ogonek* 2 (January 1948), 3.

[81] L. Rusanovoi, "Pervyi transatlanticheskii reis zakonchen," *Ogonek* 28 (July 1947), 11.

[82] "Rodnaia sovetskaia zemlia," 28.

[83] V.V. Pokshishevskii, "Shestnadtsat' stolits," *Vokrug sveta* 11 (November 1947), 2–11. See also the photos of factory workers, electric stations, and textile machines in Mirietta Shalinian, *Puteshestvie po sovetskoi armenii* (Moscow, 1951).

[84] "Tadzhikistan's Oldest City," *Pravda* (10 June 1949), 3/*CDSP* 1:24 (12 July 1949), 62.

[85] "V novoi Mongolii," *Ogonek* 51 (December 1947), 16; Aleksandr Gutorovich, "Na plotakh cherez vodopady karpat," *Ogonek* 45 (November 1947), 23; Vladimir Dmitrevskii, "Na turetskoi granitse," *Ogonek* 29 (July 1947), 7.

[86] Kelly, *Mirror to Russia*, 211.

[87] Steinbeck, *A Russian Journal*, 172. While the particular didactic intentions of the Soviet experience were unique, the fact that tourist sites were so similar was not true only of the Soviet Union. As Steinbeck wryly noted: "A visitor to [each] town in America is taken to see the Chamber of Commerce, the airfield, the new courthouse, the swimming pool, and the armory." Steinbeck, *A Russian Journal*, 172.

[88] GARF, f. 9520, op.1, d. 361, l. 10 (Report from a Georgian tourist base, 1958).

Despite all of this, the unfamiliar or "exotic" elements of the Caucasus or the Baltics could hardly be denied. The exiled Duc de Richelieu had been appointed governor of Odessa soon after its founding, and the city still resembled in architecture and layout a French provincial town.[89] So too with the "lush subtropical vegetation, the oleanders, the palm trees, the eucalyptus, the roses" of the Black Sea.[90] In addition, while promoting tourism to spaces of ethnic and cultural difference might have been intended as a way of taming these unpredictable places and minorities by Sovietizing their spaces for tourist consumption, it is not obvious that it had such an effect. In late Imperial Austria, to take one comparative example, Tyrolean peasants subject to the curiosity of foreigners "soon became aware of the distinctive elements of their particular culture."[91] As we will see in the following chapter on travel to Estonia, local peoples were able to capitalize on foreigners' curiosity, promoting and emphasizing regional cultural differences in order to attract visitors and, in some cases, to spite the Soviet center.

THE GOOD LIFE

The Soviet regime under Stalin did little to actually give its citizens a "good life," if by this we mean providing better living conditions and significantly more consumer goods, but it was aware of public discontent and increased expectations following the war.[92] We associate attention to public need with the Khrushchev era. What the history of tourism confirms, however, is that even in late Stalinism the state had to balance repression and terror with promises of significant material improvement. The promotion of domestic tourism was one way to remind Soviet citizens of the benefits of living in a socialist system, and to discourage comparisons with the more rapid economic recovery of the West. Readers of the Soviet press could compare newspaper accounts of domestic tourism, which emphasized the healing, life-giving properties of Soviet spaces, to newspaper accounts about America's "dirty and neglected" cities, which were said to be "full of rotting, messy, discarded goods, scraps of newspaper, cigarette butts and such waste."[93] Living in the West could put you "in constant danger of [your] health and life."[94] Living in the Soviet Union made you healthier and

---

[89] Kelly, *Mirror to Russia*, 192.

[90] Leder, *My Life in Stalinist Russia*, 307.

[91] Jill Steward, "Tourism in Late Imperial Austria: The Development of Tourist Cultures and their Associated Images of Place," in *Being Elsewhere: Tourism, Consumer Culture, and Identity in Modern Europe and North America*, ed. Shelley Baranowski and Ellen Furlough (Ann Arbor, 2001), 116.

[92] Brooks, *Thank you, Comrade Stalin!*, 196; Zubkova, *Russia after the War*, 97, 148.

[93] G. Rassadin and I. Filippov, "Gorod neboskrebov i trushchob: Pis'mo iz N'iu-Iorka," *Pravda* (7 April 1950), 4.

[94] Ye. Litoshko, "V trushchobakh N'iu-Iorka," *Pravda* (23 September 1952), 3.

Figure 4 Cruising in tropical waters. *Ogonek* (April 1948), back cover.

happier than ever.[95] Thus in 1946, when most Soviet citizens were still buried under snow, and urban dwellers were provisioned only on the basis of ration cards, *Izvestiia* described the energetic efforts of the city of Sochi to prepare its resorts for the coming summer season: "Spring comes early in Sochi. In the last few days the temperature has been 20 degrees. The mimosas are magnificent."[96]

There were some contradictions inherent in this appeal to consumption in a socialist society.[97] The dominant ideology of tourism was still as presented above: tourism as purposeful and patriotic. In *Tourism in the USSR*, Dobkovich contrasted the purposefulness of Soviet *turizm* with the wastefulness of "bourgeois tourism," which consisted only of "entertainment" and the "pursuit of the unusual," often degenerating into "roving (*brodiazhnichestvo*) without goal or thought."[98] But magazine advertisements suggested that Soviet tourists could not only travel, but do so in style. In contrast to prewar marketing, which was dry

---

[95] This is not dissimilar to the pacifying purposes of tourism in Nazi Germany. Shelley Baranowski, "Strength through Joy: Tourism and National Integration in the Third Reich," in *Being Elsewhere*, 215–16.

[96] "V gorode-kurote," *Izvestiia* (26 March 1946).

[97] On the conflict between communist morality and consumerism see Catriona Kelly, *Refining Russia: Advice Literature, Polite Culture, and Gender from Catherine to Yeltsin* (Oxford, 2001), especially 312–21.

[98] Dobkovich, *Turizm v SSSR*, 4.

and primarily informational (providing details about prices and routes), postwar advertising often made an connection between tourism, better and more comfortable forms of transportation, and the promise of a better and more modern future. A large, back-cover ad from *Ogonek* in 1948 showed a luxury liner cruising in tropical waters alongside palm trees.[99] The Ministry of Light Industry promoted its leather goods with an advertisement in *Vokrug sveta* depicting six elegant leather suitcases, including a steamer trunk, stacked on the front portico of a fine resort, with car and driver pictured below.[100] In June 1947, an *Ogonek* correspondent described special "comfortable" express trains designed specially to transport health resort vacationers to the Black Sea. The accompanying photos showed happy children, an eager male worker gazing out the train window, and two men in suits playing chess in a spacious cabin.[101] *Ogonek* also described with evident pride the opening of the first two public car dealerships in Moscow and Leningrad in 1947. That few could buy these cars, or that few cars were available to buy, is suggested by the fact that the stores sold motorcycles and bicycles as well as cars.[102] But the propaganda value was perhaps more important. This article was prominently located next to another on the ills of capitalist New York.

These advertisements and articles clearly suggest more than attention to material need *per se*. It is hard to argue, especially in the economically challenging conditions of postwar Russia, that elegant leather suitcases were a material necessity. What was being manipulated was public desire, and in a form inconsistent with the supposed goals of socialist advertising to teach "rational consumption," rather than to create insatiable consumer demand.[103] Why introduce the possibility of luxury cruises when so many were even unable to travel by train? Why contradict the otherwise determinedly Soviet portrayals of tourism found in earnest books and travel guides? In part, the answer was a pragmatic one: the state need for funds outweighed a commitment to ideological purity. Many of the large advertisements on the back covers of *Ogonek* and *Vokrug sveta* linked fantastical vacations with putting money aside in a state savings bank or buying a bond. This was likely meant to make the obligatory subscriptions to state bonds more palatable, though it must have been especially grating to those who had lost much of their life savings in the December 1947 currency reform, in which cash had to be exchanged at a rate of ten to one, and state bonds were suddenly worth

---

[99] *Ogonek* 18 (April 1948), back cover.

[100] *Vokrug sveta* 9 (September 1052), back cover.

[101] L. Mikhailov and A. Shin, "Passazhiry 'Chernomorskogo ekspressa,'" *Ogonek* 23 (June 1947), 10–11.

[102] "Prodazha avtomobilei, mototsiklov i velosipedov," *Ogonek* 41 (October 1947), 12.

[103] Encouraging "rational consumption" and the "rational use of leisure" were two of the policies specified in the 1957 recommendations of the Prague Conference of Advertising Workers of Socialist Countries. Philip Hansen, *Advertising and Socialism* (London, 1974), 29–30. On an earlier manipulation of public desire, see Catriona Kelly and Vadim Volkov, "Directed Desires," in *Constructing Russian Culture in the Age of Revolution, 1881–1940*, ed. Catriona Kelly and David Shepherd (Oxford, 1998), 293.

two-thirds less.[104] Tourism was a particularly useful form of state generated fantasy because vacations are so often something dreamed about, saved for, and seen as a future reward for work well done. But tourism was also useful precisely because of its indeterminate quality. After all, the state had chosen the draconian method of currency reform as a means to increase revenue when it might instead have increased the output of consumer goods. Tourism was a safer sort of "promise" than consumer goods in that its absence was not so easily noticed on local shelves.

Advertisements for luxurious tourist experiences were also examples of a different kind of postwar emphasis on "culture." In her analysis of middle-class values in Soviet fiction, Vera Dunham emphasizes a petit-bourgeois interest in freshly enameled elevators, newly waxed parquet floors, and hall lights "made in the shape of lilies," a fantasy of consumption of which tourism may surely be a part.[105] Katerina Clark's broader understanding of postwar "culture" (*kultura*) as "divans and bedspreads" but also as modernization ("a sewage system, paved roads") and politeness, is even more apt. In her study of the socialist realist novel, Clark argues that in the postwar period, "[most of the working population] sought to rise in the hierarchy of status and enjoy a higher standard of living, and to this end they endeavored to comport themselves as was deemed fit for a person of their standing."[106] It was an "official doctrine," Clark explains, that "the experience of World War II had brought about a radical change in Soviet man, who was now more sophisticated than he had been before."[107] Travel (even if not always tourism) has long been associated with "cultured" sophistication and status. In this case, both state and society may have been in agreement that tourism was desirable for the new, and supposedly more sophisticated, postwar citizen. Just what kind of tourism was ideal, as well as possible, remained a matter of debate.

SHORTCOMINGS AND DIFFICULTIES

The multiple articles and advertisements in newspapers and journals about tourism and health resorts were meant, in part, to reassure people that their material desires would be taken care of. What tourists found when they traveled was far from what was described in the fantastical advertisements and travel articles of late Stalinism, however. The numerous accounts of happy, health-giving tourist experiences contrasted with other less-satisfied reports of problems

[104] John Keep, *A History of the Soviet Union, 1945–1991* (Oxford, 1995, 2002), 23–24.
[105] Dunham, *In Stalin's Time*, 46. On lampshades and other consumer items, also see Julie Hessler, "Cultured Trade: The Stalinist Turn towards Consumerism," in Sheila Fitzpatrick, ed. *Stalinism: New Directions* (London, 2000), 182–209.
[106] Clark, *The Soviet Novel*, 197.
[107] Clark, *The Soviet Novel*, 198.

with transportation and with poor, dirty conditions. Advertisements for air travel did not mention that planes usually flew only during the day, that waits were often very long, and that in winter air travel often stopped altogether because of packed earth runways damaged by snow and mud.[108] As P. Ponomarev, Deputy to the Penza Province Soviet complained in a letter to *Izvestiia*:

Recently I had to make a flight from Penza to Molotov and back. At the Penza airport they refused to sell me a through ticket by way of Moscow under the pretext that one had to put in a request for it three days before the flight. I had to get a ticket to Moscow in the hope of attracting the attention of officials at the Vnukovo airport [Moscow]. But in Vnukovo the official on duty told me that since the ticket was not a through one I had to go back to the Bykovo airport. At the Bykovo airport there were no empty seats in the plane. I had to go back to Moscow and get a train ticket.[109]

G. Osipov took a train to the Crimea intending to spend his vacation at the rest home of the All-Soviet Radio Broadcast Committee. "The committee issues passes all over the Soviet Union," Osipov explained, "and persistently publicizes the merits of its rest homes." Osipov's Crimean vacation was far less than ideal, however.[110] In a letter to the editor of *Izvestiia*, I. Rudakov complained similarly about his experiences at the Lipetsky Spa: "I went there this year hoping to spend a profitable time resting and restoring my health. Alas, my hopes were not realized...The rooms are destitute of comfort, containing only rusty, dirty cots. Besides, they are used as passages to reach other rooms. This is not much of a rest."[111] Hotels were also a problem not only because some were unattractive, but because they had so few free rooms, many taken by permanent guests who lived there full time because of a lack of other housing.[112] According to N. Makarov, who hoped that the tourist movement would become a "mass movement," in 1951 trade union societies still had not done what they should to satisfy the Soviet people.[113]

While it is not surprising that conditions in Soviet tourist facilities and hotels were far from ideal just five years after the end of World War II, it is significant that these complaints were published in the central newspapers. This suggests that the central government wanted to inspire quick improvements in conditions by the directors of sanatoria and resorts, by local trade unions, and by the

---

[108] Gordy, *Visa to Moscow*, 354.

[109] Ponomarev, "Letter to the Editor," *Izvestiia* (28 June 1951), 3/*CDSP* 3:26 (11 August 1951), 28–29.

[110] G. Osipov, "Sanitary Shower," *Izvestiia* (5 August 1951)/*CDSP* 3:31 (15 September 1951), 31.

[111] I. Rudakov, "Neglected Resort," *Izvestiia* (22 August 1950), 2/*CDSP* 2:34 (7 October 1950), 53.

[112] Moskvin, "The Hospitality of Cities," 17. Such was also the case in postwar Germany, where hotel rooms were also often taken by long-term renters or military personnel. Koshar, *German Travel Cultures*, 178.

[113] Makarov, "For Mass Touring," 28.

directors of various responsible Ministries. It also suggests that the regime wanted people to think that they had popular everyday interests in mind, and that these interests were foiled by local "shortcomings and difficulties," not by a lack of state attention to the "needs of man."[114] Thus, a 1952 article in *Izvestiia* gave credit to the Soviet state's constant efforts to organize vacations for workers, which was said to demonstrate the "constant concern of the Communist Party and Soviet government for the welfare of the people." The article then went on to attribute problems in organizing summer vacations for workers to the Ministry of Public Health and the Central Council of Trade Unions, as well as local departments of health. The author of an unfavorable article about Crimean resorts listed those at fault by name (Comrades Golenishchev, Kirsanov, Slavshchik, and Muravyova) and accused them of visiting the Crimea not to "eliminate irregularities" but for a holiday.[115] But it was not just journalists who complained about conditions and service in health resorts and tourist bases. Letters to camp directors, and comments left in opinion books, show that tourists themselves were sometimes dissatisfied, most often with the food and with surly staff.[116] Archival documents show that problems with tourism were acknowledged at the upper levels. In September 1950, the Presidium of the Central Trade Union insisted that "improvements were necessary in transport, food, inventory, medicines, informational materials and advice."[117] "We are an extraordinary people," one Russian admitted to a visiting foreigner ten years later, "We can defeat the German armies but cannot organize the exits from a railway station."[118]

"WE KNOW THAT OUR JOURNEY MUST BE AND WILL BE THE HAPPIEST!"

In an article entitled "The Hospitality of Cities," Moskvin extolled the Soviet tourist experience: "Who does not dream of seeing something remarkable and extraordinary when he arrives in a strange town? The spirit of the traveler is open to new impressions and is always bright and friendly. When he arrives at the station and alights on the platform the new arrival, as it were, holds out his hand to a strange town and awaits a joyous handshake."[119] Moskvin's tourist sounds as if he was free, even encouraged, to seek out the unexpected and the mind-changing. But, as we have seen, postwar tourism was decidedly not about

---

[114] "Soviet Workers' Vacations," *Literaturnaia gazeta* (27 May 1952)/*CDSP* 4:23 (19 July 1952), 33.
[115] S. Makarov, "Behind a 'Favorable' Figure," *Trud* (24 June 1952)/*CDSP* 4:26 (9 August 1952), 32.
[116] See, for example, GARF, f. 9520, op.1, d. 54, l. 121; d. 35, ll. 49, 51, 61, 83, 89.
[117] Dvornichenko, *Razvitie turizma v SSSR*, 45–46.
[118] Wright Miller, *Russians as People* (London, 1960), 93.
[119] Moskvin, "The Hospitality of Cities."

forming "new impressions," but rather about internalizing official ones. Although Soviet travel was at times marketed as recreational, it was at heart "serious fun."[120] Published materials on tourism assumed (or assured?) that the lessons learned from tourism were always positive. Even the "obstacles and difficulties" admitted to occur on almost every trip served an important "moral" purpose leading to "collectivism, courage, will power, persistence, patience, endurance."[121] In the Stalinist worldview, there was no room for disappointment, frustration, or dislike of the Soviet self (just as there was no room for admiration of the capitalist other). As recorded in one post-trip report, student tourists walking through a peasant village responded to well-wishers: "We know that our journey must be and will be the happiest!"[122]

Still, the period of late Stalinism should not be seen as undifferentiated. There was a difference between the extraordinary Cold War rhetoric of 1947 and the year 1952 when there were tentative efforts at rapprochement with the rest of the world. It was Stalin who in 1952 publicly mentioned the idea of "peaceful coexistence of capitalism and communism," at an International Economic Conference.[123] As described in the introduction, recent work demonstrates that the period of late Stalinism was more fluid and dynamic than was previously thought, some of the reformist features of the Khrushchev years having their roots in the postwar era. Still, it took Stalin's death in March 1953 for possibilities for the expansion of international cultural exchange to reemerge. In his speech at Stalin's funeral, Georgi Malenkov spoke on behalf of peaceful coexistence with the West and affirmed his willingness to negotiate on European security issues.[124] By mid-1953, travel restrictions put in place in 1948, which had largely confined foreigners to Moscow, were now lifted, opening up most of Soviet Europe and Central Asia (if still not the Baltics and other transitional zones) to foreign tourists.[125] The number of Soviet visitors to foreign countries also slowly increased.[126] Most Soviet travelers were still delegates and cultural figures, but it was not only the elite who traveled. In April 1953, a month after Stalin's death, *The Times* wrote in surprise about a group of eighteen Soviet sailors who left their cargo of coal in Rouen to travel via coach to Paris.

---

[120] I have borrowed this very useful notion from Robert Edelman, *Serious Fun: A History of Spectator Sports in the USSR* (New York, 1993).

[121] Dobkovich, *Turizm v SSSR*, 3–4.

[122] GARF, f. 9520, op.1, d. 252, l. 13. "Get to know [your country] and fall in love with everything about it," concluded N.N. Mikhailov in *Nasha strana* (Moscow, 1945), 100.

[123] Margot Light, *The Soviet Theory of International Relations* (New York, 1988), 37–41.

[124] Hixson, *Parting the Curtain*, 88.

[125] "Russia: Easing Up," *Newsweek* (6 July 1953): 32. Marriages between foreigners also became easier. "The Rocky Road," *Time* (22 June 1953): 48.

[126] Rossiiskii gosudarstvennyi arkhiv noveishei istorii (RGANI), f. 5, op.30, d. 33, ll. 12–60 (Central Committee Documents about a delegation from the Antifascist committee of Soviet Women to the World Congress of Women in Denmark, 1953); op.17, d. 442, (Central Committee and VOKS documents about a delegation of Soviet artists to the World Festival of Youth in Bucharest, 1953).

"Hitherto, the crews of such Russian vessels calling at French ports have been kept on board or at least confined to the neighbourhood of the port," *The Times* noted. This time, however, they traveled to Paris, their sightseeing taking "much the same form as that of the many thousands of other Easter tourists in Paris: the Eiffel Tower, the Palais de Chaillot, the Invalides, the Arc de Triomphe, the Latin quarter, and Notre Dame and the Sacré Coeur. Returning to Rouen late last night, the captain said (in English) that they would cherish an unforgettable memory of their visit to Paris."[127] Something had changed, the nature of which is to be explored in the chapters that follow.

Travel can be about adventure, about self-discovery, about relaxation, about consumption. In the late Stalin period, however, it might best be seen as a "ritual of reassurance."[128] Tourism was a ritual of reassurance for the state: it offered a means of producing socialist-minded citizens focused internally on the advantages of the Soviet system. It may also have been a ritual of reassurance for Soviet citizens, in so far as tourism offered hope that life postwar would be an improvement on what they had thus far endured.

[127] "Russians in Paris: Tour by Ship's Crew," *The Times* (7 April 1953): 6.

[128] I have adopted the notion of travel as a "ritual of reassurance" from Linda Ellerbee's account of her adventures rafting on the Colorado River. "Our travels are not always the voyages of discovery we say we seek. Often they are rituals of reassurance." Linda Ellerbee, "No Shit! There I Was . . . " in *A Woman's Path: Women's Best Spiritual Travel Writing* ed. Lucy McCauley, Amy G. Carlson, and Jennifer Leo (San Francisco, 2000), 63.

2

Estonia as the Soviet "Abroad"

In September 1959, *New York Times* reporter Osgood Caruthers traveled to Tallinn, the capital of Estonia, nineteen years after it was forcibly annexed to the Soviet Union and just one month after Soviet authorities permitted foreign visitors to tour this long-closed city. It is evident, Caruthers concluded, that Tallinn and its sister cities in the Baltics, "have been brought fully into the new era of 'Communist construction.'" This can be seen, he writes, in the "housing that is going up at a hectic pace on the outskirts of every city, in the makeup of newspapers, in the uniformity of education...and in the emphasis placed on expanding heavy industry." Soviet homogenization was also visible in the cultures of daily life, "in tinned foodstuffs, shoes, ready-made clothing and other consumer goods, and even in hotel menus, all of which fit the general, uniform pattern to be found in Moscow and other cities up and down the vast reaches of the Soviet Union."[1] As the reference to hotel menus suggests, tourism—with its hotels, tourist bases, and iconic sites of touristic pilgrimage—was an example (but also, I will argue, a means) of the Sovietization of material culture in the different republics of the USSR. It was also evidence of the attempted Sovietization of behavior and experience: tourism in Estonia, as in the rest of the Soviet Union, was officially dedicated to strengthening the body, developing the mind, and to integrating the multi-ethnic populations of the Soviet Union.

Estonian tourism did not mean only this, however. If new, publicly funded, and prominently located hotels and monuments were sites of Sovietism, older spaces such as the medieval streets of Tallinn's Old Town, and popular, smaller spaces including cafés, were evidence of the persistence of an urban, Western-modulated Estonianism. These spaces were sometimes physically marginal, as suggested by Vasilii Aksenov's evocative descriptions of the dark niches and romantic crannies of Tallinn's ancient fortress walls and towers in his 1964 novel about Estonia, *It's Time, My Friend, It's Time.*[2] Sometimes, as Osgood Caruthers observed with surprise, "touches of the old era," lay cheek by jowl with

---

[1] Osgood Caruthers, "Soviet Transforms Baltic Lands, But Touches of Old Era Remain," *New York Times* (26 September 1959): 1–2. On the "deeply unified material culture" of Soviet imperialism see Stephen Kotkin, "Mongol Commonwealth? Exchange and Governance across the Post-Mongol Space," *Kritika: Explorations in Russian and Eurasian History* 8, no. 3 (Summer 2007): 520.

[2] Vasilii Aksenov, *It's Time, My Friend, It's Time*, trans. Olive Stevens (London, 1969), 9–12.

newer communist construction: "[M]uch of the individual color of [the Baltics'] ancient capitals—gems of medieval architecture and historic hubs of commerce" shows through "the enamel of the new Soviet culture." Tallinn's coffee houses serve "thick whipped cream in their coffee and an infinite variety of cakes and tarts to comparatively smartly dressed patrons." Monuments of the past, including handsome old houses lining "quaint narrow streets," were being restored.[3]

This chapter will argue that if, after Stalin, Sovietism still meant a standardized, often monumentalized, material and mass culture, it now also deliberately, if cautiously, included some of what had been previously excluded, namely the Westernized material and popular cultures of the Baltic states Estonia. Soviet citizens sometimes described the Soviet Union's western frontier—Estonia in particular—as the "Soviet abroad," the "Russian abroad," or simply as "our abroad" (*nasha zagranitsa*),[4] the formerly ideologically and geographically marginalized now re-imagined as a new type of "Soviet." I have focused on Estonia out of all the Baltic states as it was Estonia's combination of historic Western European architecture and contemporary "European" style that was most often marketed for tourists at home and abroad as a form of local difference now acceptable by virtue of Soviet political control.

STALINIZATION

In the 1940s and early 1950s, the Baltic republics were seen by authorities as a problem zone due to continuing popular hostility to the Soviet Union and to communist ideology.[5] The most brutal of Moscow's efforts to subdue the region was the arrest, forced collectivization, deportation, and massacre of Baltic citizens. Estonia lost approximately 100,000 people to deportations, executions, and guerrilla warfare during the war and in the postwar period. Terror was accompanied by other, less brutal, but also painfully transformative processes such as the immigration of approximately 200,000 non-Estonians (mostly Russians) to Estonia, the ideological Stalinization of schools and universities, and the implementation of a local communist government.[6]

---

[3] Caruthers, "Soviet Transforms Baltic Lands," 1–2.

[4] On the *Sovetskaia zagranitsa* see Monitor, "Privileges of the Soviet 'abroad,'" *The Times* (5 October 1964): 11. Also see V. Stanley Vardys, "The Role of the Baltic Republics in Soviet Society," in *The Influence of East Europe and the Soviet West on the USSR,* ed. Roman Szporluk (New York, 1975), 159, and Dmitrii Smirnov, "Sovietization, Terror and Repression in the Baltic States in the 1940s and 1950s: The Perspective of Contemporary Russian Society," in *The Sovietization of the Baltic States, 1940–1956,* ed. Olaf Mertelsmann (Tartu: KLEIO ajalookirjanduse sihtasutus, 2003), 55.

[5] Smirnov, "Sovietization, Terror and Repression in the Baltic States," 58.

[6] Romuald J. Misiunas and Rein Taagepera, *The Baltic States: Years of Dependence, 1940–1990* (London, 1993), 112–14, 129.

Stalinization also took place in the arenas of everyday life. As described in the previous chapter, Soviet tourism was seen as a means of integrating the body politic. A celebratory photo album assembled in 1950 on the occasion of Estonia's ten years as a part of the Soviet Union, dedicated two pages to pictures of travelers from "brother republics" voyaging to Estonia by train, plane, and ship.[7] If they now traveled for an explicitly political purpose, however, these Soviet voyagers followed long-established pre-revolutionary itineraries. At the turn of the century, Russian poets and artists spent their summers near the sea in the small towns dotting Estonia's coast.[8] By 1914, a popular summer retreat for tourists at Ust'-Narva (Narva-Jõesuu in Estonian) on the Baltic Sea attracted 14,000 summer tourists a year, many from the Imperial capital.[9] After Estonia gained its independence from the Russian Empire in 1918, travelers from the newly formed Soviet Union ceased coming, and Estonia advertised its attractions, as well as its growing number of hotels and resorts, to European tourists.[10] The interwar Estonian tourist organization, Eesti Turistide Ühing, also advertised tours abroad for Estonians to Paris, Helsinki, and Stockholm.[11] The tide reversed once again after Estonia's appropriation by the Soviet Union in 1940. The number of Soviet tourists was at first modest in part because Estonia's cities and towns, as well as its tourist bases, were so heavily destroyed during the war. (In contrast, Latvia's popular beach resort, Jurmala, was only moderately damaged. Vacationers began to visit it again as early as the summer of 1945.[12]) In 1947, the Estonian Tourist-Excursion Bureau asked the central authorities to help rebuild prewar tourist bases in cities, towns, and beach resorts.[13]

Not all travelers were from other republics. Authorities in Moscow also imagined tourism by Estonians to be a means of transforming local behavior and belief. Factory workers in Tallinn were encouraged to spend their free days following new tourist routes throughout the republic, including one that traced the path of the Soviet army in Estonia and a second that visited an historical monument located at the oil shale fields.[14] Traveling the path of the Red Army

[7] *Pevcheskii prazdnik Sovetskoi Estonii 1950g* (Tallinn, 1951), n.p.

[8] Sergei Isakov, *Russkie pisateli i Estoniia* (Tallinn, 1985), 183–85.

[9] Louise McReynolds, "The Prerevolutionary Russian Tourist: Commercialization in the Nineteenth Century," in *Turizm: The Russian and Soviet Tourist under Capitalism and Socialism*, ed. Anne E. Gorsuch and Diane P. Koenker (Ithaca, 2006), 38.

[10] Simo Laakkonen and Karina Vasilevska, "From a fishing resort to a leading Soviet health resort: Reminiscences of the social and environmental history of Jurmala, Latvia," unpublished paper, 2008; *Tallinn: Estlands pittoreska huvudstad,* folder "Turism Tallinnas," Tallinna Linnaarhiiv [Tallinn City Archive].

[11] "Kuhu reisida," folder "Turism Tallinnas," Tallinna Linnaarhiiv.

[12] Laakkonen and Vasilevska, "From a fishing resort to a leading Soviet health resort."

[13] Eesti Riigiarhiivi (hereafter ERA), arhiivifond R-2002, arhiivinimistu 1, säilitusühik 92, leht 29–32 (hereafter arhiivifond/arhiivinimistu/säilitusühik/leht) (Request from Estonian TEU to Central TEU, 1947).

[14] Gosudarstvennyi arkhiv Rossiiskoi Federatsii (hereafter GARF), f. 9520, op. 1, d. 80, l. 197 (On tourist work in Estonia, 1948).

Figure 5 Travelers from "brother republics" visiting Estonia. *Pevcheskii prazdnik Sovetskoi Estonii 1950g.*

was presumably intended to rewrite earlier commemorations of Estonian independence: as they pushed through Estonia in the latter years of the war, Soviet troops had demolished hundreds of local war memorials built between 1922 and 1940.[15]

Disappointingly, vacationers appeared to prefer urban excursions to Tallinn or trips to the seaside town of Pärnu to the more explicitly propagandistic routes suggested by Soviet planners.[16] The goal then was to make all excursions as ideologically correct as possible with the goal of creating a "proletarian sociospatial imaginary,"[17] as Robert Kaiser has described Sovietizing efforts in the Estonian border town of Narva. Vacationers debarking from the train in Tallinn were greeted by a statue of Stalin.[18] Tour guides in Pärnu were instructed to speak about plans for reconstructing the city as described in the recent five-year plan.[19] Unfortunately, Estonia's guides were said to be woefully ill-prepared for

[15] Marie Alice L'Heureux, "Representing Ideology, Designing Memory," in *The Sovietization of the Baltic States, 1940–1956,* ed. Olaf Mertelsmann (Tartu, 2003), 211.

[16] GARF, f. 9520, op. 1, d. 80, l. 153.

[17] Robert Kaiser and Elena Nikiforova, "The performativity of scale: the social construction of scale effects in Narva, Estonia" *Environment and Planning D: Society and Space* 26, no. 3 (2008): 546.

[18] Karin Hallas, ed. *20th Century Architecture in Tallinn: architectural guide* (Tallinn, 2000), 15–16.

[19] GARF, f. 9520, op. 1, d. 84, ll. 146, 162 (Note from director of Estonian TEU, 1948); d. 216, l. 194 (On the summer season in Tallinn's tourist base, 1952); d. 80, l. 153.

this kind of work. A 1946 proposed course plan prescribed classes for Estonian tour guides in the history of the Communist Party, the history and geography of the USSR, the economy of the Soviet Union and of foreign countries, and in Russian language and literature.[20] Guides were also given new scripts for old excursions. In the excursion, "Tallinn as a center of revolutionary activity," tour guides were to avoid talking about churches, instructed to speak instead about the growth of the proletariat in Tallinn, about Bolshevik revolutionary Mikhail Kalinin's activities in Tallinn between 1901 and 1904, about the "struggle" of Estonian workers against the Estonian bourgeoisie in the interwar period, and about the liberation of Tallinn from German forces in September 1944.[21] These topics were designed to help confer a long-term legitimacy for communism in Estonia. Russia's imperial past was also appropriated so as to better incorporate Estonia into the Soviet imaginary. A 1948 guide to Tallinn began with the story of Novgorod's aid to Estonia against Danish and German aggression in 1223.[22] Much was also made of the fact that Peter the Great had captured Tallinn in the Great Northern War (1700–21). He was proudly declared to have visited Tallinn on eleven occasions, during which time he established a park on the edge of the city, Kadriorg, and began the building of a palace. (The small cottage he lived in while the palace was being built was made into a museum that is still available for viewing).[23]

Estonia's own past was not entirely obliterated. In keeping with the principle of "nationalist in form, socialist in content," Estonian folk culture—music, dance, costume, and singing—was encouraged. Indeed, it was Soviet power that was proclaimed to have created the conditions necessary for the development of these popular traditions.[24] The celebratory photo volume described above was a reliquary of Estonia's folk traditions, specifically Tallinn's song festival, a tradition going back to 1865 that was appropriated by the Soviet regime and held every five years on the anniversary of the founding of the Estonian SSR. The volume included fifty pages of photographs of women and men in colorful national dress marching, singing, and dancing.[25] The public display of these traditions acknowledged Estonian specificities but the fact that many of the pictures also included larger-than-life portraits of an ever-present Stalin suggests

[20] ERA, f. R-2002, n. 1, s. 3, l.11 (Study plan for courses for tour guides, 1946).

[21] GARF, f. 9520, op. 1, d. 185, ll. 37–8 (Tallinn: Center of Revolutionary Activity, 1951); d. 216, l. 194.

[22] GARF, f. 9520, op. 1, d. 84, ll. 130–45 (Historical guide to the park Kadriorg, 1948). Much the same argument was made about excursions in Riga's Old Town. d. 185, ll. 3–29 (On excursions in Riga, 1951).

[23] GARF, f. 9520, op. 1, d. 84, ll. 130–45; *Peeter I maja-muuseum Tallinnas/Domik-muzei Petra 1-go v Talline* (Tallinn, 1956). The residential area nearby, established on the basis of the original servants' lodgings at the time of Peter, was a popular resort destination in the first part of the 20th century, when holiday homes were built there. Hallas, *20th Century Architecture in Tallinn*, 78.

[24] GARF, f. 9520, op. 1, d. 84, l. 144.

[25] *Pevcheskii prazdnik*, n.p.

that the Soviet authorities hoped to eradicate any ambiguity about who was now in control.

TRAVELING TO ESTONIA IN THE KHRUSHCHEV ERA

The use of tourism to cement Soviet identity continued after Stalin's death. Throughout the Soviet period, tourism remained, as described in the introduction to this volume, a purposeful pursuit as well as a pleasurable one. Thus the announcement, overheard on a sea resort on the Gulf of Finland in 1961, that "at seven o'clock that evening a beach lecture would be given on the international situation."[26] In 1960, the newspaper *Sovetskaia Estoniia* [Soviet Estonia] used the occasion of a group of Leningraders arriving for a vacation in Tallinn to extol the "increasing friendship" between Tallinn and the city of Lenin.[27] One of the most highly recommended tourist excursions in Narva in the 1960s was to the Kreenholm Textile Factory, which was praised as a leading textile manufacturing enterprise and an early site of socialist labor movement activity.[28]

Young people were a major focus of tourist efforts in Estonia, as they were throughout the Soviet Union. A "Young Tourist" badge was awarded to Pioneers who learned how to set up camp, ford streams, and administer first aid. Communist youth older than thirteen worked towards the badge "Tourist of the USSR," which required these skills and others, plus extensive travel.[29] In the late 1950s and 1960s, the Komsomol worked through sports organizations to develop mountaineering tours, recreational sports camps, and excursions to places of "revolutionary, war, and labor glory."[30] Encouraging Soviet patriotism was one of the main goals, as suggested by the name of one All-Union tourist expedition designed for youth: "My Country—the USSR." Like Soviet citizens everywhere, Estonians were also encouraged to travel to other republics. A short film from 1963 entitled "All-Union Tourist Route # 43," featured Estonian tourists climbing mountains in the Caucasus.[31] A later film showed a group of Estonian men climbing Mt. Lenin in celebration of the 25th anniversary of the Soviet Republic of Estonia.[32] Tourism was also meant to contribute to Estonians' knowledge of their own republic, its natural beauties and its local history, in

---

[26] Ronald Hingley, *Under Soviet Skins: An Untourist's Report* (London, 1961), 50.

[27] *Sovetskaia Estoniia* 158 (5 July 1960): 4.

[28] Kaiser and Nikiforova "The performativity of scale," 546. Reginald E. Zelnik, *Law and Disorder on the Narova River: The Kreenholm Strike of 1872* (Berkeley, 1995)

[29] L. M. Loginov and Iu. V. Rukhlov, *Istoriia razvitiia turistsko-ekskursionnogo dela* (Moscow, 1989), 39.

[30] Rossiiskii gosudarstvennyi arkhiv sotsial'no-politicheskoi istorii (hereafter RGASPI), f. 1, op. 47, d. 412 (Documents of the Department of Sport and Defense Work).

[31] Ringvaade Nõukogude Eesti, "Vsesouiznyi Marshrut No. 43," Eesti Filmiahiiv [Estonian Film Archive] (hereafter EFA), 1353/5 (1963).

[32] Ringvaade Nõukogude Eesti, "Estonian Alpinists around the World," EFA, 1703/2 (1970).

the process making them more "Soviet."[33] A 1956 Estonian newsreel showed happy young travelers setting up tents and preparing to camp on a local wooded lake.[34] A summer holiday program included camping, hiking, and meeting with well-known artists and sportsmen, activities designed to steer youth away from summer religious festivals.[35]

That said, Khrushchev-era Sovietization was not the same as Stalinization, something that held as true for tourism as it did for other aspects of daily life. Between 1956 and 1959, the majority of surviving Estonian deportees returned from the camps and from exile. The standard of living also improved significantly under Khrushchev. The function and privileges of native Estonians in the Estonian Communist Party increased, although the percentage of Estonians remained significantly below their percentage of the population. A cultural thaw facilitated an Estonian cultural renaissance and a degree of national self-realization in literature, theater, art, music, and radio broadcasting. "The decade after the thaw," Romuald Misiunas and Rein Taagepera argue, "was a time of clear re-emergence of national, Western-oriented and modernistic aspects of [local] culture."[36]

For the rest of the Soviet Union, Estonia was now newly imagined as a source of information about "Western" ways of being. Being Soviet in a de-Stalinizing Soviet Union meant that Soviet citizens were meant to learn—within limits— from encounters with other ways of being. If under Stalin, travel was a ritual of reassurance, under Khrushchev, travel increasingly presupposed leaving home for someplace different. Estonia was now portrayed in print and on movie screens as a space of safely Sovietized Western difference. As was true for so much of the Soviet experiment, however, ideals and reality could differ. The tourist experience in Estonia was often far from the comfortable, consumer-oriented tourism of capitalist countries; it was often decidedly "Soviet" in its offerings and accommodations. In addition, and importantly, not all travelers objected to this; some complained about the bourgeois individualism of Tallinn's touristic offerings, and insisted on the superiority of the Soviet model in which *turizm* was dedicated to the invigoration of the self and success of the socialist project. The tourist experience in Estonia is evidence of enthusiasm, but also of uncertainty, about Soviet Russia's relation to westernization as embodied by Estonia.

[33] GARF, f. 9520, op. 1, d. 658, l. 208 (Estonian Tourism Soviet resolutions, 1964).

[34] Ringvaade Nõukogude Eesti, no title, EFA, 957/5 (1956).

[35] GARF, f. 9520, op. 1, d. 453, ll. 8–9 (Report on Estonian tourism, 1964). This resembled efforts in the late 1920s, when proletarian tourists tried to take over pilgrimage paths for touristic purposes, one group of 650 tourists singing revolutionary songs colliding, for example, with a group of religious pilgrims walking the same path. I.I. Sandomirskaia, "Novaia zhizn' na marshe. Stalinskii turizm kak 'praktika puti'," *Obshestvennye nauki i sovremennost'* 4 (1994), 168, 171.

[36] Misiunas and Taagepera, *The Baltic States*, 179, 131–203; Toiva U. Raun, *Estonia and the Estonians* (Stanford, 1987), 201–19.

WEST SIDE STORY

The traveler riding the train from Leningrad to Tallinn in the late 1950s crossed a border, but one no longer marked by guards or passport controls. "Soldiers, sailors, workers and vacationers" rode "without question from place to place."[37] As enthusiastically described by travel writer Nikolai Mikhailov, a trip to Soviet Estonia was one of agricultural and industrial discovery: "We pass flax and potato fields, collective-farm livestock . . . excavators scooping up peat, digging ditches and straightening channels of streams." "Our train carries us westward along the Gulf of Finland," near the "large mines of Soviet Estonia" with their "cutter-loaders, belt conveyors and electric trains."[38] The traveler by bus or car was said to find it just as comfortably Soviet. According to the magazine *Turist*, all the vacationer had to do was follow Leningrad Avenue, which would deliver him right to the center of Estonia's capital city.[39]

Once the traveler arrived, however, the story of Soviet incorporation was more ambiguous. Estonia was unique in the Soviet Union due to its close and regular contact with the outside world, especially Finland. Estonians listened to Finnish radio broadcasts, which were comparatively easy to follow because of the similarity between the Estonian and Finnish languages.[40] Tallinn's citizens watched Finnish television, which included American and Western European shows.[41] In 1957, Tallinn mounted the first postwar Soviet production of a Brecht play, and in 1965, the first Soviet production of "West Side Story."[42] Although not the first Broadway musical to play in the Soviet Union—"My Fair Lady" played in Leningrad and Moscow in 1964—it was the edgier and more contemporary of the two.[43] Similarly, the first Soviet jazz festival was held in the university town of Tartu in 1964.[44] The cultural permissiveness of Estonia is perhaps best emblemized by the Soviet Estonian encyclopedia, which if dated a little later than

[37] Osgood Caruthers, "Estonians Proud of Individuality," *New York Times* (30 September 1959): 6.

[38] Nikolai Mikhailov, *Discovering the Soviet Union* (Moscow, 1965), 231–32.

[39] G. Einger, "Po Baltiiskomy pribrezhiu," *Turist* 7 (1966): 15.

[40] Vardys, "The Role of the Baltic Republics in Soviet Society," 65; *The Baltic States, 1940–1972: Documentary Background and Survey of Developments* (Stockholm, 1972), 110; Theodore Shabad, "'Bourgeois Estonia': Visitor Finds Soviet Republic Retains Individuality and Western Atmosphere," *New York Times* (19 May 1962): 4. The local KGB also complained that Estonian viewers far preferred Western films to Soviet ones. Eesti Riigiarhiivi Filiaali (hereafter ERAF), f.1, n.286, s. 20, l. 2 (Film-going among Estonians, 1964).

[41] On the importance of Finnish television as a source of information about the West, see the film *Disko ja tuumasõda* [Disco and Atomic War]. Director: Jaak Kilmi. Estonia, 2009.

[42] Misiunas and Taagepera, *The Baltic States*, 159.

[43] "'West Side Story' is Staged in Soviet," *New York Times* (31 December 1964), 11.

[44] Mark Allen Svede, "All You Need is Lovebeads: Latvia's Hippies Undress for Success," in *Style and Socialism: Modernity and Material Culture in Post-War Eastern Europe*. ed. David Crowley and Susan Reid (London, 2000), 195.

the period under review here—1968—is suggestive of the larger trend. The encyclopedia included entries on the Beatles, Radio Liberty, Brigitte Bardot, and Nikolai Bukharin.[45]

Much of this Western-inflected artistic culture was not available to Soviet tourists. Stanley Vardys suggests that Moscow permitted Estonians what it forbade others because of the language barrier, effectively confining Western ideas to the borders of Estonia (and the other Baltic republics) where they could be "tried out on a limited scale" before being permitted to enter the rest of the Soviet Union.[46] My research suggests, however, that while this was true for language-based experiences, the visual and material aspects of Estonia's Western-influenced culture and heritage—architecture, cafés, clothing, and consumer culture—were enthusiastically available for Soviet tourists both real and virtual. A trip to Tallinn combined Soviet-style smokestacks with the romantic church spires of the Old Town.

Tallinn's Old Town had remained largely unchanged in structure and street plan since its formation in the thirteenth to fifteenth centuries. The tall burgher houses with their heraldic crests and decorated wooden doors facing onto narrow cobbled streets resembled streets in Germany's Marburg or Denmark's Elsinore, not those of Moscow, Leningrad, or Kiev.[47] Tallinn's fifteenth-century Town Hall had been designed and constructed by German architects and craftsmen, the Town Hall Square on which it sits the commercial center for the Baltic Germans who in the sixteenth-century dominated Tallinn's economic and political life.[48] The dominant religious traditions, reflected in church architecture, were Lutheranism and Catholicism, a marked difference from the Orthodox material culture of Russia.

Many Soviet visitors were entranced by Tallinn's urban architecture, its Gothic churches, ancient walls, and round towers so different from what Soviet vacationers were used to. It was not only members of the intelligentsia who admired Tallinn's medieval beauties. In travel accounts published in the Skorokhod shoe factory newspaper about weekend bus trips to Tallinn, the tourists especially loved Laboratooriumi Street,[49] a winding lane running near the old city walls and ending at St. Olaf Church. Laboratooriumi Street was immortalized by Aksenov, who began *It's Time, My Friend, It's Time* with a description of its mysterious pleasures: "Moonlight spilt over the whole wall, and only the niches were in darkness. 1, 2, 3... there were eight niches in the fortress wall which ran along Laboratoorium Street. Bending double, a man could just squeeze into a niche, and yet, a long time ago, they had been designed for soldiers, and a soldier in armor had stood in each one, and there had been

[45] Vardys, "The Role of the Baltic Republics in Soviet Society," 167, and fn. 59.
[46] Vardys, "The Role of the Baltic Republics in Soviet Society," 167.
[47] Monitor, "Privileges of the Soviet 'abroad,'" 11.
[48] Neil Taylor, *Estonia: The Bradt Travel Guide* (Bucks, 2005), 106–107.
[49] *Skorokhodovskii rabochii*, Skorokhod factory, Leningrad (15 July 1966).

Figure 6 Tourists in the Old Town, 1962. With permission from the Estonian Film Archive.

room for his halberd too."[50] As this suggests, the scale of the Old Town—the narrowness of its streets, the small lanes that bent and turned, the houses that leaned over pedestrians walking below—distinguished Tallinn's city center from the monumentalism of Soviet spaces that were deliberately larger than life.

It had seemed possible postwar that the Old Town might not survive Stalinism. A Stalinist master plan for Tallinn's urban spaces approved in 1952 imagined a significantly altered city center.[51] Tallinn had been severely damaged in World War II, with close to half of the living space, and many historical monuments, destroyed by Soviet air raids during the counteroffensive against Nazi forces in 1944.[52] The phenomenal devastation of World War II and the enormous construction and reconstruction effort that took place in the postwar period encouraged and facilitated the standardization and Sovietization of public spaces. The rebuilt interior of the first building to be reconstructed in postwar Tallinn— the Estonia Theater—was strewn with Soviet symbols (and the restored exterior

---

[50] Aksenov, *It's Time, My Friend, It's Time,* 9.
[51] Hallas, *20th Century Architecture in Tallinn,* 24.
[52] Hallas, *20th Century Architecture in Tallinn,* 14. For images of the destruction, see photos available at the Tallinna Linnaarhiiv, including photos 2159, 2456, 2140.

captured for posterity in guidebooks, on postcards, and on boxes of matches).[53] By the 1950s, according to the authors of an architectural guide to Tallinn, Stalinist classicism was the norm, a style that combined "elements from the whole heritage of classical architecture" with "socialist content and nationalist form expressed by five-pointed stars, hammer and sickle and ethnic patterns."[54] The architectural value of Tallinn's historical monuments was acknowledged, but as something to be cataloged, not necessarily preserved. A 1947 illustrated guide to Old Tallinn and its "objects of note" described in detail the city's stone walls, tall medieval towers, and churches with their baroque spires. The many illustrations showed none of the wartime damage inflicted by Soviet air raids.[55] The book resembled a similar one produced about Moscow in 1947 by the Soviet Academy of Architecture, with images of the Kremlin's churches, of eighteenth-century buildings at Moscow State University, and of a rare remaining wooden house. This book concluded with a mock-up of the (never built) Palace of Soviets dominated by an enormous statue of Lenin, arm upraised.[56] Something similar was imagined for Tallinn. The Stalinist master plans for Tallinn included a massive House of Soviets scheduled to be built in Viru Square along the lines of Moscow's Stalinist skyscrapers and Warsaw's Palace of Culture. These plans were not realized, although the Stalinist regime did construct a new (and longstanding) building for the KGB on the northern edge of the Old Town.[57] Under Khrushchev, in contrast, architects and engineers began the slow restoration of Tallinn's architectural treasures. In his visit to Tallinn in 1959, Osgood Caruthers observed restorers repainting the medieval wooden shields of Estonian princes that adorned the walls of a fourteenth-century cathedral.[58] Significant restoration took longer. If in 1966, a state protection zone was established for the Old Town—the first in a Soviet-wide movement to protect historical sites and monuments—full restoration of Fat Margaret's Tower or of the spire of St. Nicholas Church took decades.[59]

Khrushchev-era authorities were eager to confirm Estonia's status as a Soviet republic and they used the Old Town to do so. On the 20th anniversary celebration of Soviet power in Estonia, Tallinn's medieval buildings were wrapped in Bolshevik images, the Town Hall draped in a gigantic poster of Lenin. In pictures of this event, it is obvious, however, that no number of posters could disguise the

---

[53] Hallas, *20th Century Architecture in Tallinn*, 15; *Tallinna juht. A User's Guide to Tallinn*, ed. Mari Laanemets and Andres Kurg (Tallinn, 2002), image 078 between pages 82 and 83.

[54] Hallas, *20th Century Architecture in Tallinn*, 15.

[55] Iulii Gens, *Staryi Tallin* (Tallinn, 1947).

[56] Iu. Savitskii, *Moskva: Istoriko-Arkhitekturnyi Ocherk* (Moscow, 1947).

[57] Hallas, *20th Century Architecture in Tallinn*, 15–16; 24.

[58] Osgood Caruthers, "Estonians Proud of Individuality," *New York Times* (30 September 1959): 6.

[59] *Tallinna juht. A User's Guide to Tallinn*, appendix, np. On the transformation of Russia's ancient monuments into tourist sites, see Anne Kropotkine, "Les ambiguités du Dégel: Que faire du patrimonie culturel?" *Cahiers du Monde Russe* 47, no. 1–2 (January/June 2006): 269–302.

uniquely European flavor of Tallinn's medieval center.[60] Indeed, authorities did not want to disguise Tallinn's European qualities; they used them in their marketing of Tallinn as a tourist destination for both Soviet citizens and foreign visitors. Soviet guidebooks, postcards, souvenirs, and documentary scenic films of Tallinn combined images of modernistic buildings and industrial achievements with pictures of the medieval Old Town, including stone gargoyles and ancient city walls.[61] Matchboxes, an informal form of souvenir, were decorated with colorful drawings of Tallinn's medieval towers, church spires, and crooked streets. Elegant blue metal containers of Tallinn cigarettes were embellished with pictures of the skyline of the Old Town.[62] A booklet of postcards from 1965 began with an image of Tallinn taken from the sea, church spires competing with industrial smokestacks. Next came a picture of Mustamäe, a Soviet district of Tallinn established in 1962 with the same five-story apartment blocks familiar from other Soviet cities of the Khrushchev era. In the rest of the booklet, images of Old Town's "Tall Hermann" Tower, the medieval town wall, and the Gothic arches of the Town Hall co-existed with postcards of a monument to the members of the First Congress of Estonian Trade Unions, of the Central Library at the Academy of Sciences, and of the modernist cinema "Cosmos."[63] The postcards combined a touristic focus on the historically picturesque with a more typically Soviet perspective that insisted on the value of the modern and the industrial.[64]

The Old Town was touristically important but as such it was also frozen in time, depicted as a "museum of medieval architecture"[65] largely devoid of ordinary people except for tourists. Pictures were central to the creation of touristic "place-myth" about Tallinn, fragmentary shots of corners, roof-tops, and spires evoking a place of observation and contemplation, not action.[66] In the twenty-minute scenic film *The Mosaic of Tallinn* [Tallinna mosaiik], visitors were shown quietly photographing and painting Old Town to the accompaniment of classical music. The images were static and staged, resembling postcards or a

[60] *Sovetskaia Estoniia* (19 July 1960), 4.

[61] *Turistskie marshruty po SSSR* (Moscow: Profizdat, 1958), photo following page 64.

[62] Images of the matchboxes can be found in *Tallinna juht. A User's Guide to Tallinn*, images 065–79 between pages 82 and 83, and of the cigarette case at the Museum of Occupation, Estonia, display case No.26 (last seen on June 2006).

[63] *Tallinn* (Tallinn, 1965).

[64] This was also true elsewhere. In late Imperial Austria, the industrial suburbs of Vienna were rarely shown; the focus was on the picturesque and on the "old, aristocratic [city] core." Jill Steward, "Tourism in Late Imperial Austria: The Development of Tourist Cultures and Their Associated Images of Place," in *Being Elsewhere: Tourism, Consumer Culture, and Identity in Modern Europe and North America*, ed. Shelley Baranowski and Ellen Furlough (Ann Arbor, 2001), 122.

[65] "Tallinn" in *The Cities of the USSR* (Moscow, 1966), n.p.

[66] My discussion is informed by David Crouch and Nina Lübbren, "Introduction," in *Visual Culture and Tourism*, ed. David Crouch and Nina Lübbren (Oxford: Berg, 2003), 5 and Eva Näripea, "Medieval Socialist Realism: Representations of Tallinn Old Town in Soviet Estonian Feature Films, 1969–1972," in *Koht ja Paik. Place and Location: Studies in Environmental Aesthetics and Semiotics* IV (2004).

photographic essay. Tallinn's real life, its "neglected backyards and worn-out patios behind the corners," was "censored," Eva Näripea argues.[67] Old-Town Tallinn resembled Victor Nekrasov's rhapsodic portrait of Italy's museum city, San Gimignano, from his 1962 travelogue *Both Sides of the Ocean*: "It is Dante. It is Boccaccio. It is the whistling of rapiers, the fluttering of capes, silk ladders hung down from balconies, the dying sound of lutes, the hollow steps of the night watch on the cobbled walks, the trembling flame of lanterns blown by the wind."[68] Nekrasov's literary portrait of Italy's landscape is consistent with official and popular Soviet admiration for the historical, non-living Europe of the Middle Ages and Renaissance. This admiration was of a profound, but academic and artistic kind.

Ironically, however, even as the Old Town was safely situated in an aesthetic European past, its Westernized aspects were made a part of the story of Soviet progress. Estonia was simultaneously un-Soviet and would-be Soviet. Soviet authorities, Näripea asserts, used the "ideologically conflicting heritage of the Old Town"—its European imagery—in the "service of Soviet propaganda." The Westernized aspects of Tallinn's Old Town were woven into a new story about the international texture of the Soviet Union.[69] The Western heritage of Estonia's capital city, together with a higher standard of living, as described below, was deployed to help sell the Soviet Union to both domestic and foreign tourists as successful, contemporary, picturesque (and, for foreign travelers, a good place to spend hard currency). Soviet representations of Estonia's beautiful Old Town reversed those of a prewar tourist brochure, which showed Estonia connected to Western Europe via ships and planes and with nothing except an unmarked train track connecting it to Russia.[70] Tourism, as Näripea argues, "amplified the symbolic value" of Tallinn's historical monuments for both ideological and economic needs.[71]

"WOULD YOU LIKE SOME STRAWBERRIES? WE ARE SERVING THEM WITH CREAM"

In *The Mosaic of Tallinn*, Estonia's particularities were signaled by references to the Old Town's medieval architecture, but also to consumer plenty through

---

[67] Näripea, "Medieval Socialist Realism," 130. Warsaw's Old Town was also turned postwar into "a historical city core rather than treated as a living, animated place." David Crowley, *Warsaw* (London, 2003), 51.

[68] Nekrasov, *Both Sides*, 26–27.

[69] Näripea, "Medieval Socialist Realism," 126 and Eva Näripea, "Turistlik eskapism ja sümfoonilised variatsioonid: Tallinna vanalinn vaatefilmides 1960–1970. aastail," *Kunstiteaduslikke Uurimusi* 2–3 (14) (2003): 88.

[70] *Tallinn: Estlands pittoreska huvudstad.*

[71] Näripea, "Medieval Socialist Realism," 123.

images of shiny shop windows, well-dressed women and children, plentiful food in stores, and attractive outdoor cafés.[72] The city's modern housing complexes, factories, and shopping streets were shown full of people strolling, talking, eating, consuming, and working, all to a soft jazz accompaniment.[73] An article in *Pravda* entitled "Love and beautify your city!" praised Tallinn for its exemplary (and singular) efforts at municipal improvement: "Here one's attention is attracted not only by the original architecture, but also by the cleanliness [and] order." The residents of Tallinn were reported to spend much of their free time caring for their city, planting tens of thousands of trees in the suburbs and around the premises of factories and enterprises.[74]

Cafés were a point of particular pride in Tallinn; local tourist literature bragged that "coffee conquered Tallinn in 1702, even earlier than it did Paris."[75] Cafés were found in crooked medieval houses in the Old Town and in contemporary rooms in the newer parts of town. The tiny Café Gnome, with its excellent coffee, was so small that patrons had to drink quickly, relinquishing their spots to the crowds wanting access.[76] In coffee houses such the Pegasus and the Old Thomas, on the other hand, travelers and locals alike could linger over a cup of coffee and a sweet pastry.[77] The Pegasus Café, "a favorite haunt of the Bohemian public" in the 1960s, was stylishly outfitted with a three-story spiral staircase and with wall lights laid out in geometric groupings. The presence of the café, located in the Writers' House, a postwar building constructed along one whole side of the medieval quarter, was indicated by a neon sign of a coffee cup with steam swirling upwards.[78] Drinking coffee rather than tea again distinguished the Estonians from their neighbors to the east; Estonians, like Scandinavians and Germans, were coffee drinkers, unlike the tea-drinking Russians.

For a visiting British reporter there was something "un-Soviet" about Estonian restaurants and cafés.[79] He described his surprise at a waiter's "courteous offer" of strawberries and cream at the end of one dinner. For this traveler who was "used to indifference and interminable waiting at more expensive hostelries in other parts of the Soviet Union," the "idea of service and the appetizing cuisine" was evidence of Estonia's "more prosperous and better ordered life than in Russia."[80] Russians, he argued, did not disagree: "A sophisticated Muscovite

---

[72] *Tallinna mosaiik* [The Mosaic of Tallinn] Director: Andrei Dobrovolski. Tallinnfilm, 1967, EFA, 1744/1-11.

[73] *Tallinna mosaiik.*

[74] "Love and beautify your city!" *Pravda* (6 October 1965)/*Current Digest of the Soviet Press* (hereafter *CDSP*) 17, no. 37 (1965): 40.

[75] Shabad, "'Bourgeois Estonia," 4.

[76] H. Khrabrova, "Druz'ia, muzyka i kofe," *Ogonek* 26 (21 June 1959): 21.

[77] Shabad, "'Bourgeois Estonia," 4; G. Einger, "Po Baltiiskomy pribrezhiu," *Turist* 7 (1966): 15.

[78] Hallas, *20th-Century Architecture in Tallinn*, 34–35; *Tallinn.*

[79] Monitor, "Privileges of the Soviet 'abroad,'" 11.

[80] Monitor, "Privileges of the Soviet 'abroad,'" 11.

Figure 7 Enjoying one of Tallinn's cafés. *Ogonek* (June 1959), 20.

hearing my impressions agreed. 'Oh, yes,' he said, 'you have been to what we call our *Sovetskaia zagranitsa* (our Soviet 'abroad')'."[81]

Moscow's press saw it differently. *Ogonek* admitted that the pleasures of Tallinn's cafés—their "cosiness," "aromatic coffee," twenty types of "warm pirozhki" and fifteen kinds of rolls—could be enjoyed "nowhere else but in Tallinn," but the journal located Tallinn solidly within the Soviet sphere. The best of all the coffee houses, according to *Ogonek*, was the Café "Moscow."[82] Still, if Tallinn's coffee houses were Soviet by virtue of their geopolitical location, the central press did admit that they were as of yet unique. Tallinn's cafés were a model to be adopted elsewhere in the Soviet Union, a vision of the Soviet future. "Come along with us to visit Tallinn's cafés," the article in *Ogonek* concluded, "to see how well Soviet people enjoy themselves, and open something similar in your own towns!." In a 1959 letter published in *Komsomolskaia pravda*, G. Rybakov, a Leningrad engineer, urged something similar. He described his feelings about the state of cafés in Leningrad versus those in Tallinn, saying that he felt "ashamed for my native Leningrad. We have only two or three cafés—the Northern Café, the Comfort Café—where one can sit and listen to music." "Even these are more like restaurants," Rybakov complained, "they serve alcoholic beverages and hot dishes.

[81] Monitor, "Privileges of the Soviet 'abroad,'" 11.
[82] Khrabrova, "Druz'ia, muzyka i kofe." The "Moscow" was the renamed Kultas's Café, which first opened in the 1930s. Hallas, *20th Century Architecture in Tallinn*, 39. For a more recent history of the Moscow Café in the 1980s as "the headquarters of the punkers" with their "spikes and rivets" see *Tallinna juht. A User's Guide to Tallinn*, 67.

Of course, you can order a cup of coffee too, but you feel very uncomfortable with your cup of coffee when there are copious platters and bottles on the tables around you." Instead, Rybakov asks, why can't we have "cafés [like those in Tallinn] where one could look at the latest magazines and newspapers, cafés with a television lounge; cafés with dancing...cafés where one could play chess and checkers; cafés where people of the same occupation could gather." Such cultured gathering spots were especially necessary, Rybakov argued, because Soviet citizens were soon to be given two days off a week, thus making the "problem of leisure" even more urgent than before.[83]

Rybakov's letter, unsurprisingly, reflected official policy. In 1959, the Central Committee of the Soviet Union passed a resolution encouraging the development of public eating facilities, including cafés.[84] In the USSR, as in Western Europe and North America, a cup of coffee had become a sign of the modern life. Soviet authorities could not resist adding the pedagogical to the pleasurable, however. Youth cafés (*molodezhnoe kafe*), fourteen of which were opened in Leningrad in 1963 alone, were a place to drink coffee, eat a small snack, or have a glass of wine, but were also meant to make young peoples' leisure time more cultured. Poets read their newest creations, intellectuals gave lectures about contemporary music and art.[85] The architecture of cafés, too, was purposefully contemporary, with exposed bricks and metal. Here Tallinn's cafés were again a model for the rest of the Soviet Union, adorned with the kinds of "simple unstained woods and terra-cotta lamp fixtures," that Khrushchev-era designers intended for the rest of the USSR even if they often failed to achieve the desired effect, ending up instead with the "gaudy plastics and elaborate indirect lighting" so prevalent in Russian interiors of the period.[86]

225 FOOD SHOPS: CONSUMER CULTURE

It was not only Tallinn's cafés that were seen as a model of consumer culture. "The accent is on public service in the Soviet Union these days, and all eyes are on Tallinn," Theodore Shabad, a *New York Times* journalist reported in 1965. "Whenever the talk turns to cafés, repair shops or attractive window displays, someone is likely to say, 'Now, when I was in Tallinn....'" Estonian authorities were proud of their offerings, publishing a commercial directory of eighty pages that listed "everything from taxi stands to veterinary clinics."[87] In this city of

---

[83] G. Rybakov, "In the Editor's Mail: Over a Cup of Coffee," *Komsomolskaia pravda* (5 February 1959)/*CDSP* 11, no. 8 (1959): 35.

[84] See the entry on "obshchepit" in N. Lebina, *Entsiklopedia banal'nostei. Sovetskaia povsednevnost': Kontury, simvoly, znaki* (St. Petersburg, 2006), 266.

[85] See the entry on "molodezhnoe kafe" in Lebina, *Entsiklopedia banal'nostei*, 237–38.

[86] Monitor, "Privileges of the Soviet 'abroad,'" 11.

[87] Shabad, "Bourgeois Estonia," 4.

300,000 people there were "288 stores selling manufactured goods of all kinds, 225 food shops, 245 street-corner kiosks that may offer anything from newspapers to candy, 21 pharmacies and 373 'public eating establishments.'"[88] Soviet shopper-travelers to Estonia agreed with the *New York Times* journalist, seeking out, for example, Danish-style furniture, which was made in Estonia and publicized in Soviet design magazines, but infrequently available elsewhere.[89] Even when the goods were the same in Tallinn as they were elsewhere in the USSR, the displays were often more attractive and more individualistic. Estonian shoppers listened to the sounds of Glenn Miller over department-store sound systems.[90]

Estonia's offerings were numerous only in contrast to other parts of the Soviet Union, of course. Although the Baltic republics were the most industrialized and modernized parts of the Soviet Union, stores experienced the short supplies and long lines typical of the rest of the USSR.[91] Souvenirs were among those items sometimes difficult to find. In 1962, the Estonian Soviet of Ministers instructed the relevant ministries of culture and art to produce more souvenirs reflecting local industries and talents, and more postcards of local sites.[92] (The absence of place-specific souvenirs was true throughout the Soviet Union. One Canadian traveler complained in 1960 that the souvenirs for sale in Yalta were the same he had seen in Moscow, Leningrad, Kiev and Odessa.)[93] That said, for Soviet tourists the lack of souvenirs may not have been dire. Visitors were often happiest with a bottle of the Estonian liquor *Vana Tallinn*.[94] In general, however, Soviet travelers to Estonia were looking for everyday items, for radios and other electrical equipment, and for clothing, for which the Baltics were a land of plenty in contrast to other regions of the USSR. Tourists from other parts of the Soviet Union devoured Tallinn's offerings to the detriment of the local population, whose own access to goods was, according to Misiunas and Taagepera, significantly offset by the influx of shoppers from elsewhere.[95]

Articles in the Moscow press described Tallinn "as a model of Soviet provision for the daily needs of the citizen."[96] A modern, Tallinn-inflected Sovietism was shown to inject just the right amount of contemporary style into Khrushchev-era fashions. A series of articles published in *Nedelia* in 1962 about the importance of satisfying women's consumerist demands for lingerie, hosiery, hair salons, and beautiful clothing praised Tallinn as a model. The authors compared Tallinn's

[88] Shabad, "'Bourgeois Estonia," 4.

[89] Monitor, "Privileges of the Soviet 'abroad,'" 11.

[90] Osgood Caruthers, "Estonians Proud of Individuality," *New York Times* (30 September 1959): 6; Shabad, "'Bourgeois Estonia," 4.

[91] Misiunas and Taagepera, *The Baltic States*, 186; Kevin O'Connor, *The History of the Baltic States* (Westport, CT., 2003), 136–37.

[92] ERA, f. R-2002, n. 1, s. 156, l. 30 (On improving the sale of souvenirs, 1962).

[93] Larry Wills Henderson, *A Journey to Samarkand* (Toronto, 1960), 76.

[94] Smirnov, "Sovietization, Terror and Repression in the Baltic States," 56.

[95] Misiunas and Taagepera, *The Baltic States*, 186.

[96] Shabad, "'Bourgeois Estonia," 4.

worthy attention to women's consumerist demands to the inadequacies of Moscow and Leningrad, with their "tawdry" fashions (a "riot of bad taste"), lack of hairdressing salons, and disinterested, sometimes hostile, service staff.[97] Still, although readers must have understood that it was Tallinn's Western-influenced culture that was responsible for its attention to consumer demand, Tallinn's successes are again described as Soviet ones. Estonian clothing designer Annika Burlako believed, according to the article, that the secret of beauty lay in "the ability to dress with taste and at the same time in accordance with one's character, work and pocketbook, that is, to dress rationally."[98] These ideals were fully in accordance with officially promoted standards of beauty and dress.

What it meant to dress "rationally" was not always obvious, however. Again, Tallinn served as an example. A 1961 article from *Komsomolskaia pravda* condemned Sochi's Young Communists for harassing a visiting tourist from Estonia (a member of the Tallinn City Komsomol to boot) for wearing a "bright sports shirt" produced at Tallinn's Klementi Mills. "[Decent] young men wearing brightly colored shirts and young women wearing slacks" are "hunt[ed] down" by Sochi's street patrols, *Komsomolskaia pravda* complained. Although "it was not Soviet but foreign tailors who first began to make the narrower trousers," *Komsomolskaia pravda* insisted, "it is no sin for us to borrow whatever is beneficial and comfortable from abroad" as long as it does not veer into excess. The polite Komsomol member from Tallinn in his contemporary looking "bright sports shirt" epitomized Khrushchev-era modernity, avoiding the excesses of both the too-Western—those youth who dress "so as to stand out from the crowd"—and the too-Stalinist, namely the old-fashioned, overly aggressive, and poorly dressed young guards from Sochi, who wore "plaid shirts in the dullest tones" and "heavy, unattractive shoes."[99]

THE HOTEL TALLINN

Hotels provided another opportunity to display contemporaneity. The Hotel Tallinn, built in 1963 just below the Old Town, was featured in an exuberant one-minute Estonian newsreel. The film proudly displayed the lobby, the restaurant, the kitchen, and a few of the 160 rooms. It described the hotel as a destination for visitors from around the world. "Welcome to the Hotel Tallinn!" the film exulted.[100] The Hotel Tallinn reflected a Khrushchev-era commitment

[97] "It is difficult to be beautiful," *Nedelia* (September 9–15, 1962)/*CDSP* 14, no. 38 (1962): 11–29.

[98] "It is difficult to be beautiful," 11–29.

[99] N. Kolesnikova, "Patrol in Knee Pants. Concerning a Southern City, Maturity of Views and the Young Communists' Battle for Good Taste," *Komsomolskaia pravda* (13 December 1961)/*CDSP* 12, no. 51 (1961): 19–20.

[100] Ringvaade Nõukogude Eesti, "Hotel Tallina," EFA, 1464/7 (1964).

to a new, modernist architectural style for tourist attractions and facilities. Under Stalin, Soviet hotels and sanatoria (as well as factories, post offices, party buildings, and train stations) were adorned with Roman colonnades, Greek columns, and marble arches.[101] The Kharkov train station, as wonderingly described by visitor Laurens van der Post, looked like a "Greek temple from the outside" and a "marble palace" from the inside with "a huge chandelier outshining anything in Versailles."[102] Khrushchev's campaign against Stalinist classicism encouraged in its place a contemporary, minimalist style, which was distinguished from the heavy ornateness of Stalinist architecture by its attention to simple, clean lines. If new in style, it was still standardized. The Scandinavian-influenced architecture of Khrushchev modernism, with its lack of ornamentation, extensive glass surfaces, and minimalist furnishings, could be found on new buildings everywhere, ranging from the Pioneer Palace on Moscow's Lenin Hills to the Kosmos Cinema in Tallinn.[103] Notably, it was the Hotel Tallinn that was one of the first examples of minimalist modernism in Estonia.[104] The Hotel Tallinn added to a small inventory of prewar Estonian hotels such as the Palace, the Imperial, and the Bristol. (The changing names of these hotels reflect the changing times: the Hotel de St Petersburg opened in 1850, was remained the Bristol in the mid-1930s, and after Soviet control, the Toomie. The Imperial was renamed The Balti.)[105] The Hotel Tallinn was featured in a booklet of postcards aimed at international visitors who were, in 1959, newly permitted to stay in Tallinn, Riga, and Vilnius. The hotel was a showcase of Khrushchev-era Soviet design; the postcard shows an austere five-story building with a concrete canopy.[106]

Another new style, the international style of the high-rise, was also used for Tallinn's hotels.[107] One of the most important of these was the twenty-two-story, 463-room Intourist hotel, the Viru Hotel, which though built in the late 1960s reflected the internationalist plans of the Khrushchev era in design and in dedication to tourism. Its central location, in Viru Square on the edge of Old Town, was the same spot—significantly—that had been proposed in late Stalinism for the building of a House of Soviets. The excellent views of the city center visible from its windows could be seen as a symbol of hospitality. Its verticality (unique for the time), and the fact that it was surrounded by a busy intersection

---

[101] Laurens van der Post, *Journey into Russia* (London, 1964), 115.

[102] Soviet infrastructure, on the other hand—lavatories, waiting-rooms, and restaurants—was often inadequate, with people camped out night and day in train station waiting rooms. See van der Post, *Journey into Russia*, 198.

[103] Hallas, *20th Century Architecture in Tallinn*, 97; *Tallinn* (Tallinn, 1965); Susan E. Reid, "The Pioneer Palace in the Lenin Hills, Moscow, 1962," in *Picturing Russia: Explorations in Visual Culture*, ed. Valerie Kivelson and Joan Neuberger (New Haven, 2008), 218–23.

[104] *Tallinna juht. A User's Guide to Tallinn*, Appendix, np.

[105] Tallinna Linnaarhiiv, f. R-98, n. 1, s. 106, ll. 1, 19 (Tallinn hotel inventory, 1956) and private correspondence with Andres Kurg.

[106] *Tallinn*.

[107] Hallas, *20th Century Architecture in Tallinn*, 16–17.

Figure 8 Hotel Tallinn.

and a parking lot, suggest that it was also intended to isolate foreigners.[108] In most ways, as the authors of a recent travelers' guidebook to Tallinn's Soviet past explain, the high-rise hotel "was nothing that extraordinary; similar giants of that decade can be found in at least every capital of the other former Soviet republics."[109] What was different, they argue, was that it was built by the Finns, which meant that the hotel could boast of "foreign quality and rare finishing materials" unlike those found in any other Intourist hotel.[110] In the Viru Hotel, as in so many other arenas of Tallinn's material culture and daily life, the Soviet and the "foreign" combined in a mix unique to Estonia.

---

[108] Hallas, *20th Century Architecture in Tallinn*, 44–45.
[109] *Tallinna juht. A User's Guide to Tallinn*, 101.
[110] *Tallinna juht. A User's Guide to Tallinn*, 101.

EAST SIDE STORY

If some of the new infrastructure was directed towards satisfying the domestic traveler, much of it was dedicated to pleasing the increasing numbers of international tourists. In 1965, a regular boat service between Helsinki and Tallinn was reestablished, enabling close to 10,000 mostly Finnish travelers to visit Tallinn that year, and almost twice as many the year following, on trips ranging from three and a half hours to four days.[111] Ordinary Soviet tourists, in contrast, did not have access to either the Hotel Tallinn or the Viru Hotel. First-class Soviet hotels did not often admit private citizens off the street. Instead, in Tallinn as in Moscow, rooms were allocated through official channels for official business.[112] Price was not the issue; Soviet hotel prices were set very low, aimed at domestic users traveling on official business who were granted a per diem of just two rubles sixty kopecks, a price unchanged since 1953.[113] Foreign visitors, on the other hand, often received preference at first-class hotels because they paid in hard currency.[114] At the Hotel Viru, both bookings and payments were arranged through Moscow, with the profits remaining in Moscow; hotel workers themselves did not know how much the rooms cost. The only thing that was managed locally was profit from hotel restaurants.[115]

If Soviet hotels were promoted both domestically and internationally as sites of Soviet modernity, the fact that first-class hotels were populated by foreigners meant that they were also, contradictorily, portrayed as dangerous places of bourgeois decadence. The Soviet press described speculators and "parasites" swarming around hotels "planning their deals and spending their free hours and filthy lucre."[116] Aksenov's depiction of a Tallinn hotel in *It's Time, My Friend, It's Time* is a good example of the ambiguous positioning of the Soviet hotel, and perhaps particularly the Estonian hotel, as a site of both enviable modernity and dangerous cosmopolitanism, of Estonia as both un-Soviet and über-Soviet. In the beginning of the novel, the young hero Valya stumbles out of

---

[111] Unlike Soviet tourists, Finnish visitors were not impressed by the consumer goods available for sale in Estonia, criticizing the lack of variety, the long lines, and the low quality of items for sale. Nor were they interested in guided tours of Tallinn's attractions. They came to see their relatives, to enjoy the city's inexpensive bars and restaurants, and to make a little money on the black market. ERA f. R-2288, n. 2-c, s. 4, l. 19; s. 9, ll. 10–13; s. 12, ll. 1–4; s. 19, ll. 1–23 (On work with foreign tourists, 1965, 1966). Only the capital cities of the Baltics were open to foreign visitors.

[112] George Feifer, *Russia Close-up* (London, 1973), p. 119.

[113] As journalist George Feifer explained in reference to Moscow's Rossia Hotel, because "both giver and taker of the per diem allowance [were] *au fond* state agencies," hotels could not charge anything in great excess of the allowance. Feifer, *Russia Close-up*, 110–11.

[114] Feifer, *Russia Close-up*, 111. On the money made from foreign tourists in Tallinn's hotels, see ERA, f. R2288, n. 2-c, s. 19, l. 32.

[115] Correspondence with Andres Kurg as informed by Sakari Nupponen, *Viru hotell ja tema aeg* (Tallinn, 2007).

[116] Feifer, *Russia Close-up*, 120.

the Old Town searching for his estranged wife, a Soviet film star: "At last I could see the sixteen-storied hotel through a veil of branches. All of the ground floor was lit up; light poured from the windows of the restaurant and the café. I walked to the edge of the pavement, leant against the barrier, and took stock. A queue waiting for taxis swayed drunkenly. Cars came up, one after the other. Ten paces from the public laboratory, the old Jewish shoe-cleaner slept in his chair."[117] The hotel is where Tanya, together with the film's producer and director, live, enjoy life, and drink champagne. It is the opposite of the rough-hewed, but indubitably Soviet housing of the Siberian community where Valya and Tanya happily end up at the conclusion of the story.

Soviet tourists did stay in hotels, but they were rarely like the Viru Hotel or even the Hotel Tallinn. The problem of adequate lodging for Soviet tourists was acute in Tallinn and a source of frequent, outraged complaint. Tourists were supposed to be housed in the Tallinn *turbaza*, located in a set of three former merchant houses dating from the fourteenth century on Pikk Street, in the Old Town. Today, the buildings house one of Tallinn's finest, and most expensive, small hotels (the website of which acknowledges with pride the guild elders and burgomasters who once lived there, but says nothing about its incarnation as a Soviet *turbaza*).[118] In 1960, however, the conditions were far less pleasant. Preserved even at that time as an architectural monument, the building had plenty of character but, according to many tourists, not much charm. They complained about the "damp, gloomy, and dark" conditions.[119] Still, due to Tallinn's desirability, the *turbaza* was frequently overflowing, especially in summer when travelers from all over the USSR eager to visit Tallinn sometimes arrived a few days earlier than scheduled hoping to snag one of just over 100 spots, a number increased from just thirty spaces in 1955.[120] Excess tourists were housed in the dormitories, in school classrooms, and in some instances, in the sleeping wagon of a train parked at Tallinn's train station.[121] Those without showers, which presumably meant everyone not in the *turbaza*, were instructed to visit a nearby *bania*, ten minutes away from the center by foot, or three stops by tram.[122]

Adding to the challenges were the number of tourists who traveled independently to Estonia, i.e. without a prearranged voucher for accommodations and food. "Wild tourism" was increasingly common throughout the Soviet Union as

[117] Aksenov, *It's Time, My Friend, It's Time*, 17–18.

[118] See "history" at www.threesistershotel.com.

[119] ERA, f. R2002, n. 1, s. 211, l. 4 (Description of Tallinn tour base, 1964); s. 257, l. 16.

[120] ERA, f. R-2002, n. 1, s. 257, l. 50 (Estonian response to a letter of complaint, 1966); ERA, f. R-2002, n. 1, s. 156, l. 47 (Lack of accommodations in Tallinn, 1962); s. 92, l. 35 (Tallinn tourbase, 1955).

[121] ERA, f. R-2002, n. 1, s. 200, l. 9 (Serious deficiencies in the organization of tourist excursions to Moscow, 1964); s. 257, l. 16 (Letter of complaint); GARF f. 9520, op. 1, d. 631, l. 202 (Plenum report, 1964).

[122] ERA, f. R-2002, n. 1, s. 257, l. 15.

the gap between propaganda about tourism (promises about which encouraged more and more citizens to travel) and a continuing lack of adequate infrastructure expanded. In 1951, when domestic tourism was still occasional, especially to areas only recently incorporated into the USSR, all of the tourists staying in Tallinn's *turbaza* traveled there independently.[123] In 1957, forty-four percent of all tourists to Estonia still traveled independently—without a voucher—in contrast to seventeen percent to the Black Sea Coast, seven percent to the North Caucasus, and just four percent to Moscow.[124] Some vacationers snagged a place in the city center. Others camped on the nearby beach of Pirita where from their vantage point they could see Tallinn's suburbs, again a very different landscape than that found elsewhere in the USSR, with their compact, one- or two-story little homes, some accompanied by a one-car garage.[125] Vacationers arrived by bus and by train, and some via hitchhiking, which was especially popular in the Baltics. Hitchhiking enthusiasts purchased special coupons for two rubles that were then good for 1,000 km of travel with willing truck drivers, private vehicles still being rare. The "Autostop" movement first took off among Leningraders in 1961, with Estonia among the most popular of places to hitchhike, as the roads were in good condition and the destinations desirable and close together.[126]

It should be noted that the poor lodging in Tallinn was not exceptional; grumbling about tourist bases and hotels was common throughout the Soviet Union. Vladivostok's Cheliushkin Hotel was despairingly said in one report to have "streams of water pouring from the ceiling" that "flooded the beds when it rained."[127] Especially evident in Estonia, however, was a conflict between the rough and ready *turizm* encouraged and practiced in many other parts of the USSR, and the desire for relaxing and entertaining leisure and culture associated with Tallinn. In response to complaints from tourists that they had to eat in a cafeteria that was a ten- to fifteen-minute walk from their dormitory, officials of the Estonian Tourism Soviet grumpily responded that "this should not be a hardship for *tourists*," defending their inadequacies on the dubious grounds that Soviet *turisti* should not expect (or even desire) the same luxuries as bourgeois tourists.[128]

[123] ERA, f. R-2002, n. 1, s. 40, l. 114 (Tallinn tour base).

[124] GARF, f. 9520, op. 1, d. 357, l. 1 (On fulfilling plans for tourist-excursion work, 1957); f. 9520, op. 1, d. 313, ll. 12–13 (On fulfilling plans for tourist-excursion work, 1955).

[125] Out of 350,000 square meters of housing constructed in Estonia between 1959 and 1963, almost a third of it was private. Monitor, "Privileges of the Soviet 'abroad,'" 11.

[126] Open Society Archive, Budapest (hereafter HU OSA), Records of Radio Free Europe/Radio Liberty Research Institute (hereafter RFE/RL), Soviet Red Archives, 1953–1994, Old Code Subject Files, 300-80-1, Container 1048, (Hitchhiking in the USSR, 1962); GARF, f. 9520, op., 1, d. 453, ll. 2–3; Theodore Shabad, "Hitchhikers get a lift in Soviet," *New York Times* (12 April 1964): 10; entry on "avtostop" in Lebina, *Entsiklopedia banal'nostei*, 40–41; Lewis H. Siegelbaum, *Cars for Comrades: The Life of the Soviet Automobile* (Ithaca, 2008), 219.

[127] Yu. Lvov, "Brief and to the Point," *Izvestiia* (June 16, 1953), 2/*CDSP* 5:24 (July 26, 1953), 41.

[128] ERA, f. R-2002, n.1, s. 257, l. 15. Italics in original.

That said, efforts were made in Estonia, as they were elsewhere, both to improve tourist conditions and to encourage more people to participate. A 1962 *perestroika* of tourism work throughout the Soviet Union led to a reorganizing of central, republic-level, and regional tourist-excursion bureaus into central, republic-level, and regional tourism soviets headed by a new Central Soviet for Tourism. Local tourist clubs were established in order to encourage the mass development of tourism.[129] In Estonia this led, according to archival sources, to an increase in local tourist activity from some 36,600 people involved in tourist work in 1963 to almost double that in 1964.[130] In 1963, the number of tourist camps rose to forty-eight as compared to just eleven in 1962.[131] Tourist clubs were established in Estonian cities, including Tallinn and Tartu, but also in smaller towns such as the border town of Valga and the heavily industrialized, oil-shale town of Kohtla-Järve. Clubs were meant to meet two times a week in order to provide guidance and material assistance to tourists, including tents, sleeping bags, and coupons for hitchhiking. New and better tourist materials in Russian and in Estonian were (supposed to be) prepared including brochures about Estonia's revolutionary history, pamphlets about Estonia's architectural and natural attractions, maps showing Estonian auto-tourism routes, and shiny new stickers advertising Estonia's major cities to be stuck on cars and suitcases.[132] Challenges continued. Estonian authorities still complained, in terms very like those of their compatriots in other Soviet republics, about deficiencies among tourist club cadres, about the lack of seminars and other educational materials for instructors and guides, and about a lack of monetary and material resources.[133]

For all of its problems, urban Tallinn had the advantages of the exotic pleasures of the Old Town, of cafés, and of shops. The tourist experience of rural Estonia was without these advantages. Few of the most common tourist routes in Estonia included significant time at the seashore. Although located on the Baltic Sea, Tallinn was a largely urban destination: most of the seaside was closed to nonmilitary uses, with the exception of the suburb Pirita and the Ferry Terminal.[134] Significant time at the beach appears to have been largely reserved for those visiting sanatoria and health resorts at Pärnu and Haapsalu, a reason why many who visited there ostensibly for medical cures were in fact enjoying vacations.[135] In contrast, common tourist itineraries like Travel Route #21 included three days in Tallinn (with city excursions, a visit to Peter the Great's

---

[129] GARF, f. 9520, op. 1, d. 447, ll. 1–33; Loginov and Rukhlov, *Istoriia razvitiia turistsko-ekskursionnogo dela,* 41; V.A. Kvatal'nov and V.K. Fedorchenko, *Orbity 'sputnika:' iz istorii molodezhnogo turizma* (Kiev, 1987), p. 26.

[130] GARF, f. 9520, op. 1, d. 658, l. 207.

[131] GARF, f. 9520, op. 1, d. 543, ll. 1–18 (On tourism work in Estonia, 1964); d. 678, l. 98.

[132] GARF, f. 9520, op. 1, d. 572, l. 20 (Plan for tourist literature, 1963–1965).

[133] GARF, f. 9520, op. 1, d. 658, ll. 202–204. See, for example, complaints about tourist bases in the Far East, d. 680, l. 69 (Report by an inspector to the Amur region, 1964).

[134] *Tallinna juht. A User's Guide to Tallinn,* appendix, n.p.

[135] GARF, f. 9593, op. 8, d. 50, ll. 3–31 (Report on medical activities of sanatoria, 1960).

house in Kadriorg Park, and a brief trip to the sea at Pirita), six days at the "picturesque" Aegviidu-Neliiärve tourist base located on the banks of a small lake fifty-six kilometers from Tallinn, and three days at the university town of Tartu, with a visit to the library, a tour of the main university buildings, and a trip to the ethnographic museum.[136] Vacationers could also travel from Leningrad to Tallinn for three- to five-day bus trips, tour eight locations in Estonia for eighteen days as part of Trip Route #84, or visit Estonia as part of a larger and longer tour of the Baltics.

For vacationers to Aegviidu-Neliiärve, a common destination on most tourist routes in Estonia, the Estonian tourist experience was decidedly different than for visitors to Tallinn. The tourist base was located in the woods on the shores of a lake. The fashionable wooden building at the heart of the tourist base was constructed before the war in the period of Estonian independence; Soviet authorities later added tents designed to hold up to 260 people. Vacationers were invited to swim, fish in the lake, hike, visit a nearby collective farm, and participate in evening talent shows.[137] At one evening event in 1953, an Estonian tourist played the accordion and sang songs about peace while another vacationer read out loud a poem by Mayakovsky. Nearby excursions included bus trips to collective farms.[138]

The photographic record shows a beautiful building and a peaceful lake. Many travelers to Aegviidu-Neliiärve complained about the offerings, however. They objected that there was nothing interesting to do, that the tents were wet, the weather cold, the toilets unsanitary, the camp workers "rude," and the food "boring." There was no bus in which to take excursions, the guides were "uneducated," the director of the *turbaza* was drunk. To be sure, some reported that they had a good time, and that the excursions and the food were satisfactory. Other tourist bases, one at Kubija for example, were said to be very good. In general, however, it appears that rural Estonia was not the "window to the west" that some Soviet tourists might have hoped for.[139]

Contradictorily, for some travelers, the tourist experience in either rural or urban Estonia was not Soviet enough. Estonia was too independent, inadequately aware of its subordinate status in a Soviet empire. "[The guides in Tallinn] didn't show us a single museum or exhibit about the achievements of the national economy of the Estonian Republic, about the maturing of Soviet Estonia," one group of Russian tourists loudly protested in an angry letter to the Central Tourist-Excursion Bureau in 1960.[140] Evident in some cases were ethnic tensions

[136] ERA, f. R-2002, n.1, s. 128, ll. 6–7 (Description of Tourist Route No.21, 1959).

[137] *Turistskie marshruty po SSSR* (Moscow, 1958), 65–66.

[138] ERA, f. R-2002, n. 1, s. 211, l. 6 (Description of tourist base, 1964); GARF, f. 9520, op. 1, d. 262, ll. 144–46 (Report of Estonian TEU, 1953).

[139] GARF, f. 9520, op. 1, d. 572, l. 44 (Estonian Tourism Soviet resolution, 1963); ERA, f. R-2002, n.1, s.155, ll. 8, 15 (Letters); s. 211, l.145: s. 257, ll. 80–81 (Letter, 1967).

[140] ERA. f. R-2002, n.1, s. 142, l. 56 (Letter, 1960).

Figure 9 The tourist base at Aegviidu-Nelijärve. With permission from the Estonian Film Archive.

between Russians and Estonians. A Russian-speaking tourist from Kiev was incensed at the poor treatment she and other Russian speakers received from guides and bus drivers in their mixed group of Estonian and Russian tourists. A thirty-minute description of touristic sites in Estonian was said to have been distilled to just a few words in Russian: "On the right a burial mound, on the left a lake." It was horrible," she wrote, "horrible that after twenty-three years of Soviet power in Estonia, during which nothing but good has been done for this small country" we should suffer such treatment. "Why such ingratitude?" she demanded.[141] As this outrage suggests, language was a point of particular frustration for some non-Estonian visitors. The persistence of Estonian and apparent unwillingness to use Russian was seen to be emblematic of an unhealthy amount of nationalist pride.

Some tourists hoped for a different kind of Sovietism. They expected, and missed, the carefully scheduled group activities common to most Soviet tourist experiences, grumbling that they were left too often to their own devices, especially while in Tallinn. As one tourist bitterly wrote home: "In the evening we went on the first excursion around the city's historical sites. It lasted for two hours. That was it. Nothing more. Today there is only a trip to Kadriorg Park,

[141] ERA, f. R-2002, n.1, s. 257, ll. 82–84.

and tomorrow to the beach. This is, of course, very little to do each day, it takes up only one half to two hours. The rest of the time there is absolutely nothing to do. The people at the *turbaza* told us to enjoy their restaurants and cafés. All of the tourists rebelled, swearing at the administration. . . . it is beyond belief."[142] For this tourist, and for others whose frustrations are preserved in the archives, the leisurely and self-directed pleasures of Tallinn's cafés and street life were not what they understood tourism to be. They had paid for scheduled group activities. That self-directed pleasures were considered by some to be anti-Soviet is suggested by the protests of one group of Moscow tourists who especially objected to their leisurely, open-ended schedule in Tallinn given that it was the anniversary of the Russian Revolution.[143] For these representatives of Soviet centralism, Estonia's pleasures came a distant second to celebrations of history, collectivity, and power.

"WE ESTONIANS FIND IT DIFFICULT TO LEARN RUSSIAN"

In 1964, a British reporter described a series of "clearly unfriendly remarks" in Lithuanian directed at a "busload of loud Russian tourists armed with cameras piled into the Baroque church of Peter and Paul in Vilnius during Mass."[144] Hostility to visiting tourists was not peculiar to the Baltics, of course. A Russian woman who lived in Anapa as a child remembered the crowds of vacationers in her area in the summer, so many that it could be hard to shop for basic food items. "There were sometimes too many people and too much noise, in cafés and in restaurants," she complained. "There was always a huge line for milk, for bread in the summer time."[145] On the other hand, some benefited from the tourist traffic, making extra money by renting rooms for the summer to vacationers.[146] Relationships were not always hostile. A Latvian woman remembered with fondness a family from Moscow that stayed with her every year.[147]

Still, like the Lithuanians described above, Estonians sometimes resented visiting Russians and preferred foreign tourists to Soviet ones. In the early 1960s, when a visiting English journalist was told that there was no room available in a restaurant in which vacant seats were "plainly visible," a Russian

---

[142] ERA, f. R-2002, n. 1, s. 257, l. 16 (Letter, n.d.).

[143] ERA, f. R-2002, n. 1, s. 200, l. 9 (On serious deficiencies in the organization of a tourism excursion to Tallinn, 1964).

[144] Monitor, "Regionalism replaces Nationalism," *The Times* (6 October 1964): 13.

[145] With thanks to Catriona Kelly for this material from her interview project, CKQ-Ox-03, PF 10 (B), 6–7 (June 2003).

[146] Ronald Hingley, *Under Soviet Skins: An Untourist's Report* (London, 1961), pp. 43–44.

[147] Laakkonen and Vasilevska, "From a fishing resort to a leading Soviet health resort." Also see Christian Noack, "Coping with the Tourist: Planned and 'Wild' Mass Tourism on the Soviet Black Sea Coast," in Gorsuch and Koenker, *Turizm.*

official candidly told him: "You must have been taken for a Russian—you should talk to them in English."[148] The Russian hero of *It's Time, My Friend, It's Time* resorts to English when seeking to weasel a bottle of vodka out of a tired Estonian shop assistant closing her doors: "'O meesees, geev me pleez uwon battel vodka." It worked: "She looked at me intently, and then she let me in, taking me for a foreigner."[149] This was not exclusive to Estonia; foreign tourists were better treated than Soviet ones at almost every level of the tourist experience. But while the decent restaurants, better-quality Intourist hotels, and special hard-currency stores provided for foreigners were, for the Soviet state, a means of pulling in hard currency, the preference for Western tourists in Estonia may have had nationalist significance. In response to a *New York Times* reporter, who in 1962 asked about the relative absence of Russian heard on the streets or in shops, an Estonian woman explained frankly: "We Estonians find it difficult to learn Russian. German and English are so much easier."[150]

Indeed, the history of Soviet tourism in Estonia suggests ways in which the peoples of the Soviet republics may have used tourism as a means to push the boundaries of permissible nationalism. Historians of capitalist tourism have described local peoples emphasizing regional cultural differences in order to attract visitors and money.[151] The development of tourism in turn-of-the-century Austria, as described by Jill Steward, was part of the making of regional and ethnic identities that contributed to the "forces of fragmentation that threatened the Habsburg Empire."[152] Opportunities for regional independence were more circumscribed in the Soviet Union and in the socialist periphery, where so many aspects of tourism, and of life, were heavily centralized and controlled. But they did exist. In the mid-1960s, a Lithuanian tourist club at the Kaunas Polytechnic Institute used tourism to "research the customs and traditions of [Lithuania], safeguard monuments of national freedom, and to refute efforts of Sovietization and loss of national identity." One of the (unwritten) purposes of the tourist club was "to be physically and spiritually prepared for the struggle for the freedom and independence of the Motherland Lithuania."[153]

Tallinn's Old Town is a good example of such activity in Estonia. If the Old Town was an example of "staged authenticity"—photographs, postcards, and guidebooks used to mark certain touristic sites as both important and

[148] Monitor, "Regionalism," 13.
[149] Aksenov, *It's Time, My Friend, It's Time*, 14.
[150] Shabad, "'Bourgeois Estonia," 4.
[151] Steward, "Tourism in Late Imperial Austria," 116.
[152] Steward, "Tourism in Late Imperial Austria," 108.
[153] Egidija Ramanauskaité, "Lithuanian Youth Culture versus Soviet Culture," in *The Baltic Countries under Occupation: Soviet and Nazi Rule, 1939–1991*, ed. Anu Mai Kõll (Stockholm, vol. 23, 2003), 325. On the ways in which tourism threatened (and supported) the agenda of socialist authorities in the GDR, see Scott Moranda, "East German Tourist Itineraries: In Search of a Common Destination," in Gorsuch and Koenker, *Turizm*.

"authentic"[154]—it was also a site of resistance to Soviet staging. The Old Town was an example of what Tim Edensor has called an "iconic site" and was vulnerable to multiple meanings. In his work on tourism in India, Edensor explores the ways in which iconic sites can be "claimed by competing groups, who invest them with meanings which are attuned to their political project or identity." Foreign tourists are told stories in books and by guides about the Taj Mahal similar to those found in the stories of British colonial administrators and travelers. For Indian visitors, on the other hand, "the site represents national pride."[155] Such was the case too for Warsaw's Old Town, which although rebuilt as a cleaned-up and Sovietized "simulation" of an historic center, was one of the rare places in Warsaw where "residues of the [pre-communist] past" were found.[156] Tallinn's Old Town offered a similar alternative to the uniformity of new residential and industrial districts. It also became, as described by Eva Näripea, "a tactical means of opposing the imported Soviet culture." Heritage protection for the Old Town was one of the few means for Estonians to stress their "belonging" to the "European, not Russian cultural realm" and by this to emphasize "the unjust and violent intervention of the Soviet occupation."[157]

ESTONIANIZATION

In *Imperial Eyes: Travel Writing and Transculturation*, Mary-Louise Pratt describes the imperial metropole's "obsessive need to present and re-present its peripheries and others continually to itself." For the eighteenth-century European explorers that Pratt analyzes, travel writing was "heavily organized in the service of that imperative."[158] In the twentieth-century Soviet Union, tourism was similarly organized. As described in this chapter, tourism was intended to help incorporate Estonia's regional distinctions into the larger whole of the Soviet Union. In contrast to the eighteenth-century European imperial powers, however, which were "habitually blind[ed] to the ways in which the periphery determin[ed] the metropolis,"[159] Khrushchev-era authorities consciously deployed images of a Estonian periphery in order to shape the Soviet center. The Baltic borderlands, Estonia especially, held a unique place in the Soviet imagination. In contrast to the Soviet Union's southern republics—the Caucasus in particular—that were often imagined as a "zone of violence," a closed space,

---

[154] On staged authenticity see Dean MacCannell, *The Tourist: A New History of the Leisure Class* (Berkeley, 1976, 1999), chp 5.
[155] Tim Edensor, *National Identity, Popular Culture and Everyday Life* (Oxford, 2002), 46–47.
[156] Crowley, *Warsaw*, 54.
[157] Näripea, "Medieval Socialist Realism," 131, 133–34.
[158] Mary Louise Pratt, *Imperial Eyes: Travel Writing and Transculturation* (London, 1992), 6.
[159] Pratt, *Imperial Eyes*, 6.

or, at best, as a "parallel civilization,"[160] the Baltics were frequently imagined as superior by virtue of their association with the "West." This was risky. "Hybridity breeds uncertainty," Deborah Cherry writes about the French relationship to its Algerian colony. Images and understandings "forged in an encounter between several cultures and patched together from disparate, dissident elements" often "jostle against, add to, replace, and break into one another," evidence of the "uncertainty and precariousness" of authority.[161] In the mid-1960s, Alexander Solzhenitsyn wrote *The Gulag Archipelago* while hiding amongst friends in Estonia: "For the first time in my life I felt as if I were safely abroad, as though I had left the USSR."[162]

In the Khrushchev era these risks were minimal, however. The appropriation of Estonia's "Western" qualities appeared to many to be a positive change following the xenophobia of late Stalinism. In addition, importantly, there was no doubt as to who held power. The term *nasha zagranitsa* [our abroad] implied a wistful longing for the abroad, but also a proprietorial colonialism. Admiration of Estonia was justified by virtue of the republic's location within Soviet borders: medieval European architecture, comfortable cafés, and Finnish-built hotels were burnished to a fine Soviet sheen. It was the center that determined which aspects of Estonian Westernism would be enthusiastically adopted, magnanimously tolerated, or forcibly suppressed. It was the center that appropriated Estonia's resources—the oil shale fields but also the Old Town—not Estonia that willingly bestowed them. And it was travelers from the center who confirmed their sovereignty, even in their admiration, by publishing their accounts of travel to the margins in the central press.

The relationship remained a fraught one, however. We have seen that some were made uncomfortable by the ambiguity implicit in official admiration for the cultured pleasures of the periphery. The Russian–Estonian relationship overturned the more usual narrative in which the larger, dominant power is the giver of civilization to the smaller, subordinate one. The success, or not, of the Sovietization of Estonia—of which tourism was a part—is a matter of ongoing historiographical and political debate. Less contentious, perhaps, is that the Soviet Union was never successfully Estonianized. Russia and the other republics largely failed to incorporate the kinds of Estonian difference imagined by some to be superior. Although Estonia moved from being a region to be suspicious about to a region to admire, it remained a Soviet abroad, on the periphery, rather than at the center, of what it meant to be Soviet.

---

[160] Bruce Grant, *The Captive and the Gift: Cultural Histories of Sovereignty in Russia and the Caucasus* (Ithaca, 2009), chp 6.

[161] Deborah Cherry, "Algeria In and Out of the Frame: Visuality and Cultural Tourism in the Nineteenth Century," in Crouch and Lübbren, *Visual Culture and Tourism*, 55–56.

[162] Alexander Solzhenitsyn, *Invisible Allies* (Washington, D.C., 1997), 54.

3

"What Kind of Friendship is this?:" Tourism to Eastern Europe

In 1956, the residents of the city of Gorky heard the following announcement on the local radio: "At the height of the summer season every worker in Gorky dreams of how best to spend his holiday. One dreams of going to the Crimea, another of the southern shores of the Caucasus, and the third, choosing a different path for his vacation, goes on a tourist trip abroad."[1] The most common destination for the Soviet international tourist was Eastern Europe. Although front-page stories in the press described with evident pride the number of new and exotic countries Soviet citizens could now visit—Iceland, Luxembourg, and Thailand to mention only a few—many of these destinations were open only to members of the Soviet political, scientific, athletic, and cultural elite.[2] In contrast, Eastern Europe was now available to a new category of tourists who, if still largely from the middle rather than from below, nonetheless represented a sea change in regime attitudes toward international travel.

This chapter explores what Soviet tourists to East European countries saw, bought, and how they behaved. It uses the practices of sightseeing and consumption to explore the relationship between Soviet center and East European periphery. Soviet tourists traveling to capitalist countries were expected to defend themselves and the reputation of the Soviet Union against clearly articulated differences. But what about Eastern European countries: were tourists traveling to an other, or to an extension of the Soviet self? In the official imagination, as presented in published travel accounts, Eastern Europe was often presented as a younger and less advanced version of the Soviet self. Tourists to this Eastern Europe were going back in time to visit an imaginary, younger, historical self—an imagining that was used to help justify Soviet domination over the socialist periphery. Questions of production and consumption, however, made this relationship more complex. East European countries—especially East Germany, Poland, and Czechoslovakia—were also portrayed as the acceptably socialist

---

[1] Gosudarstvennyi arkhiv Rossiiskoi Federatsii (hereafter GARF), f. 9520, op. 1, d. 316, l. 48 (Text for a radio announcement on tourist trips abroad).

[2] "International Tourism on a New Scale," *Literaturnaia gazeta* 1 (6 May 1958) / *Current Digest of the Soviet Press* (hereafter *CDSP*) 10, no. 18 (11 June 1958): 25.

home of modernist style. Indeed, Soviet modernization depended on exchange between the USSR and its satellites, including the import of Czech furniture and design and East German plastics.[3] Tourists to this Eastern Europe were moving forward in time to experience what the Soviet Union might become in the future.[4]

"TRAVEL TO FOREIGN COUNTRIES...
HOW EASY IT HAS BECOME!"[5]

In a 1956 interview, a resident of Kamchatka in the Soviet Far East described his surprise at ending up on a trip abroad. "It happened completely unexpectedly. We were talking with a woman who turned out to work for the regional trade union council. Talk turned to tourist trips. She told us that going on a tourist trip really was possible."[6] The Kamchatka interviewee was not the only person to question the idea of travel abroad after so many years of living behind closed borders. Indeed, this interview was part of a 1956 propaganda campaign launched because the new plan for international tourism had not been fulfilled the year previous. Pressured by a 1956 resolution from the Presidium of the Central Trade Union, which outlined "deficiencies in trade union efforts to organize tourist travel abroad," local trade union officials anxiously wrote to central authorities to describe their efforts to increase international tourism.[7] To encourage people to sign up for travel abroad, those returning from trips were asked to describe their voyage by giving lectures, making a contribution to wall

---

[3] Susan E. Reid and David Crowley, ed. *Style and Socialism: Modernity and Material Culture in Post-War Eastern Europe* (Oxford, 2000).

[4] Throughout this chapter I use the term "Eastern Europe" to refer to those countries between the USSR and Western Europe that were within the Soviet sphere of influence. Soviet sources on international tourism, in contrast, most often referred to these nations as "socialist countries" in pointed contrast to tourism to and from "capitalist countries." Soviet tourism to both Poland and England was considered tourism to a "foreign" (*zarubezhnyi*) country, but Poland was less foreign by virtue of being "socialist." I have not adopted this terminology in part for the practical reason that by the end of the Khrushchev era, socialist tourism also included travel to places like Cuba, but also because I do not want to privilege the ideological definition of this liminal space. By so often referring to "Eastern Europe" as a whole, however, I recognize that I risk (as do so many Soviet sources) suggesting that it was a single entity. In reality, of course, the construction of an Eastern European and/or socialist identity was a gradual and often contested process. On the term "Eastern Europe" in the context of travel writing see Alex Drace-Francis, "Towards a Natural History of East European Travel Writing," in *Under Eastern Eyes: A Comparative Introduction to East European Travel Writing on Europe,* ed. Wendy Bracewell and Alex Drace-Francis (Budapest, 2008).

[5] This quotation is from the journalist interviewing the Khamchatka tourist described below. GARF, f. 9520, op. 1, d. 316, ll.128–129 (Transcript of broadcast, 1956).

[6] GARF, f. 9520, op. 1, d. 316, l. 129.

[7] GARF, f. 9520, op. 1, d. 316, l. 41(On fulfilling the plan for sending Soviet tourists abroad, Gorky Oblast, 1956); d. 317, l. 16 (On fulfilling the plan for travel abroad, Leningrad Oblast, 1956); l. 1 (On fulfilling the plan for sending Soviet tourists abroad, Lvov Oblast, 1956) and V.V. Dvornichenko, *Vazvitie turizma v SSSR (1917–1983 gg)* (Moscow, 1985), 49.

newspapers, participating in photo exhibitions, or speaking on radio and television.[8] Local newspapers ran frequent articles about travel such as one by *Sovetskaia Moldavia* that described the tours to socialist countries now available: "After June 1 [1956] another twelve-day tour of Romania will be organized. The program of the trip includes historical, architectural and artistic monuments of Bucharest, visits to industrial enterprises and the Museum of the Romanian Workers' Party."[9]

Some people may have had to be convinced that they now really could apply to travel abroad. Others may have been hesitant because of the cumbersome application process, more cumbersome even than the already strenuous process for applying for a voucher for travel to a domestic health resort. For the first few years following the introduction of international tourism, problems with the application process were said to be a main reason why the plan for the number of tourists was not fulfilled.[10] The primary responsibility for organizing these processes and for sending people abroad fell to Intourist and to the Tourist Excursion Bureau (Turistsko-ekskursionnoe upravlenie, hereafter TEU) of the All-Union Central Council of Trade Unions (Vsesoiuznyi tsentral'nyi sovet professional'nykh soiuzov, hereafter VTsSPS).[11] The Komsomol's Bureau of International Youth Tourism, or "Sputnik" as it was commonly called, was responsible for youth. The TEU worked on a local and regional level with people hoping to travel abroad.[12] Intourist and Sputnik, together with the Ministry of Foreign Affairs, were responsible for establishing monthly and yearly plans for travel abroad and for deciding where tourist groups would travel and what their itineraries would be.[13] They established connections with foreign travel agencies who provided for tourists when abroad. Together with the Ministry of Foreign Affairs, they processed the forms necessary for vacationers to get foreign visas as well as the "foreign" passports required of most citizens leaving the Soviet

---

[8] GARF, f. 9520, op. 1, d. 468, l. 75 (Report to a TEU meeting on foreign travel, 1961).

[9] "Foreign Tourism," *Sovetskaia Moldavia* (5 May 1956) / *CDSP* 8, no. 19 (20 June 1956): 23.

[10] See, for example, GARF, f. 9520, op. 1, d. 317, l. 24.

[11] Rossiiskii gosudarstvennyi arkhiv noveishei istorii (hereafter RGANI), f. 5, op. 30, d. 113, l. 35. On border controls, see Andrea Chandler, *Institutions of Isolation: Border Controls in the Soviet Union and Its Successor States, 1917–1993* (Montreal and Kingston, 1998).

[12] In 1962, the VTsSPS reorganized the central and local level TEU organizations into central and local level tourism councils. G.P. Dolzhenko, *Istoriia turizma v dorevoliutsionnoi Rossii i SSSR* (Rostov, 1988), 121.

[13] GARF, f. 9612, op. 1, d. 387, ll. 1–6, 16 (Materials about the activities of Intourist, 1957). Also see the list of meetings, exchange agreements with foreign countries, and advertising, all to be arranged by Sputnik, in Rossiiskii gosudarstvennyi arkhiv sotsial'no-politicheskoi istorii (hereafter RGASPI), f. m-5, op. 1, d. 2, ll. 168–73 (Preparing for the summer tourist season, 1959). In 1955, Intourist was accepted as a member of the International Union of Official Travel Organizations (IUOTO); in 1956 it became a member of the Regional Commission on Tourism in Europe. V.M. Ankudinov, "Vazhnaia forma mezhdunarodnogo obsheniia," *Mezhdunarodnaia zhizn'* 12 (1959): 96.

Union.[14] Intourist and Sputnik were also responsible for the many small but important details of travel; they oversaw, for example, the manufacture of suitcase labels and of small gifts and lapel pins to be given away as gifts.[15]

Applicants for tourism abroad had to navigate multiple levels of bureaucracy. Adults generally applied first to the trade union of their factory or institution, while young people applied to their local or city level Komsomol organization.[16] After a preliminary vetting, applications were forwarded to one of the nine *oblast* party committees (*obkoms*) where commissions made up of obkom, trade union, and KGB representatives determined who would travel abroad, paying special attention, as will be described in Chapter Four, to those who hoped to be accepted for travel to capitalist countries.[17] Once a group of lucky people had been accepted for travel abroad, a list of these people, together with character assessments, completed questionnaires, medical forms, and adequate payment to be deposited in Intourist's State Bank account, were forwarded to Intourist.[18] Screening by those at the top was not always done to the satisfaction of those at the bottom, as in the case of the Moscow Oblast Council, which in 1957 complained that their recommendations were not always taken into account: people whom they thought deserving and appropriate were not always given permission to travel.[19]

Many of those who traveled in the 1950s and 1960s via Intourist were from privileged groups who often, but not always, had party connections: academics, cultural workers, factory managers, party functionaries.[20] Of the tens of thousands of tourists traveling via Intourist to Eastern Europe in 1961, about 40 percent were party members and 17 percent were workers.[21] In part, it was that these individuals were most likely to satisfy the political and educational requirements necessary for travel abroad.[22] It was also that Soviet intellectuals based in the large urban centers of Moscow and Leningrad were, especially at first, most likely to want to travel abroad, being more likely to have maintained a

[14] GARF, f. 9612, op. 1, d. 387, ll. 1–6, 16 (Intourist activities, 1957); Ankudinov, "Vazhnaia forma," 97.

[15] RGASPI, f. m-5, op. 1, d. 2, l. 73 (Preparing for the summer tourist season, 1959).

[16] "Tickets for Tourist Travel," *Leningradskaia pravda* (16 May) /*CDSP* 8, no. 20 (27 June 1956): 35; GARF, f. 9612, op. 1, d. 387, ll. 25–26 (Foreign documents for Soviet citizens traveling abroad); RGANI, f. 5, op. 30, d. 161, l. 35 (Meeting of the Cheliabinsk KPSS obkom, 1956); RGASPI, f. m-5, op. 1, d. 52, ll. 21–22 (Instructions on formulating documents and sending young tourists abroad). Rural applicants applied through their regional Soviet of workers' deputies.

[17] RGANI, f. 5, op. 30, d. 161, ll. 35–36; GARF, f. 9520, op. 1, d. 390, l. 28 (Report on Uzbek tourism, 1961).

[18] GARF, f. 9612, op. 1, d. 387, ll. 1, 34.

[19] GARF, f. 9520, op. 1, d. 317, l. 34 (Sending people abroad, 1957).

[20] See, for example, the discussions in GARF, f. 9520, op. 1, d. 390, l. 34 (Report at a conference on international tourism, 1961); d. 319, l. 86 (Report from the Moscow City Soviet Trade Union at a conference on international tourism, 1961).

[21] GARF. f. 9520, op. 1, d. 432, ll. 3, 29.

[22] RGANI, f. 5, op. 30, d. 161, l. 35.

sense of cultural connection to non-Soviet spaces. At issue was also the problem of *blat* (connections). Making one's way through the snares and thickets of applying for travel abroad demanded the kind of well-massaged and careful connections with party and trade union hierarchies that privileged elites were most likely to have. It sometimes happened that after receiving information about possible trips abroad, local trade union and party organizations themselves chose the "best comrades" for trips abroad, encouraging them to assemble the necessary documents.[23] Finally, intellectual workers and high-ranking people also had more vacation time. In 1958, approximately 40 percent of workers still had just twelve days of vacation a year, which meant that many were unable to go on Intourist tourist trips abroad as these trips were often more than two weeks long.[24]

The application process was meant to ensure that applicants had a proper "political understanding and moral quality," a good relationship to work, and were active participants "in social life."[25] To assist in the evaluation process, Soviet citizens wishing to travel abroad to socialist countries had to fill out three pages of forms about their personal and work history, including information about nationality, party membership, previous trips abroad, and foreign languages.[26] Knowing how to fill out these forms—how to reproduce the kind of authoritative language required—was necessary but not sufficient. Applicants also had to provide a character reference (*kharakteristika*) from their place of work or the secretary of their local party organization.[27] Recommendations typically summarized information about education, nationality, profession, party or Komsomol membership, and described individual achievements and qualities. G., captain of a fishing boat, party member since 1961, and "Hero of Socialist Labor" since 1963, was recommended for travel abroad by the Secretary of the Sakhalin Oblast Komsomol.[28] P., a scientific worker in the department of applied hydrodynamics, was recommended for a trip abroad due to her energetic work habits in areas of societal importance, her "active participation" in public work (including a position as editor of the institute's wall newspaper), her party membership, and her position as secretary for ideological work in the party bureau of the Institute of Hydrodynamics.[29]

The complexities of the application process meant that approval sometimes took a very long time, especially as trade union organizations often lacked staff

[23] GARF, f. 9520, op. 1, d. 390, l. 27.

[24] GARF, f. 9520, op. 1, d. 438, l. 101 (TEU meeting on international travel, 1961). Some 12 percent of Soviet citizens, presumably the higher ranking ones, had more than twice as many vacation days: over 24 days a year. *Trud v SSSR: Statisticheskii sbornik* (Moscow, 1988), 106.

[25] GARF, f. 9612, op. 1, d. 387, l. 33 (Requirements for travel abroad, 1957).

[26] GARF, f. 9612, op. 1, d. 387, ll. 34, 37–39 (Copies of questionnaires for travel abroad, 1957).

[27] GARF, f. 9520, op. 1, d. 316, l. 46 (Requirements for travel abroad, 1956); d. 391, ll. 104–105 (TEU conference on foreign tourism, 1961).

[28] RGASPI, f. m-5, op. 1, d. 222, l. 72 (Character reference).

[29] RGASPI, f. m-5, op. 1, d. 222, l. 78 (Character reference).

adequately trained in the processes required to send people abroad.[30] A group of tourists from Astrakhan Oblast who applied to go on a trip to Czechoslovakia in August 1956 were forced to delay their trip until late September because it took almost two months for their documents to be approved. Nine out of the fifteen tourists were unable to travel because of the change in dates.[31] Aleksandr Konstantinov described the complex and obstructive process he went through to go to Eastern Europe in 1969: "You had to have six copies of your character recommendation, a document called a *kharakteristika*, signed by the Komsomol leader, trade union leader, and head of the Communist Party at the institute, strictly in that order, and then by the same three officials at the university, using carbon paper. They could make you return even if there was a single typing mistake, and the next party meeting might be a month and a half away. Incidentally, this was their 'Catch 22.' They rarely turned down people directly, but made you return over and over again for signatures."[32] As a delegate from the Moscow Oblast Soviet to a Tourist Excursion Bureau conference admitted, there were many people who wanted to travel, but "we don't take all who so desire."[33]

For some people, the cost of travel abroad could also be a deterrent. In 1959, an excursion to Romania cost 1122 rubles.[34] In contrast, a twenty-day trip to Sochi was half that, just 560 rubles. For only 360 rubles, one could enjoy a ten-day sightseeing trip in and around Moscow.[35] When the average wage of a Soviet industrial worker in 1955 was just over 9,500 rubles a year, a trip to Eastern Europe could be well out of reach: a sixth of his or her annual salary.[36] Although the real wages of Soviet workers increased in the late 1950s due to an increase in the minimum wage in 1957 and to a relatively constant cost of living, such that people then had slightly more discretionary income to spend on luxuries such as tourism, it was still not enough for some ordinary workers.[37] Money was even more of a problem for agricultural workers. Intellectual workers, on the other hand, may not have made more money in salary than industrial workers— historian Evgeniia Gutnova complained about the extraordinary cost of trips abroad in her memoir[38]—but they could earn more money on the side from consulting, tutoring, and renting extra rooms. All of this meant that on Intourist

[30] GARF, f. 9520, op.1, d. 316, l. 42 (Report, Gorky Oblast Council of Trade Unions, 1957).
[31] GARF, f. 9520, op.1, d. 316, l. 13 (On the work of sending Soviet tourists abroad, Astrakhan Oblast, 1956).
[32] Donald J. Raleigh, ed. and trans., *Russia's Sputnik Generation: Soviet Baby Boomers Talk about Their Lives* (Bloomington, 2006), 52.
[33] GARF, f. 9520, op. 1, d. 391, l. 145.
[34] GARF, f. 9520, op. 1, d. 430, l. 187.
[35] *Turistskie marshruty po SSSR* (Moscow, 1958), 340, 342, 348.
[36] On the average wage see Abram Bergson, *The Real National Income of Soviet Russia Since 1928* (Cambridge, 1961), 422.
[37] Janet G. Chapman, *Real Wages in Soviet Russia since 1928* (Cambridge, MA., 1963), 181–84.
[38] E.V. Gutnova, *Perezhitoe* (Moscow, 2001), 315.

organized trips the number of *rabochie* was still far fewer than some authorities desired.[39]

While Intourist recognized the importance of travel to Eastern Europe and hoped to facilitate travel by workers, it was unwilling to lower its prices. In 1961, the chairman of Intourist, V.M. Ankudinov argued that the existing prices for travel via Intourist to Eastern Europe were already at the margin of what Intourist could afford.[40] This appears to be true, although financial details are scattered and sketchy. Intourist did not control the cost of travel once the vacationer arrived abroad; East European countries charged different prices for hosting Soviet visitors. In 1955, the Polish travel agency, Orbis, charged 800 rubles for a first-class hotel and food for a ten-day trip, while Bulgaria asked for just 420 rubles. Romania required 600 rubles for bus transport, in contrast to Hungary's travel agency, Ibusz, which charged just 160 rubles.[41] Intourist passed this price difference on to the traveler.[42]

Trade unions did want more working-class people to travel. To facilitate this, in 1956 the VTsSPS began offering a stipend of 70 percent toward the cost of a tourist trip abroad for low-paid factory and white-collar workers.[43] In 1958 the TEU developed non-hard-currency exchanges between Soviet trade union organizations and the trade unions of East European countries. By 1961, there were exchanges with ten different countries, the vast majority of which were to health resorts and rest homes. By traveling to a sanatorium or rest home for relaxation and healing rather going on a tourist excursion, participants were more likely to be allowed to travel for longer due to medical necessity.[44] Still, although the purported goal of these exchanges was to increase the number of workers who traveled abroad, in 1961 the TEU complained that these trips still "looked more like Intourist groups than trade union groups."[45] Archival records for individual trips suggest that on some exchanges, between 50 and 85 percent of the participants sent to Eastern Europe each year on non-hard-currency exchanges for were

---

[39] In 1963, authorities tried to "fix" this problem by arguing that the percentage of workers was 43 percent if one included engineers and technical workers. GARF, f. 9520, op. 1, d. 613, l. 18. Also see RGASPI, f. m-5, op. 1, d. 52, l. 33 (Composition of Soviet youth groups abroad, 1959); d. 158, l. 119 (On international tourist trips of Soviet youth from 1958–1962).

[40] GARF, f. 9520, op. 1, d. 391, l. 169 (Report to TEU conference on international travel, 1961).

[41] RGANI, f. 5, op. 30, d. 113, l. 48 (Costs of tourist trips, 1955).

[42] RGANI, f. 5, op. 30, d. 113, l. 66.

[43] RGANI, f. 5, op. 30, d. 225, l. 53. The tourists also received a 50 percent discount on train travel within the Soviet Union. GARF, f. 9520, op. 1, d. 391, l. 4.

[44] The perceived difference between tourism and travel for healing and relaxation is clear from the 1955 resolution on travel, the draft version of which recommended that Soviet citizens traveling to sanatoria and rest homes in socialist countries be allowed to travel on internal Soviet passports. This proposal does not appear to have been accepted in 1955. RGANI, f. 5, op. 30, d. 113, l. 35.

[45] GARF, f. 9520, op. 1, d. 391, l. 20.

workers,[46] but even on trips that were designated for workers and other low paid travelers, non-workers appear to have taken advantage of a system extraordinarily dependent on personal connection and *blat*. This should not surprise us. The same was true for domestic travel to Soviet health resorts when, as Diane Koenker has argued, "even early on in the Soviet period, connections mattered more than medical status or social position" for travel to sanatoria.[47]

That said, these processes did get easier. In 1956, when the idea of holiday travel abroad was brand-new, the bureaucratic process for tourism resembled that for the diplomat, foreign trade expert, or cultural figure applying to go abroad in the 1920s for work-related reasons.[48] Not so ten years later. In 1965, Czechoslovakia and the USSR abolished the need for visas for travel between the two countries.[49] A year later, for the first time, about 1,000 people traveled independently, i.e. without a group, on vacation to Bulgaria, Romania, Hungary, Czechoslovakia, Poland, the GDR, and Yugoslavia.[50] Beginning in 1967, the international year of the tourist as declared by the United Nations, Soviet tourists were allowed to travel to most Eastern Europe countries using only their internal

[46] GARF, f. 9520, op. 1, d. 422, ll. 3, 4, 6, 54 (On Soviet tourists traveling for healing and to socialist countries in 1961); op. 2, d. 26, l. 17 (On sending Soviet workers abroad for healing and rest to socialist countries, 1964); op. 1, d. 613, l. 18 (Information on international tourism, 1963); d. 432, l. 4; d. 691, ll. 144–46 (On fulfilling the plan for rest, 1963).

[47] Diane P. Koenker, "Mending the Human Motor," unpublished paper, 30.

[48] Michael David-Fox, "From Illusory 'Society' to Intellectual 'Public': VOKS, International Travel and Party-Intelligentsia Relations in the Interwar Period," *Contemporary European History* 11, no. 1 (2002): 16–22. In early Soviet period (1919), passport control was under the direction of the People's Commissariat for Foreign Affairs which issued "passports only to persons whose departure raised no objection from the People's Commissariat of Internal and Military Affairs." Beginning in May 1922, application to travel had to be accompanied by a certificate from the GPU "attesting to the absence of legal obstacles to travel." In 1922, control over passports was transferred to Commissariat of Internal Affairs. In June 1925, the USSR issued a Statute on Entering and Leaving the USSR describing three kinds of passports—diplomatic, service, and civil. There were severe penalties for leaving the USSR without permission. Under Khrushchev there was more travel abroad, although the Khrushchev Statue on Exit and Entry from June 1959 was on paper very little different from the 1925 laws, differing "only in its updated terminology, increased detail, and a revised categorization of passport-holders." Mervyn Matthews, *The Passport Society: Controlling Movement in Russia and the USSR* (Boulder, 1993), 22–26, 37.

[49] Open Society Archive, Budapest (hereafter HU OSA), Records of Radio Free Europe/Radio Liberty Research Institute (hereafter RFE/RL RI), Soviet Red Archives, 1953–1994, Old Code Subject Files, 300-80-1, Container 1049.

[50] GARF, f. 9520, op. 2, d. 28, l. 33 (Trip report, Bulgaria, 1966); "Our Hospitality," *Izvestiia* (28 October, 1966), 4/*CDSP* 43 (1966): 22. In 1964 Soviet travel authorities began to consider permitting individuals to travel to socialist countries as independent tourists without preset itineraries (something that was already happening between some east European countries). Erokin agreed that such a topic should be discussed as part of a larger question about developing various new forms of tourism, but reminded delegates that individual tourism was not yet part of current practice. GARF, f. 9520, op. 1, d. 613, ll. 5–7 (Conference of travel bureaus of socialist countries, GDR, 1964).

Soviet passports and a tourist voucher.[51] More and more people traveled to Eastern Europe, millions each year by the 1970s.

"OUR HEART IS ONE HEART"

Before they left, tourists learned about what they might see and were told how to feel about it. The many accounts about travel to Eastern Europe published in Soviet journals and magazines emphasized East Europeans' warm welcome of their Soviet visitors. "As soon as they found out we were Russian, the Czechs tried to do something nice for us," gushed one young traveler on a 1962 Soviet radio broadcast.[52] Sunny travel essays about tourist trips to Bulgaria were popular versions of more conventional political articles on Soviet–Bulgarian friendship, the Soviet tourist receiving in miniaturized form the wildly enthusiastic greeting Khrushchev was said to have received on his 1962 trip to Bulgaria.[53] Soviet military and economic domination were re-presented as liberation and rebuilding, resembling what Mary Louise Pratt has called "anti-conquest," or the strategies "whereby [colonial powers] seek to secure their innocence in the same moment as they assert [their] hegemony."[54] Pratt is referring to travel and travel writing by the European bourgeoisie, but Soviet travel writing served much the same purpose, instructing citizens at home and abroad that the Soviet domination of Eastern Europe was both necessary and just. Tourism, together with published travel accounts about these trips, helped make Eastern Europe part of a new Soviet imaginary at home, reinforcing authoritative discourses about Soviet superiority and control.[55] "It's good that Russians again come to our country!" one Yugoslav citizen was said to have exclaimed in a 1956 travel account published in *Ogonek*: "Your country is big, powerful, while ours is small. But our heart is one heart, a Slavic heart, and between us, as between brothers, there is much that is shared, much as if between relations."[56] In trip accounts, Eastern European regimes were presented not as other but as younger, less advanced, versions of the Soviet Union. Indeed, so much was said to be shared

---

[51] HU OSA, RFE/RL RI, Soviet Red Archives, 1953–1994, Old Code Subject Files, 300-80-1, Container 1049; Jill. A. Lion, "Long Distance Passenger Travel in the Soviet Union," Paper prepared for the Research Program on Problems of International Communication and Security, MIT, October, 1967, 54.

[52] RGASPI, f. m-5, op. 1, d. 95, l. 43 (Radio broadcast transcript, 1962).

[53] "Dobre doshli, sovetskie brat'ia!" *Ogonek* 21 (May 1962): 2–3.

[54] Mary Louise Pratt, *Imperial Eyes: Travel Writing and Transculturation* (New York, 1992), 7.

[55] In this, Soviet tourism resembled British travel to India, for which travel books, exhibitions, newspaper reports, and children's literature helped create a "British imaginary" of India. Inderpal Grewal, *Home and Harem: Nation, Gender, Empire and the Cultures of Travel* (Durham, 1996), 87.

[56] K. Cherevkov, "Leningradtsy v Iugoslavii," *Ogonek* 25 (June 1956): 4. That this rhetoric was only partially successful is suggested by the fact that in 1960 Yugoslavia was still classified as a capitalist country in a list of Komsomol travel destinations. RGASPI, f. 5, op. 1, d. 52, l. 9. (Composition of Soviet youth tourists to capitalist countries in 1960.)

Figure 10 Soviet tourists presenting a pin to their Czech guide. *Puteshestvie v stranu druzei* (Leningrad, 1959), 76.

between the older and wiser Soviet Union and its less experienced "blood brother" that any significant expression of ethnic or national difference was often eclipsed in favor of a shared socialist/working class identity.[57] It is as if these accounts were trying to soften not only existing differences that might get in the way of fraternal relations, but also older ethnic (Slav/non-Slav) and historical differences and perceptions.

Many aspects of the East European tourist experience confirmed conservative discourses about a friendly and fraternal, but fundamentally unequal, relationship between a superior imperial metropolis and the socialist periphery. Most important in this respect was the role of the Red Army in "liberating" the region from Nazi occupation. The obligatory excursion in Berlin was to Treptower

[57] The term "blood brother" was a common one. See, for example, M. Bugaeva, "U Bolgarskikh druzhei," *Ogonek* 37 (1956): 5. Sometimes they were "sisters" as in the case of the book, *Sestra moia Bulgariia* (Moscow, 1963).

Park, where travelers visited the Soviet War Memorial, an enormous twelve-meter-high statue of a soldier cradling a baby in his arms while crushing a swastika underfoot. "The most impressive place we saw [on our tour of Berlin] was the monument to the Soviet war," effused one Komsomol trip leader. "Our delegates brought wreathes to lay down. Around us we saw many, many tourists, Germans from other cities, children. They were all coming to pay honor, to respect and grieve."[58] Tourism was also used to confirm the industrial prowess of a modern Soviet Union, as exemplified by large construction projects of postwar rebuilding. Travelers to Warsaw visited the enormous socialist realist skyscraper, the Stalin Palace, which was said to embody all of the Soviet Union's many gifts to Poland, as well as its brotherly superiority. The concert halls demonstrated Soviet concern for the cultural life of Polish citizens, while the meeting rooms provided a space for political gatherings, including the meetings of the Polish Communist Party.[59] Not all tourist excursions were serious: purpose and pleasure could coexist. On a cruise down the Danube (Dunav) River, the voyagers pretended to cross the Equator, celebrating "Neptune's Holiday" onboard ship.[60] Still, many of the sites were determinedly socialist. On this twenty-day cruise on the Danube, tourists visited the tomb of Bulgarian leader Giorgii Dimitrov, a cemetery of Soviet soldiers killed in the liberation of Belgrade, and a Prague museum dedicated to Lenin.[61] A group of thirty-three tourists from Rostov traveling to Romania were shown a tractor factory and an oil refinery in addition to museums and parks.[62] Vacationers in Poland saw historical and cultural monuments in the cities of Gdansk, Stalinograd, Krakow, and Zakopane, as well as a shipbuilding wharf and the metallurgical plant of Nowa Huta.[63] Many of these sites were Stalinist, meaning both the heroic past of revolutionary construction, and a more recent Stalinist past evident in those countries, such as the GDR, that had resisted Khrushchev's de-Stalinization.

The experience of travel often challenged Soviet narratives of military and industrial superiority, willing subordination, and socialist fraternalism, however. For one, itineraries for Soviet tourists were set in significant part by East European tourist organizations. East European organizations generally wrote the texts for advertisements and brochures about travel in their country, which were then translated into Russian to be distributed to Soviet tourists. They hired local guides to accompany Soviet tourists. Although the President of Intourist

[58] RGASPI, f. M-5, op. 1, d. 171, l. 46 (Trip report, GDR, 1963). See also *Turistskaia poezdka v Germanskuiu Demokraticheskuiu Respubliku* (Moscow, 1959), 3. In countries other than Germany, local heroes were sometimes honored alongside Soviet ones. GARF, f. 9520, op. 1, d. 405, l. 11 (Trip report, Bulgaria 1961); l. 61 (Trip report, Hungary, 1961).

[59] L. Kudrevatykh, "Na ulitsakh Varshavy," Ogonek 16 (April 1956), 6.

[60] GARF, f. 9520, op. 1, d. 954, l. 20 (Program for tourists on Dunav cruise, 1966).

[61] GARF, f. 9520, op. 1, d. 954, l. 20.

[62] GARF, f. 9520, op. 1, d. 405, l. 1 (Trip report, Rumania 1961).

[63] "Every worker can spend his leave abroad," *Trud* (6 May 1956), 3/ *CDSP* 8, no. 18 (13 June 1956): 20.

Figure 11 Visiting a memorial to Soviet soldiers in Belgrade, ca. early 1960s.

defended this practice ("Only the country which takes our tourists can guarantee what it is in a position to show") others complained that East European tourist agencies did not exert sufficient control over either guides or itineraries.[64] For some Soviet authorities, and perhaps some tourists, there was too much attention paid to historical and religious sites of the pre-socialist (and often nationalist) world and not enough visits to the contemporary products of Soviet socialist industrialism.[65] The Secretary of the Ukrainian Soviet of Trade Unions complained about visits to the "old ruins of Roman Catholic churches" instead of "excursions to enterprises and organizations."[66] Our tourists want to see contemporary, Eastern Europe, a Gorky official argued similarly.[67]

[64] GARF f. 9612, op. 1, d. 561, l. 5 (Report by Intourist representative in Bulgaria); d. 391, l. 170.
[65] GARF f. 9520, op. 1, d. 391, l. 43.
[66] GARF f. 9520, op. 1, d. 391, l. 43.
[67] GARF, f. 9520, op. 1, d. 316, l. 42. There is some evidence that Soviet workers traveling on non-hard-currency exchanges did visit more factories than those traveling with Intourist. See d. 26, l. 17.

Of particular threat to Soviet strategies of representation was the infiltration of local guides, who were necessary as "translators" of language but also of local sites and experience. Trip leaders complained about young guides who emphasized their pre-socialist heritage as a way to assert their independence and to deny the authority of the USSR.[68] While published travelogues emphasized East Europeans' warm welcome of their Soviet visitors (accounts frequently began with a rhapsody to the unseasonably warm weather or to the spring flowers greeting their arrival), in practice, Soviet tourists were voyaging as colonizers among people who were not always pleased to see them.[69] One Czech guide openly expressed his preference for capitalist countries because of their "higher standard of living," and because capitalist countries were "fighting for peace," while the USSR had "acted aggressively for many years."[70] A Romanian train conductor forced Soviet tourists with assigned seats to give up their places to Romanians saying that they also wanted to travel: "It's our territory, our power."[71] Not surprisingly, given that much of this tourism followed closely on the Soviet suppression of the Hungarian revolution in 1956, Hungary was an especially challenging destination because of the anti-Soviet insults tourists sometimes confronted.[72] "The guides were very poorly prepared, except for their ability to speak Russian, and could say absolutely nothing about what they showed us," complained one trip leader. "Most of the time they could say something about kings and queens, but not a word about revolutionary events in the country, about the heroes of the people's uprising, about the workers' class war for freedom, or about the freeing of their country from capitalist oppression. This created the impression that Hungarian guides were ashamed to speak of these topics and of the events of 1956. They said nothing about the contemporary position of Hungary, about the large social reforms which have taken place in the past few years in the country."[73]

It was for this reason, in part, that a tourist's time was highly structured ("bus here, bus there," observed one former tourist), closely chaperoned, and in a group. Official evenings of friendship were encouraged, but even among socialist brothers this was still friendship at a distance: after one evening party a worker was censured for sitting with the Hungarian musicians rather than staying with his own group.[74] Trip leaders complained about tourists who met up with the

---

[68] GARF, f. 9520, op. 1, d. 504, l. 88.

[69] On the warm greetings, see K. Cherevkov, "Leningradtsy v Iugoslavii," *Ogonek* 25 (June 1956): 4 and V. Soloukhin, "Bolgarskie vstrechi," *Ogonek* 51 (December 1956): 15.

[70] GARF, f. 9520, op. 1, d. 504, l. 89 (On improving work in international tourism, Ukrainian section).

[71] GARF, f. 9520, op. 1, d. 405, l. 16.

[72] GARF, f. 9520, op. 1, d. 391, l. 156.

[73] GARF, f. 9520, op. 1, d. 504, l. 88.

[74] GARF, f. 9520, op. 1, d. 422, l. 10. Also see GARF, f. 9520, op. 1, d. 430, ll. 111–12. The quote "bus here, bus there" is from an interview with Valeriia Emmanuilovna Kunina, who

"wrong people," and slipped out at night to go to bars.[75] Travelers were likewise discouraged from meeting with relatives or friends. When a few Soviet citizens on a trip to Poland asked to be freed from the scheduled itinerary so that they could see their relatives, they were denied permission, with only one finally receiving approval to spend a night with relatives in Gdansk.[76] Trade union and tourism officials emphasized, in contrast, the educational and professional contacts Soviet worker-tourists could make, anxious about more informal, less regulated types of contact with East Europeans.[77]

Travel to Eastern Europe also provided opportunities for encounters with Western items and ideas, particularly in Poland, Czechoslovakia, and Germany. In Poland, magazines available at corner kiosks, such as *Dookoła Świata* [Around the World], reported on Western culture, including French fashion and American jazz. Travelers could listen to Polish radio stations that played French and American jazz.[78] In 1957, tourists to Warsaw who managed to find a free evening could see performances of Eugène Ionesco's *The Chairs,* Samuel Beckett's *Waiting for Godot* or Jean-Paul Sartre's *The Flies.*[79] Works by James Joyce, Aldous Huxley, and Agatha Christie were also available in Polish translation.[80] Some East European countries were also more open to international exchanges and tourism than was the Soviet Union; in 1957 the Ford Foundation began providing fellowships for East Europeans to study in Western Europe and the United States. There were, admittedly, limits to this kind of encounter. One was the group experience; another was language. Although Joseph Brodsky learned Polish so as to take advantage of the "window onto Europe" that Poland provided, few more ordinary tourists knew the local languages of the countries to which they traveled.[81]

Despite the controls, Soviet citizens were being permitted, indeed even encouraged, to cross long-closed borders. Challenges to Soviet ideological and political superiority could be disturbing, but the benefits of travel were thought to outweigh potential risks, at least for some members of the citizenry. Indeed, the vice-president of Intourist warned tourists not against the dangers of difference and deviance, but of thinking oneself superior. We have to guard against the know-it-alls, Erokhin argued in 1962, the "tourist who upon arrival in a country,

although thrilled to have traveled abroad noted that her time was highly structured. Interview, Moscow, July 2004.

[75] GARF, f. 9612, op. 1, d. 561, l. 79.

[76] GARF, f. 9520, op. 1, d. 425, l. 6 (Trip report, Poland, 1961)

[77] GARF, f. 9520, op. 1, d. 391, l. 45.

[78] David Crowley, "Warsaw's Shops, Stalinism and the Thaw," in *Style and Socialism: Modernity and Material Culture in Post-War Eastern Europe,* ed. Susan E. Reid and David Crowley (Oxford, 2000), 41; K.S. Karol, *Visa for Poland* (London, 1959), 178; John Kenneth Galbraith, *Journey to Poland and Yugoslavia* (Cambridge, 1958), 72.

[79] Karol, *Visa for Poland,* 178.

[80] Karol, *Visa for Poland,* 185.

[81] Joseph Brodsky as cited in Richmond, *Cultural Exchange and the Cold War,* 202.

takes on the role of a person who doesn't ask questions, but only answers them."[82] There were things to learn from younger "brothers," especially, as we will see below, in the realms of consumption and culture. If in a 1957 issue of *Vokrug sveta,* Vadim Safonov began his account of a trip to Bulgaria, with a recitation of the pleasures of home, he also described the excitement of crossing previously closed borders into a new country, and possibly a new way of thinking.[83] Exposure to difference, be it controlled, was now part of what made a good Soviet citizen.

SHOPPING ADVENTURES

One of the major attractions of travel abroad was the opportunities it provided for viewing and purchasing goods unavailable at home. It was in the street market and the clothing store that Soviet tourists traveled most definitively to the future of a modernizing socialist society. Tourist Karpeikina wandered though one store in Poland with "wide open eyes." "We don't have the kind of children's goods that they have in Poland," she remarked.[84] Thirty years after a trip to the GDR, Soviet cardiologist V.I. Metelitsa still remembered mistakenly trying to buy a dress for a ten-year-old daughter in a maternity shop: "In our country I couldn't even imagine that such a specialized shop could exist."[85] Some of the most enticing materials were available on the black market. Soviet tourists to Poland could shop for blackmarket goods, everything from cosmetics to dinner jackets to razor blades, at Warsaw street markets.[86] Most stores were state-run, but there were also "private shops, hidden away in small lanes, that sold all kinds of things."[87] In Germany, before the construction of the Berlin Wall in 1961, American food, clothing, and music circulated on both sides of a divided country.[88]

All of this was despite the fact that the socialist part of Berlin suffered from shortages in comparison to its capitalist neighbor, as did other East European countries.[89] In 1954, East Germans queued for cabbage, tomatoes, and onions.[90] Ten years later, both the German *Handelsorganisation* (HO) stores

---

[82] GARF, f. 9520, op. 1, d. 468, l. 55; f. 9612, op. 1, d. 387, l. 4 (Intourist statement on Soviet tourism, 1957).

[83] Vadim Safonov, "U bolgarskikh brat'ev," *Vokrug sveta* 9 (September 1957): 4.

[84] GARF, f. 9520, op. 1, d. 425, l. 7.

[85] V.I. Metelitsa, *Stranitsy zhizni* (Moscow, 2001), 317. This trip took place in 1971.

[86] Crowley, "Warsaw's Shops, Stalinism and the Thaw," 37. Also see Karol, *Visa for Poland,* 180.

[87] Kudrevatykh, Na ulitsakh Varshavy," 7.

[88] Uta G. Poiger, *Jazz, Rock, and Rebels. Cold War Politics and American Culture in a Divided Germany* (Berkeley, 2000), 2; Bernard Newman, *Berlin and Back* (London, 1954), 121.

[89] Newman, *Behind the Berlin Wall,* 78. Also see Iu. Korol'kov, "V Germanii cherez desiat' let," *Novyi mir* 5 (May 1961): 133.

[90] Newman, *Berlin and Back,* 113.

Figure 12 Dubrovnik street market, ca. early 1960s.

and co-operative stores in the GDR were still the butt of jokes about poor-quality goods.[91] Still, even if the material goods they sold were limited, as described by David Crowley, East European stores offered possibilities for shopping adventures different from those at home: "Not only did the [Polish] street market offer the opportunity to engage the senses in direct and prohibited ways—fingers to touch, eyes to range over and compare all the goods on display—but it was an 'adventure' made up of chance encounters with things. The fact that many of these things came from 'beyond the iron curtain' added to their appeal as 'forbidden fruit.'"[92]

Looking and touching was often a Soviet tourist's only form of consumption. "Our tourists behave badly in stores, looking at everything, pricing it and buying nothing," worried the Soviet embassy in Prague. "All of this creates a very bad impression among those nearby and among salespeople."[93] In the early 1970s, East Berlin crystal and dishware stores took to posting signs in Russian saying

[91] Newman, *Behind the Berlin Wall*, 78.
[92] Crowley, "Warsaw's Shops, Stalinism and the Thaw," 39.
[93] GARF, f. 9520, op. 1, d. 580, l. 128.

"Do Not Touch"[94] Tourists looked and touched rather than bought because they received only a small amount of hard currency with which to make purchases. Travelers on a twelve-day Intourist excursion to the GDR could withdraw eighty-four German marks from the State Bank foreign exchange post in Brest before crossing into Eastern Europe, the equivalent of about 217 rubles.[95] This was enough to buy two pairs of nylons, one lesser quality wool dress, or three or four linen sheets, but not enough to buy a watch and far too little for a radio set.[96] To increase how much they could buy, vacationers sometimes brought items of their own to sell or trade, most often Soviet watches or cameras. Comrade Galkina from Moscow sold her camera in Austria and used the money to buy two blouses.[97] The exchange may not have made sense financially: in 1954, a new portable camera of the Leica type cost 713 rubles while a silk blouse cost 138 rubles.[98] But cameras had become readily available in the USSR beginning in the mid-1930s, while good quality blouses were hard to find.[99] Some tourists were accused by Soviet officials of traveling for the sole purpose of speculating, such as one Comrade Mikhailova from Leningrad Oblast, who was said to have traveled to Poland in order to make money from selling watches.[100] A few tourists managed to get together enough money to buy large amounts of goods to sell at home. One of the first Soviet tourists found bringing in contraband was caught at customs in March 1962 smuggling in ninety pairs of nylon stockings hidden in a suitcase with a false bottom.[101]

It is not surprising that Soviet officials condemned "profiteering," but they were also anxious about other, less marginal forms of consumption. "The majority of [problems abroad] happen in connection with the incorrect expenditure of foreign currency, and inappropriate behavior in stores," insisted Comrade Serov, a Novosibirsk delegate to a Trade Union Excursion Bureau meeting on foreign travel.[102] Serov gave as an example a young female researcher who bought "some kind of curtain in Germany" which she carried along with her "for the entire itinerary."[103] Serov's chosen target—a young woman—is illustrative of the type of tourist thought most likely to consume at the expense of other activities. Young people in general were often considered a risk in trips abroad,

[94] V.I. Metelitsa, *Stranitsy zhizni* (Moscow, 2001), 317.
[95] *Spravochnik: Ob usloviiakh i marshrutakh*, 39, 89. Also see GARF, f. 9520, op. 1, d. 438, l. 93 on where tourists could receive their hard currency.
[96] Newman, *Behind the Berlin Wall*, 29. The prices of items in the GDR are from 1964.
[97] GARF, f. 9520, op. 1, d. 430, l. 11.
[98] Chapman, *Real Wages in Soviet Russia since 1928*, 193, 195.
[99] Jukka Gronow, *Caviar with Champagne: Common Luxury and the Ideals of the Good Life in Stalin's Russia* (Oxford, 2003), 61.
[100] GARF, f. 9520, op. 1, d. 430, l. 111 (On the inadequate behaviour of Soviet tourists abroad in 1960). See also GARF, f. 9520, op. 1, d. 438, l. 118 (Report to TEU conference, 1961).
[101] RGASPI, f. m-5, op. 1, d. 158, l. 122 (On international tourist trips of Soviet youth from 1958–1962).
[102] GARF, f. 9520, op. 1, d. 468, l. 78.
[103] GARF, f. 9520, op. 1, d. 468, l. 78.

when "in view of the absence of certain life experiences" they "sometimes wrongly value[d] foreign lifestyles"[104] But it was women who were believed especially likely to abandon the ideologically appropriate group excursion for glitter of the shop window. Anxieties about women's supposedly natural and uncontrollable urge to consume are not exclusive to tourism, of course, nor to the Soviet Union.[105] But, according to Susan Reid, in this period of some ambiguity about satisfying consumer demand, Soviet authorities were especially worried about "Soviet citizens', and especially *women's*, potential for excessive, unwarranted consumerism."[106] As historian Mary Louise Roberts has reminded us, "commodities do not, in themselves, encourage one to be accountable or responsible to any set of political ideals."[107] But for the Khrushchev regime, according to Reid, "once unleashed" women's "insatiable desire" to consume threatened to become "the Achilles' heel of socialism."[108] With this in mind, it is not surprising perhaps that there was more anxiety about consumption on trips to Eastern Europe than on trips to Western Europe or North America: in 1961, close to 60 percent of tourists on hard-currency trips to Eastern Europe were female.[109] So too on Sputnik trips, where on many trips 70 to 80 percent of the participants were female.[110] On trips to capitalist countries, in contrast, there were almost always more men than women.[111]

That the high-ranking party members and elite scientific and cultural figures who went on trips to capitalist countries were usually male is not surprising. It is less obvious why there were more women than men on trips to Eastern Europe. Galina Tokareva, a long-time Komsomol member, argued that more women traveled to Eastern Europe because they were more likely to be party and Komsomol activists.[112] As an example she described her own frequent excursions to Eastern Europe as a trip leader for children and youth traveling to international youth camps. Her enthusiastic portrayal of *turizm* as a form of political activism is consistent with official Soviet understandings of tourism as purposeful. And yet, tourism was also a nod to individual consumer desire. Indeed, it is also possible that more women traveled to Eastern Europe via the urban

[104] GARF, f. 9520, op. 1, d. 438, l. 185.

[105] Mary Louise Roberts, "Gender, Consumption, and Commodity Culture," *American Historical Review* 103, no. 3 (June 1998): 817–44.

[106] Susan E. Reid, "Cold War in the Kitchen: Gender and the de-Stalinization of Consumer Taste in the Soviet Union under Khrushchev," *Slavic Review* 61, no. 2 (Summer 2002): 240. Emphasis in the original.

[107] Roberts, "Gender, Consumption, and Commodity Culture," 842.

[108] Reid, "Cold War in the Kitchen," 240.

[109] GARF, f. 9520, op. 1, d. 432, ll. 2–3; d. 375, l. 8.

[110] RGASPI, f. m-5, op. 1, d. 158, l. 121.

[111] Of 228 tourists to the United States in 1961 traveling with Intourist, 144 were men, and eighty-four women. To "capitalist" countries as a whole in 1960, 51.7 percent of travelers were men, and 48.3 percent women. See GARF. f. 9520, op. 1, d. 432, ll.1, 29. The same was true for youth travel. RGASPI, f. 5, op. 1, d. 52, l. 9 (Youth tourists to capitalist countries in 1960.)

[112] Interview with Galina Mikhailovna Tokareva, Moscow, July 2004.

itineraries of Intourist and Sputnik precisely because it was such a good way to shop. There is some suggestion in the sources that men preferred more sporting forms of tourism, including hiking and camping, a difference satirized in a 1959 cartoon showing an unhappy woman sheltering with her husband under a tent in the rain. The caption ran: "Travel with you again to the south? Never!"[113] Significantly, there were more men than women on many of the non-hard-currency programs favored by workers, especially those staying at East European Houses of Rest, which were again places for outdoor activities. Local reports from 1964 show the same trend with women outnumbering men on the Intourist trips, and men outnumbering women in the trade union exchanges.[114] Consumption reveals the contradictions inherent in sending people abroad to further the collective cause of Soviet socialism, and then giving them hard currency, even if in limited amounts, to satisfy individual desires while there.

"WHAT KIND OF FRIENDSHIP IS THIS?"

The tourist experience was not always a pleasant one. For West Europeans and North Americans traveling to Warsaw, Prague, and Bucharest, the sometimes drab and dirty conditions of streets, hotels and city were offset by the adventure of traveling behind the Iron Curtain. British traveler May MacKintosh was disappointed to find Romania more modern than she had hoped: "There is something mysterious, almost cloak and daggerish, about swooping down from the darkness on a new country, and it is in the nature of a let-down to find that the airport reception hall at Constanza is a model of modernity." She was reassured to find that the airport hall "did not exist the week before and that the blaze of lights, like an electrical Niagara, beyond Constanza, could only be reached over a tortuous, bumpy road."[115] For Soviet tourists, who were less likely to romanticize the visual and material poverty of state socialism, the bumpy roads or poor conditions of Romanian resorts were sometimes intolerable, especially when they had hoped for better. Although foreign, Soviet tourists were still fraternal, this meant that as in many families, the best was reserved for guests, while the family had to make due with the leftovers.[116]

---

[113] *Krokodil* no. 21 (30 July 1959): back page. Women also may have been especially fond of cruises. Of 3,000 people going on boat trips on the Danube in 1961, over 60 percent were female. GARF. f. 9520, op. 1, d. 432, l.64 (Numbers and categories of tourists going abroad in 1960 and 1961).

[114] GARF, f. 9520, op. 1, d. 422, l. 54; d. 682, ll. 28–29, 71, 102–104, 110–14 (Local reports on tourism, 1964). This was not universally so. See d. 26, l. 20 (Soviet tourists to Bulgaria, 1964).

[115] May MacKintosh, *Rumania* (London, 1963), 91. The idea of the East European hotel as a site of mystery is an old trope. See Maria Todorova, *Imagining the Balkans* (New York. 1997), 15.

[116] Local citizens were treated no better. The Hotel Bristol in Warsaw was, like Intourist hotels in the Soviet Union, reserved for Western visitors. See the description of trying to get a room at the Hotel Bristol by the former Polish citizen turned French journalist. Karol, *Visa for Poland*, 171–72.

Capitalist visitors were wined and dined in ways inaccessible to Soviet tourists. In Romania, British travelers were directed "to hotels which [were] carefully vetted and judged as being up to Western standards;" they were "up-to-date," and "modernistic," "situated amid cool green lawns and thickly blooming flower beds."[117] A group of British tourists returning to Bulgaria for a second summer holiday on the sea said they hoped to return every year as their holiday was "damn good value for the money."[118] Soviet tourists did not always feel the same. On Mamaia, on the Black Sea Coast, each country was assigned its own hotel: "the Yalta for the Russians, the Palace for the Finns, the Modern for the British."[119] Arriving in Varna, a Bulgarian coastal resort town, one group of Soviet tourists was told that although they were expected, there were absolutely no hotel spaces available. Offered no transport, they made their way by city bus to a hotel some fifteen kilometers outside of the city. There too they were told that there was no room, as the hotel was full of German tourists. The Soviet men ended up sleeping on the street, while the women slept in bunks.[120] The issue in part was that Soviet tourism did not provide the same hard-currency benefit as tourism by West Europeans or North Americans. In addition, it was seen by some locals as yet another way in which the USSR took economic advantage of Eastern Europe. In 1959, a group of Soviet tourists to Bulgaria was forced to sleep in the woods on the outskirts of town with no water and nothing to eat because the hotel management said it was "not prepared" for a non-hard-currency exchange, presumably preferring to reserve its rooms for paying customers.[121] "What kind of friendship is this," one tourist to Albania muttered, "All it means is that they don't give a damn about taking care of us."[122]

A group of tourists that traveled from Moscow to Poland and Czechoslovakia by bus were exhausted by the end of their holiday. "Almost all of the tourists talked about how they traveled, about all of the problems," reported the trip leader. "The bus was not ready, in L'vov and Minsk the hotels weren't ready, for six hours the group sat and waited, the bus always broke down. . . . everyone had really wanted to come on this trip, but because of these inadequacies their pleasures were dashed."[123] One group to Bulgaria was so upset by repeated inconvenience (late breakfasts, no porters for luggage, etc.) that a "special rest" had to be organized for them.[124] This was all too similar to what some travelers

---

[117] MacKintosh, *Rumania*, 47.
[118] Arnold L. Haskell, *Heroes and Roses: A View of Bulgaria* (London, 1966), 133.
[119] MacKintosh, *Rumania*, 94.
[120] GARF, f. 9520, op. 1, d. 375, l. 8.
[121] GARF, f. 9520, op. 1, d. 375, l. 8.
[122] GARF, f. 9612, op. 1, d. 372, l. 8.
[123] GARF, f. 9520, op. 1, d. 468, l. 24.
[124] GARF, f. 9520, op. 1, d. 405, l. 8 (Trip report, 1961).

Figure 13 The Hotel Moskva in Prague. *Puteshestvie v stranu druzei* (Leningrad, 1959), 36.

had experienced at home in the Soviet Union. When one group traveling from Moscow to Hungary was told only at the very last minute that their train to Hungary was delayed and would leave the next day, they were forced to "chase from one end [of Moscow] to the other to find a place to spend the night.[125] Groups slept in the Moscow train station when Intourist failed to find hotel rooms, or on the streets of L'vov when the same happened there.[126] In 1963, the vice-chairman of the Central Soviet for Tourism sent 54 pages of complaints about inadequacies in foreign tourism to the Chairman of Intourist, V.M. Ankudinov.[127]

Some of the problems were related to the magnitude of postwar reconstruction. In East Berlin, the new "Stalinallee" was a massive boulevard of socialist realist proportions but many other buildings had yet to be repaired. Eighty-five percent of Warsaw's buildings had been destroyed. If the capital city was determinedly and quickly rebuilt, many of Poland's smaller towns long remained

---

[125] GARF, f. 9520, op. 1, d. 405, l. 116 (Trip report, Hungary, 1961); GARF, f. 9520, op. 1, d. 317, l. 12.
[126] GARF, f. 9520, op. 1, d. 405, l. 23 (Trip report, Bulgaria, 1961); GARF, f. 9520, op. 1, d. 317, l. 5.
[127] GARF, f. 9520, op. 1, d. 618 (Complaints about inadequacies in services provided for Soviet citizens traveling abroad, 1963).

in ruins. The Baltic Sea resort in Kolberg was deserted in 1961, with empty beaches and only the "skeleton-like remains" of the resort hotel.[128] "We are building everywhere," a representative of Orbis, the Polish travel organization told one Western guest, "Poland will soon become a major tourist destination."[129] But if in 1960, Warsaw's Hotel Bristol, in which most Western foreign guests were hosted, was still surrounded by scaffolding, the conditions for Soviet tourists were even more challenging. It is not surprising in this context that some destinations were more popular than others. Yugoslavia was very popular, Romania and Bulgaria less so, and Albania least desirable as it was said to be a "hard country" in which to travel.[130] Germany was described as grim by one traveler in the late 1960s: "Everything was far more serious in the GDR than it was back home. We did everything with humor and they were so serious about things."[131] The GDR, still in the grip of Stalinism, was "far more 'in the dark' than we were." Poland, in contrast to both the GDR and the Soviet Union, was described as an appealingly "free country."[132] Of course, the history of the war also influenced Soviet feelings about Germany. When traveling in the GDR, Soviet travelers sometimes provocatively sang patriotic songs from the Second World War.[133] As this suggests, Eastern Europe was not a single, undifferentiated entity.

In almost every case, however, despite all of the challenges, for the vast majority of tourists, the difficulties were a disappointment but not a fatal one. Most travel reports, even when they described problems, were positive both about conditions and about the experience of their tourists. The number of Soviet tourists to Eastern Europe each year continued to increase. There is every reason to believe that most of those who were able to travel were delighted to do so despite sometimes challenging conditions and mixed reception.

"GREASY BEAVER COATS [AND] HATS WITH EAR FLAPS:" SELLING THE SOVIET UNION

Soviet tourists were not only consuming Eastern Europe, but selling the Soviet Union. With their "words, conversations, and personal contacts, [tourists] are

---

[128] Charles Wassermann, *Europe's Forgotten Territories* (Copenhagen, 1960), photo essay between pages 175 and 209.

[129] Wassermann, *Europe's Forgotten Territories*, 8. On the destruction of Polish towns and resorts, also see Frank Gibney, *An Informal Guide to Poland* (New York,1958).

[130] GARF, f. 9520, op. 1, d. 391, l. 151.

[131] Raleigh, *Russia's Sputnik Generation*, 42.

[132] Raleigh, *Russia's Sputnik Generation*, 42.

[133] Aleksei Popov, "Sovetskie turisty za rubezhom: ideologiia, kommunikatsiia, emotsii (po otchetam rukovoditelei turistskikh grupp)," *Istorichna panorama: nayk. statei*, vol 7 (Chernovci, 2009), 51.

invaluable propagandists for our successes, our politics, and our Marxist-Leninist ideology," argued one Intourist representative to Bulgaria.[134] Soviet tourists did not always live up to expectations. Tourist authorities were ambivalent about sending Soviet citizens abroad not only because of the potential for unregulated experiences, but because of the uncultured impressions travelers sometimes conveyed of themselves and, by extension, of the Soviet Union. Much of the behavior condemned by authorities violated cultural norms (*kul'turnost'*). Catriona Kelly has described the virtual "torrent" of advice books appearing in the Khrushchev era, proscribing appropriate forms of "cultured behavior" in an ever-widening arena of subjects.[135] As portrayed in these books, the ideal Soviet man or woman of the 1950s had "a developed taste in curtains and wallpaper, an eye for elegant dress, good table manners, and refined speech."[136] The cultured individual also knew how to dress and behave while traveling abroad. Proper behavior and dress for tourists were described in articles such as one called "Happy Trails" that ran in a Moscow fashion magazine in the early 1960s.[137] In large part there was little specifically Soviet about this advice, which often resembled Europe-wide advice about appropriate behavior. In a report to a Tourist Excursion Bureau meeting about international travel, Alekseeva, a tourist expert, was dismayed, for example, by ill-mannered Soviet tourists to Eastern Europe who did not know what to do with the lemon on their fish.[138] There was also a long history of pre-revolutionary anxieties about Russian inferiority in comparison to European standards of cultured behavior, and specifically about the behavior of Russian tourists abroad. In his 1857 novella *Asia*, Ivan Turgenev mocked the growing numbers of vulgar, pleasure-seeking Russian tourists abroad who lacked the sophistication and cultivated manners of the gentlemen traveler.[139]

The superior and cultured narrator of Turgenev's novel identifies, and thereby avoids, ordinary Russian tourists abroad "by their walk" and "the cut of their clothes."[140] In the 1950s, too, clothing was a particularly important marker of cultural sophistication or ignorance, a point of some irony given Soviet official anxiety about excess consumption, often of clothing, as described above. In a report to a 1962 meeting on international travel, Erokhin, the vice-chairman of Intourist, fretted about the poor dress of Soviet tourists: "Our tourists, arriving for vacation were dressed such that we felt badly for Soviet man, not because he doesn't have the money necessary to purchase a swimming suit, but because

---

[134] GARF, f. 9612, op. 1, d. 561, l. 82.

[135] Kelly, *Refining Russia*, 320.

[136] Kelly, *Refining Russia*, 321.

[137] As described in GARF, f. 9520, op. 1, d. 468, l. 14.

[138] GARF, f. 9520, op. 1, d. 468, ll. 12–13.

[139] Susan Layton, "The Divisive Modern Russian Tourist Abroad: Representations of Self and Other in the Early Reform Era," *Slavic Review* 68, no. 4 (Winter 2009), 856–59.

[140] Layton, "The Divisive Modern Russian Tourist Abroad," 858.

although literate and cultured in all other ways, he does not know how to dress or conduct himself properly."[141] "There was an exceptionally good group that went to Czechoslovakia; it was obvious that they were all working people," Erokhin continued, "but some arrived in greasy beaver coats, hats with ear flaps, and boots with the trousers tucked in. They looked like illustrated caricatures of the typical Soviet man."[142] Despite the exceptional "goodness" of these working class tourists, their working-class style was embarrassing. Articles in the popular *Concise Encyclopedia of Home Economy* advocated simple blouses for women with loose, comfortable skirts, or, as an option for outdoor activities, capris.[143] Alekseeva complained about Soviet women who ignored such advice. "How can you figure out who are our tourists in a foreign country?" she asked. Our "women waste lots of money sewing dresses [and] expensive silk dressing gowns, when maybe a simple cotton dress would be better."[144] The ideal tourist-citizen dressed in a measured but modern style, avoiding both the "Soviet" dress of the obviously working class, and the vulgarity of the aspiring elite.

Tourists who dressed inappropriately posed multiple threats to Soviet attempts to sell the superiority of the Soviet Union. In part, their inattention to contemporary styles suggested the cultural backwardness of the USSR. Their clothes also challenged the Soviet presentation of self as economically prosperous. "The men wore some kind of knitted underwear [to the beach]," Erokhin wrote about one group to Eastern Europe, "It had once been black, but had faded to grey; one end hung below the knees, and the other rode up God knows where."[145] Erokhin worried about the impact of such dubious costumes on non-Soviet observers: "At this same moment, tourists from Poland and the GDR arrived and we felt pained to the depths of our souls looking at our good, deserving people who for their work, their role in the world, deserve to be looked at with admiration, not with ridicule."[146] By showing up in their underwear, tourists revealed the dirty reality of life in the Soviet Union, where it could be difficult to buy a swimsuit. Concerned about the international reputation of the USSR, as well as the personal dignity of the Soviet tourist, Erokhin admitted that consumer conditions were less than adequate and suggested that tourist organizations should sell swimsuits to departing travelers so that "our people aren't left in such bad straits."[147] Better pre-trip education that would discuss appropriate "norms of behavior for Soviet people" was an additional solution.[148] Tourist officials in Latvia produced a film on etiquette meant to help

[141] GARF, f. 9520, op. 1, d. 468, l. 82.
[142] GARF, f. 9520, op. 1, d. 468, l. 84.
[143] *Kratkaia entsiklopediia*, 977.
[144] GARF, f. 9520, op. 1, d. 468, l. 15.
[145] GARF, f. 9520, op. 1, d. 468, l. 82.
[146] GARF, f. 9520, op. 1, d. 468, l. 82.
[147] GARF, f. 9520, op. 1, d. 468, l. 83.
[148] GARF, f. 9520, op. 1, d. 391, l. 94; d. 405, l. 2 (Trip report, 1961).

prepare tourists to go abroad, which demonstrated, among other skills, "how to behave while eating, how to use a spoon, fork, and knife."[149] Once abroad, less worldly tourists were also encouraged to "watch the group leader, [and] watch the guide," and to "keep a close eye on what experienced comrades are doing."[150] In these reports, we hear the voice of the educated Soviet member of the intelligentsia embarrassed by Soviet citizens less "cultured" than he or she. Unwittingly, they also replicate the superior voices of Western travelers to the Soviet Union, who in their travel accounts often commented on poor service in Soviet restaurants and hotels and on the "truly pathetic dresses and shoes" Russian women wore.[151]

It is notable that all of the examples of uncultured behavior provided by Erokhin and Alekseeva were about tourism to socialist countries. This may have been because those traveling to capitalist countries were more likely to be from highly educated classes presumed to be more cultured: opening up new possibilities for tourism to a wider spectrum of people led to increased anxiety about these people when they traveled. The Soviet project of ideological and economic domination in Eastern Europe also made authorities sensitive to the cultural position of tourists in countries under Soviet control. In order to preserve Soviet moral and cultural authority, tourists from the USSR needed to appear at least as cultured as those they were visiting. It was "uncomfortable," Alekseeva reported, when Soviet tourists did not have any money to pay for a coat check at theaters: "We aren't so poor that we can't pay for the coat check." Trip leaders need a little change, she concluded, so that "our tourists can freely use the things that tourists from other countries are able to use."[152] The Soviet Union was not alone among colonizers in its effort to look good in front of the "natives" of course.[153] The difference is that Eastern Europe was imagined by Soviet observers as more "Western" (and thus more "modern") than the USSR even as it was politically dominated and economically plundered. In Soviet travel accounts the most positive differences mentioned about Eastern Europe were the "cultured" behaviors of modernity that had long been positively associated with the "West." A travelogue in *Ogonek* described the streets of Warsaw as admirably quiet and "disciplined." Pedestrians were said to cross the road "only at crosswalks and only with a green light."[154] A 1960 article in *Novyi mir* described with loving enthusiasm the "attentive," "calm" and "attractive cordiality" of a café waiter in Czechoslovakia.[155] The Soviet Union was by implicit if unstated

[149] GARF, f. 9520, op. 1, d. 468, ll. 12–13.

[150] GARF, f. 9520, op. 1, d. 468, l. 13.

[151] Gunnar D. Kumlien, "Fashion à la Russe" *The Commonweal* (17 January 1958): 402.

[152] GARF, f. 9520, op. 1, d. 468, l. 16.

[153] Grewel, *Home and Harem*, 93.

[154] Kudrevatykh, "Na ulitsakh Varshavy," 7; Ia. Fomenko, "Predvesenii Budapesht," *Ogonek* 13 (March 1958): 4.

[155] I. Radvolina, "K druz'iam v Chekhoslovakiiu!" *Novyi mir* 5 (May 1960): 146.

comparison understood to be less decorous, less polite, and less "civilized," even as these qualities were now central to what it meant to be Soviet.

Soviet experts assumed that Soviet tourists were embarrassed by their lack of knowledge about how to behave and dress. But how did Soviet tourists themselves feel about what was appropriate? Were the workers sporting hats with ear flaps themselves embarrassed, wearing them only because they had no other alternative? Or did they think these hats warm, comfortable, and perfectly suitable? Some tourists surely tried their best to imitate foreign fashions. Khrushchev's peasant upbringing and lack of education made him anxious not to be humiliated in his international encounters with Western leaders; he consulted others with more international experience than he about what to wear to the Geneva summit of July 1955 and had a suit custom-made for his meeting with the Queen in Britain in 1956.[156] But others actively refused the recommendations of authorities. "One woman, large, middle-aged, went out in a tight skirt, high-heeled shoes, a black hat and gloves. It was summer time. She was told to 'take off the hat,' but she just responded, 'Let them go ahead and look at us.'" The tourist was not bothered, but Alekseeva was. "If tourists wear modest clothes even to the theater, then that won't be noticed," Alekseeva concluded. "But if a large woman wears a dress with ruffle, overly adorned, then people will laugh at her."[157] Erokhin argued that wearing the "wrong" clothes reduced the mood of a "good, kind man," to "some kind of clodhopper who feels ashamed."[158] But we need not assume that travel experts were correct about this. Perhaps the resistance to changing clothes was a defiant assertion of self in the face of comparative poverty and desperation? Maybe the "large, middle-aged woman" in a "tight skirt" was not resisting "bourgeois" norms, but the sometimes self-serving notions of polite and cultured behavior imposed from above? We know that tourists sometimes resented the authority of trip leaders, who were said to occasionally rebuke comrades "in inappropriate and untactful ways, often yelling loudly."[159] One group sent a letter of complaint to Intourist about their trip leader, who upon meeting them belligerently declared: "I am considered an important worker at MOSPS [the Moscow Soviet of Trade Unions] and can purge and clear each of you out thoroughly."[160] "We constantly felt as if we were dangerous characters, if not almost criminals, thanks to the sick fantasies of our leader!"[161]

Sending Soviet citizens to the ambiguous space of Eastern Europe had both advantages and risks. The regime had long acknowledged that there was much to be learned from the technological achievements of the "West." But what

---

[156] William Taubman, *Khrushchev: The Man and his Era* (New York, 2003), 350, 356.
[157] GARF, f. 9520, op. 1, d. 468, l. 15.
[158] GARF, f. 9520, op. 1, d. 468, l. 84.
[159] GARF, f. 9520, op. 1, d. 430, l. 98 (Letter of complaint to Intourist).
[160] GARF, f. 9520, op. 1, d. 430, l. 98.
[161] GARF, f. 9520, op. 1, d. 430, l. 98.

happened when these achievements and other material advantages were also evident in the socialist, but non-Soviet "East?" The risk was believed limited, in that those sent abroad were supposed to be "suitable people" who would "uphold the prestige and interests of their government."[162] They were supposed to return home restored but not transformed. And indeed, many tourists may have combined enthusiasm for a regime now trusting them enough to allow them to travel with pleasure at what they could consume. For some, more goods did not necessarily mean that life was better. As Susan Reid has argued about the Soviet perception of the American Exhibition in Moscow in 1959, not everyone thought material goods were what mattered most.[163] Some Soviet tourists to East European countries, both in the Khrushchev era and later, internalized official conceptions of themselves as superior representatives both of the world's first socialist country and the country that had freed Eastern Europe from fascism.[164] Still, experiencing at first hand the relative ideological freedoms and material superiorities of socialist countries like Poland surely made many tourists question the supposed superiority of the Soviet Union, increasingly so as Khrushchev-era promises turned to Brezhnev-era disappointments in the 1970s.[165] If, in theory, the material superiorities of many East European countries might be taken positively as evidence that socialism and consumerism could coexist, in practice, it was hard to explain why the socialist younger brother was so much better off than his elder sibling.

---

[162] GARF, f. 9520, op. 1, d. 390, l. 9.

[163] Susan E. Reid, "Who Will Beat Whom? Soviet Popular Reception of the American National Exhibition in Moscow, 1959," *Kritika* 9, no. 4 (Fall 2008): 855–904.

[164] See discussion in Alexei Popov, "Tenevye storony zarubzhnogo (Byezdnogo) turizma v Sovetskom Soiuze (1960–1980-e gg.)" *Kultura narodov Prichernomoria* no. 152 (Simferopol 2009): 151–55.

[165] John Bushnell, "The 'New Soviet Man' Turns Pessimist," in *The Soviet Union since Stalin*, ed. Stephen Cohen, Alexander Rabinowitch, and Robert Sharlet (Bloomington, 1980).

4

Performing on the International Stage: Tourism to the Capitalist West

In the early 1960s, Intourist published a guidebook for Soviet tourists setting off by cruiseship to see Copenhagen, London, Paris, Rome, and Athens. The guidebook, *A cruiseship trip around Europe,* described the typically touristic—the Eiffel Tower and the Roman Colosseum—but emphasized the political; the description of each port of call was prefaced with an analysis of the country's political system, the relative strength of the local Communist Party, and the most important local industries. The main purpose of tourism, as described in this guidebook, was for the Soviet tourist to "to talk about his country, his city, about the achievements of his great country with love and warmth—to tell the truth about Soviet people and to leave behind a good impression of himself."[1] This chapter explores the performative function of Soviet tourism to Western Europe, what we might call a theater of diplomacy. Consistent with the Khrushchev-era policy of peaceful coexistence, the tourist was sent abroad as an envoy for cordial, if careful, relations between socialist East and capitalist West. International tourism was a means of promoting a new, post-Stalin, Soviet self. Tourists sang "Soviet" songs in trains and on buses, handed out thousands of souvenir pins, Palekh (lacquer) boxes, and postcards, met with foreign dignitaries and journalists, answered questions, and gave lectures. Like the exhibits at the Soviet Pavilion at the Brussels World's Fair in 1958, Soviet tourists to capitalist countries were on display for curious viewers who were eager for a glimpse behind a newly-opened Iron Curtain.

Scholars have explored the political and performative function of travel, especially colonial-era practices of "discovery" and "exploration" used to lay claim to peoples and territories.[2] Greg Dening describes late eighteenth century missionary and ethnographic encounters between Europeans and Pacific islanders as a form of theater in which "[g]overnment, law, property, and fire, civilization, God—were represented . . . in gesture, stylized action, and all the

---

[1] *Kruiznoe puteshestvie vokrug Evropy na teplokhode "Estoniia,"* (Intourist brochure, 1961), 3.
[2] See, as just one example, the discussion in Amitav Ghosh, "Foreword," in *Other Routes: 1500 Years of African and Asian Travel Writing,* ed. Tabish Khair, Martin Leer, Justin D. Edwards, and Hanna Ziadeh (Bloomington, 2005), ix.

props of flags and weapons."[3] Less has been said about nineteenth- and twentieth-century *tourism* and performance, and most of this has focused on the "performances" the tourist himself sees, experiences, and consumes while traveling. Dean MacCannell has applied Erving Goffman's theatrical metaphor about the "social performances" of service personnel in reception offices and hotels, to what he describes as the "staged authenticity" of tourist attractions.[4] Jane Desmond writes about the performative display of bodies for tourist consumption, ranging from Hawaiian dancing to the Orca whale acts at Sea World.[5] Robert Rydell, and others, have explored the staged displays of World's Fairs and exhibitions.[6] Far fewer scholars have explored the performative elements of the tourist experience itself. Judith Adler has written about the "styles" of what she calls the "performed art" of travel, including the styles of the medieval pilgrimage, the "sentimental" journeys of late eighteenth-century travelers, and the aristocratic Grand Tour.[7] Tim Edensor explores the "expected and 'appropriate'" actions and duties expected of tourists, including "things which *must* be seen, photographs which *have to be* taken, souvenirs and postcards which *need* to be acquired, the *imperatives* to sample a range of cultures and commodities." "As a highly directed operation, with guides and tour managers acting as choreographers and directors, many performances are repetitive, specifiable in movement, and highly constrained by time," Edensor concludes.[8]

The travel practices of Soviet tourists were also culturally determined, their viewing practices and their behaviors mediated by guidebooks and by travel accounts. But unlike most tourism elsewhere, Soviet performances were more than culturally mediated; they were politically motivated and determined. The typical French tourist to Florida follows the well-worn path of lying on the beach, visiting Disney World, and buying a postcard of Key West. But she does not see this as a performance (even if we might), nor was she explicitly trained by the French government on how to behave. Indeed, she is likely to see a trip to Florida as a chance to "get away from it all," to act in ways different from the

[3] Greg Dening, "The theatricality of observing and being observed: Eighteenth-century Europe 'discovers' the ? century 'Pacific'," in *Implicit Understandings: Observing, Trip Reporting, and Reflecting on the Encounters between Europeans and Other Peoples in the Early Modern Era*, ed. Stewart B. Schwartz (Cambridge, 1994), 455.

[4] Dean MacCannell, *The Tourist: A New Theory of the Leisure Class* (Berkeley, 1999), ch. 5.

[5] Jane C. Desmond, *Staging Tourism: Bodies on Display From Waikiki to Sea World* (Chicago, 1999). Also see, S. Coleman and M. Crang, eds., *Tourism: Between Place and Performance* (New York, 2002).

[6] Robert W. Rydell, *All the World's a Fair: Visions of Empire at American International Expositions, 1876–1916* (Chicago, 1984); Ellen Strain, *Public Places, Private Journeys: Ethnography, Entertainment, and the Tourist Gaze* (New Jersey, 2003), chp. 2.

[7] Judith Adler, "Travel as Performed Art," *The American Journal of Sociology*, 94: 6 (May 1989): 1366–91.

[8] Tim Edensor, "Staging tourism: tourists as performers," *Annals of Tourism Research* 27, no. 2 (April 2000), doi:10.1016/S0160-7383(99)00082-1.

usual, to take on a new role.[9] In contrast, Soviet tourism in Western Europe was explicitly theatrical, and tourists were expected to stay in character at all times. In large part, the importance of performance stemmed from the insecurities and competition of the Cold War. However, the Cold War deployment of tourism also built on the purpose-driven function of Soviet *turizm* in contrast to leisure-driven capitalist *tourism*. Proletarian tourists of the 1920s and 1930s also served as "ambassadors of socialism," although in their case as colonializing superiors from the center traveling to less cultured others in the Soviet periphery. They were, as described by Diane Koenker, "encouraged to conduct cultural work among the inhabitants of the villages they passed through," going out on their tours "armed with gifts of cultural significance—notebooks, pencils, pens, and primers in the local languages."[10] This understanding of *turizm* makes explicit 20th-century tourism's broader connection to the missionizing and civilizing travel of the early modern period.

In the 1950s, the primary target of Soviet gifts—now souvenir pins and *matroshka* (nesting) dolls[11]—was Western Europe. This audience differed from most in the colonialized peripheries. If the USSR, after World War II, was recognized as a world power, it was more tendentiously a cultural power. Tourism was a part of a Cold War "Cultural Olympics," however, tourism as a form of cold war diplomacy differed from other forms of cultural contest in that it required relatively ordinary citizens—in contrast to the more usual delegates, artists, and scientists—to perform Soviet identity on the basis of modest train-ing.[12] This had the advantage of appearing less practiced. Theatricality is especially intense, however, "when the moment being experienced is full of ambivalences"[13]—as was very much the case for Soviet travelers to Western Europe. On their travels to see the sites of Western Europe, Soviet tourists were objects of intense observation. Soviet tourists to Scotland were photo-graphed by other tourists to Scotland, who found them as interesting, if not more so, than the Scottish sites they had come to see.[14] The first group of Soviet tourists to Italy in 1956 were followed everywhere by photographers and

---

[9] Edensor, "Staging tourism: tourists as performers."

[10] Diane P. Koenker, "The Proletarian Tourist in the 1930s: Between Mass Excursion and Mass Escape," in *Turizm: The Russian and East European Tourist under Capitalism and Socialism*, ed. Anne E. Gorsuch and Diane P. Koenker (Ithaca, 2006), 128.

[11] Gift-giving was considered so important that in 1954, the Ministry of Culture proposed establishing a special fund to provide travelers (at this point only delegates) with appropriate gifts. Rossiskii gosudarstvenii arkhiv noveishei istorii (hereafter RGANI), f. 5, op. 30, d. 70, ll. 69–70 (October 1954).

[12] David Caute, *The Dancer Defects: The Struggle for Cultural Supremacy during the Cold War* (Oxford, 2003), 3.

[13] Dening, "The theatricality of observing and being observed," 454.

[14] Gosudarstvennyi arkhiv Rossiiskoi Federatsii (hereafter GARF), f. 9612, op. 1, d. 478, l. 47 (Trip report about a group from the Armenian Society for friendship and cultural relations with foreign countries traveling to Great Britain, 1961).

journalists.[15] The novelty of Ivan and Olga seeing the sights and shopping for souvenirs led some West European locals to enthusiastically prepare for their new Soviet visitors. In 1957, when fewer than 500 Soviet tourists had thus far visited Italy, the Vatican City excitedly prepared a guidebook in Russian for the "influx" of almost 5,000 tourists they hoped for in 1958.[16] If the tourists were received with curiosity, and even some enthusiasm, however, they were also received with wariness, with what Paul Ricoeur has called a hermeneutics of suspicion: the struggle to see behind the "veil," to uncover the hidden agenda projected to lie behind the surface of behavior.[17] Such efforts to see behind the veil were especially intense in a world defined and divided by the closed "curtain" from which these tourists had so unexpectedly just arrived.

A WORKING VACATION

Tourists to Western Europe were on a vacation, but it was a working vacation. As such, authorities were very selective about who traveled. A group of Soviet tourists visiting Great Britain included, among others, the Minister of Finance for Lithuania, the Chief architect for the city of Yerevan, the Headmistress of Kiev Boarding School no. 24, the Head of the Department of Diagnostics of the Tadzhik Hospital no. 1, an Actor in Moscow's Maly Theater, a Lecturer in the Department of English of the Maurice Thorez Pedagogical Institute, the Chairman of the Vladimir Ilyich Collective Farm, and a former member of the "Women's Bomber Squadron."[18] Of close to 400 tourists on a month-long trip around Europe on the cruise ship *Victory* in the fall of 1961, only two were workers. The rest consisted of engineers, educators, medical professionals, white-collar workers, scientists, writers, artists, and a few privileged housewives."[19] Not surprisingly, given these elite professions, thirteen of the eighteen tourists were men, a gender imbalance that distinguished these trips from tourism to Eastern Europe.[20] The elite nature of these groups was recognized

[15] Open Society Archive, Budapest (hereafter HU OSA), Records of Radio Free Europe/Radio Liberty Research Institute (hereafter RFE/RL RI), Soviet Red Archives, 1953–1994, Old Code Subject Files, 300-80-1, Container 1048 (February 1956).

[16] "Vatican Guide Book in Russian: Free Issue to Tourists," *The Times* (24 December 1957): 5.

[17] Paul Ricoeur, *Freud and Philosophy: An Essay on Interpretation* (New Haven, 1970).

[18] "Name List," found in"SCR Events 1960s," [British] Society for Cultural Relations with the USSR (hereafter SCR Archive).

[19] GARF, f. 9520, op. 1, d. 420, l. 6 (Trip report, European cruise, 1961). There was the occasional group of industrial or agricultural workers: in 1964 one group of 29 people traveled to England by the invitation of a "workers group for non-student, and non-hard currency exchange." Rossiiskii gosudarstvennyi arkhiv sotsial'no-politicheskoi istorii (hereafter RGASPI), f. m-5, op. 1, d. 197, l. 15 (Report to Sputnik, 1964); ll. 81–82 (Trip report, England, 1964).

[20] "Name List," found in "SCR Events 1960s," SCR Archive. Similarly, in a list of people traveling with Sputnik to capitalist countries in 1960, 772 of them were male and 590 of them were female. Cruise ship trips sometimes differed. On one trip in 1961, for example, 59 percent of

by West European authorities. The British Foreign Office instructed those locals who were hosting Soviet visitors not to offer them vodka, as many of them "think this is a working-class drink, and prefer wine."[21]

Groups made up of the professional elite provided, in the words of one trip leader, "the possibility to conduct discussions . . . on any topic."[22] The need for the tourist of the 1950s and 1960s to be able to conduct discussions with educated foreign elites distinguished them from the (very rare) international tourist of the 1930s. In 1930–31, two groups of the worker elite, the *udarniki* (shock workers), had the opportunity to travel to Europe on the cruise ships *Abkhaziia* and *Ukraina*.[23] They met with European workers at factories and other industrial sites in a period when the Soviet Union was much admired for its industrial prowess and full employment.

In contrast, the international tourists of the 1950s and 1960s had to sell the Soviet Union to curious but often well-educated and sometimes hostile audiences. Theirs was a collective performance of a different kind in which tourist-educators, artists, scientists, and representatives from various Soviet national republics combined in an ensemble meant to display and perform a new internationalist, post-Stalinist Soviet identity. As such, especially valuable were what the Director of Intourist, N.V. Popovoi, called "specialized tourist groups," groups whose expertise in industry, agriculture or the arts, would best be able to influence European opinion about Soviet achievements. When art historian Mikhail German applied to join a group traveling to France, he hoped that they would take him as a "young specialist" on French art.[24] Discounted trips were also authorized for tourist groups traveling under the auspices of the All-Union Society for Friendship with Foreign Countries (VOKS).[25] Evgeniia Gutnova was an historian of Britain, but her first successful application to travel was as a member of the "USSR–Great Britain Friendship Society."[26] Particularly desirable, as evident in the composition of the group traveling to Great Britain described above, was ethnic and national diversity. Although the earliest groups

---

the passengers were women and 41 percent were men. GARF, f. 9520, op. 1, d. 420, ll. 5–6 (Trip report on a cruise around Europe, 1961). An exception was travel to Finland, which while a "capitalist" country was seen as a friendlier, and perhaps less politically important, destination. On Sputnik trips, groups traveling to Finland had the highest percentage of working class and female youth. RGASPI, f. m-5, op. 1, d. 52, l. 9 (List of youth tourists traveling to capitalist countries, 1960).

[21] The National Archives, London, Foreign Office, FO 371 122948 (On the treatment of Soviet delegations to the UK, 1956).

[22] RGASPI, f. m-5, op. 1, d. 159, l. 31 (Trip report, England, 1962).

[23] V.A. Kvatal'nov and V.K. Fedorchenko, *Orbity "sputnika:" iz istorii molodezhnogo turizma* (Kiev, 1987), 25; Koenker, "The Proletarian Tourist in the 1930s," 131.

[24] Mikhail German, *Slozhnoe proshedshee: Passé composé* (St. Petersburg, 2000), 414–15.

[25] "O napravlennii Soiuzom sovetskikh obshchestv druzhby i kul'turnoi sviazi c zarubezhnymi stranami," Soviet Archives, http://psi.ece.jhu.edu/>~kaplan/IRUSS/BUK/GBARC/pdfs/peace/ct184-61.pdf.

[26] Evgeniia Vladimirovna Gutnova, *Perezhitoe* (Moscow, 2001), 315.

sent abroad in the mid-1950s were from Leningrad and Moscow, soon tourists were deliberately selected so as to make diversity a part of the spectacle.[27] Of the group to Great Britain, seven tourists were from Moscow, five from the Baltic republics, the rest from Ukraine, the Caucasus, and Central Asia.[28]

Getting to Western Europe required exemplary credentials, a squeaky clean past, political connections, and (usually) previous travel without incident to Eastern Europe. Applicants for travel to capitalist countries had five pages of forms to fill out that included questions about family and work history, violations of Soviet law, family members living abroad, and family members interned abroad during the war.[29] Superiors at work and in party and Komsomol organizations were interviewed about potential travelers.[30] Finally, aspirants also needed a certificate of good health, the successful achievement of which required them to pull the necessary strings. "They gave the certificate only reluctantly even to healthy people," Mikhail German remembered. "One could be fit for military service but not fit for travel abroad."[31] The entire process made candidates very nervous. German recalled it with displeasure:

A young-looking man with the last name of 'Ivanovich' (all of these types are Ivanovichs), very self-satisfied, smiling, inscrutably-sleek, gave me an unprecedented questionnaire printed on stark white paper. In my whole life I had never filled out such a questionnaire. Despite the fact that Stalin had died long ago, to write about the repression of my relatives was terrible, especially as I had managed not to write about it earlier. In addition I knew a bit about relatives of my father living in France, Switzerland and the States. I tried not to remember anything about them.[32]

It was so common for permission to be refused, or documents to be delayed, that people applying to go abroad sometimes did not tell even their closest friends and relatives about their plans until the day before departure.[33]

---

[27] GARF, f. 9612, op. 1, d. 373, l. 1 (Trip report, Great Britain, 1956); RGASPI, f. m-5, op. 1, d. 174, l. 33 (Trip report, France, 1964). Also see the list of tourist destinations organized according by regions in RGASPI, f. m-5, op. 1, d. 52, ll. 4–7 (List of tourist trips by Soviet youth abroad, 1960).

[28] "Name List," found in "SCR Events 1960s," SCR Archive.

[29] GARF, f. 9612, op. 1, d. 387, ll. 34, 37–39 (Questionnaires for travel abroad, 1957). On the character assessment see also, GARF, f. 9520, op. 1, d. 391, ll. 104–105 (TEU conference on international tourism, 1961).

[30] RGASPI, f. m-5, op. 1, d. 168, l. 1–3 (On serious insufficiencies on sending Soviet youth on tourist trips abroad, 1963); German, *Slozhnoe proshedshee*, 415.

[31] German, *Slozhnoe proshedshee*, 415. Applicants for trips abroad joked: "If I can live here, why would I get sick abroad?"

[32] German, *Slozhnoe proshedshee*, 415. The feeling was much the same for Aleksandr Aleksandrovich Konstantinov in 1980. "We all got called in by the Central Committee of the CPSU [Communist Party of the Soviet Union]. I got summoned too. There was a Central Committee instructor named Chebotarev. I remember it well. I remember the long corridors, the rugs, the green walls, and the plain black letters in which their names were written. And I remember that man, Chebotarev, and the way he looked at me." Donald J. Raleigh, ed. and trans., *Russia's Sputnik Generation: Soviet Baby Boomers Talk about Their Lives* (Bloomington and Indianapolis, 2006), 45.

[33] Gutnova, *Perezhitoe*, 324.

The privileging of travel to Western Europe for members of an elite class resembled, in many ways, the gross inequality and special access to goods and services of the 1930s, when it was only the elite, be they shock workers or high-ranking party cadres, who consistently had access to regular supplies of good food and clothing while others lived in hunger.[34] So too after the war, in what Vera Dunham has called the "Big Deal."[35] Entitlement and privilege continued in the Khrushchev era, evident in the response of a group of violently upset tourists who complained to the Communist Party Presidium when their cruiseship itinerary was changed en route from Stockholm and Copenhagen to Helsinki and Turku.[36] Traveling to Western Europe also required the necessary financial resources; historian Evgeniia Gutnova complained about the extraordinary cost of trips abroad in her memoir.[37] That said the problem was not as great as might be expected. While a fourteen-day itinerary to New York, Washington, Chicago, Dearborn, and Niagara Falls cost over 6000 rubles,[38] trips to Western Europe sometimes cost not much more than a trip to Eastern Europe. An excursion to Sweden in 1956 was 2390 rubles, which was about the same as a trip to the GDR and less than the cost of a trip to Poland the year previous.[39] Still, the cost of travel to capitalist countries was a dilemma. As an agency designed in part to make money for the regime through the acquisition of international capital obtained from tourists visiting the Soviet Union, Intourist could not use up all of the hard currency it acquired for the state on touristic reciprocity, especially to capitalist countries.[40] "For now," the Chairman of Intourist, Ankudinov argued in 1961, the hard currency Intourist acquired should be "spent on what is regarded as expedient, for example on the purchase of chemicals, on goods dearly needed."[41]

However, if social distinctions based on status and on economics continued after Stalin's death, there were differences too. To emphasize only the elite aspects of this travel is to miss how remarkable it was for *anyone* to travel as a

---

[34] Jukka Gronow, *Caviar with Champagne: Common Luxury and the Ideals of the Good Life in Stalin's Russia* (Oxford, 2003), 36.

[35] Vera S. Dunham, *In Stalin's Time: Middle-Class Values in Soviet Fiction* (Cambridge, 1976), 5, 17.

[36] GARF, f. 9520, op. 1, d. 420, ll. 17–18 (Trip report, Baltic cruises, 1961).

[37] Gutnova, *Perezhitoe*, 315.

[38] *Spravochnik: Ob usloviiakh i marshrutakh puteshestvii sovetskikh turistov za granitsu* (Moscow, 1960), 28, 156.

[39] GARF, f. 9520, op. 1, d. 316, l. 45 (Information for tourists traveling from Gorky Oblast to Sweden, 1956); RGANI, f. 5, op. 30, 113, l. 48 (1955).

[40] See the discussion of Intourist as a commercial venture in Shawn Salmon, "Marketing Socialism: Inturist in the Late 1950s and Early 1960s," Gorsuch and Koneker, *Turizm*, 190–92.

[41] GARF, f. 9520, op. 1, d. 391, l. 183 (Report to TEU conference on international travel, 1961). To bolster its accounts, Intourist applied a surcharge of 20 percent for tourists traveling to capitalist countries, plus the usual 6 percent to the VTsSPS. In addition, tourists paid to have their foreign passports formulated: 400 rubles in the case of a 1956 trip to Sweden. On the debit side, Intourist allowed each tourist traveling to Sweden to exchange seventy-seven rubles into hard currency, which was a small amount for Soviet tourists, but not insignificant perhaps for a regime short on hard-currency. GARF, f. 9520, op. 1, d. 316, l. 45.

tourist to the capitalist West. In his memoirs, German, himself admittedly a member of the cultural elite, describes in detail and with still palpable wonder the voyage of each person he knew who traveled to Europe beginning in 1956.[42] "Only party members went, having put in great effort, and with connections. But they went."[43] And they returned as objects of great fascination and envy. When German was told that he would be allowed to travel to Paris, he was bowled over: "It was unreal. It seemed that there was nothing else that I would ever need in this world!"[44]

TOURISM AS THEATER

Tourism joined other Soviet cultural offensives aimed at Western Europe. In the late 1950s, more international radio broadcasts—in German, Italian, French, English, Spanish, Swedish, and Finnish—were directed at Western Europe than at any other part of the non-socialist world.[45] Soviet news and culture magazines—the pictorial magazine *Culture and Life*, the news review *International Affairs*, and the magazines *Soviet Literature*, *Soviet Screen*, *Soviet Youth*, and *Soviet Woman*—were meant to educate Europeans (and others) about Soviet achievements.[46] The Soviet pavilion at the 1958 Brussels World's Fair was another effort to promote the USSR as modern, industrialized, ethnically diverse, and ideologically superior. Visitors were meant to feel awed on arrival as they entered a main hall which included enormous bronze sculptures of a male worker and female peasant, red banners running floor to ceiling, and—as a focal point at the far end—a sculpture of Lenin posed in front of a backdrop of the Kremlin. The two floors of the 269,000-square-foot pavilion emphasized industry, heavy machinery, and scientific accomplishments, with displays of the latest Soviet car, working replicas of an oil drill and coal mine, and exhibits about space exploration.[47] The focus on industrialization stood in notable contrast to the American

---

[42] German, *Slozhnoe proshedshee*, 263–64.
[43] German, *Slozhnoe proshedshee*, 283.
[44] German, *Slozhnoe proshedshee*, 426.
[45] 287 broadcast hours per week in 1957 in Europe in contrast to 193 hours in the Near East, South Asia and Africa, 126 in North America, and 35 in Latin America. "Soviet Propaganda and World Public Opinion since the Twentieth Party Congress," Confidential Trip report, USIA Office of Research and Intelligence, 14 July 1958, National Archives and Records Administration (hereafter NARA), RG 306, Box 15, S-10–58, 9.
[46] "Communist Media Activities in 1957," USIA Office of Research and Intelligence, January 15, 1958, NARA, RG 306, Box 16, S-2–58, 6: "Communist Propaganda Activities in Western Europe during 1959: A Brief Survey," USIA Office of Research and Intelligence, 23 February 1960, NARA, RG 306, Box 1, R-7–60, 25–26.
[47] "Brussels asks World to its Fair," *Life* 44, no.13 (31 March 1958): 23, 27; "Pavilion of the U.S.S.R. A Guide," NARA, RG 43, Box 5, BEG 401; "Incoming telegram (from Brussels), Department of State, 1 August 1957," NARA, RG 43, Box 5, BEG 401; Postcards, U.S.S.R.

Figure 14 The Soviet pavilion at the Brussels World's Fair. With permission from the Larry Zim World's Fair Collection, Archives Center, National Museum of American History, Smithsonian Institution.

Pavilion, which emphasized the pleasures of daily life and the provision of consumer goods (including propeller beanies and mail order catalogs).[48]

In contrast to radio programs, magazines, and the Brussels World's Fair, tourists presented the human face of Soviet socialism. Like these other efforts, however, their performance was also highly scripted. They were individuals at service to the Soviet *kollektiv*, a group traveling together, resembling in their organization and socially valued function other types of Soviet collectives: production-based, educational, artistic, and military.[49] As at the Brussels World's Fair, some of the achievements they spoke about were industrial: tourist-engineers visited European factories and spoke about Soviet ones. Other achievements were cultural. Tourists literally performed on behalf of Soviet socialism: they played the piano, sang opera, read poetry, and danced. Harold Shukman,

Pavilion, Larry Zim World's Fair Collection, 1841–1988, Archives Center, National Museum of American History, Smithsonian Institution Libraries, Box 48, Box 80.

[48] "Communist Propaganda and the Brussels Fair," 22 January 1958, USIA Office of Research and Intelligence, NARA, RG43, Box 5, BEG 401, 12; "Performing Arts Program USSR in Belgium," 23 September 1957, NARA, RG 43, Box 5, BEG 401.

[49] Oleg Kharkhordin, *The Collective and the Individual in Russia: A Study of Practices* (Berkeley, 1999), 87–88.

who worked as a British guide and translator for Soviet tourists in the 1950s, remembered having to schedule recitals at the last minute to accommodate tourists who had asked upon arrival in the UK to perform for British audiences. One of his groups included a female singer who had been a Stalin Prize winner, a ballet duo from the Bolshoi ballet, and a professional pianist. The group, according to Shukman, had a prearranged program designed to showcase Soviet abilities.[50] Not every group was so talented. "We sang our songs, performed our dances," one trip report noted, but it would be even better if future groups included "professionals."[51]

Tourists also acted on behalf of Soviet Union when they gave lectures and met with high-ranking politicians, educators, and legal professionals. Darya Smirnova, a member of the Presidium of the Supreme Soviet of the USSR and a weaver at the Trekhgornaia textile mill in Moscow, was typical. She visited with Major-General Dimoline, Secretary of the Inter Parliamentary Union, and spoke to students at Holburn College.[52] Question and answer sessions were a common form of interaction. Tourists told audiences that the Soviet Union was a peace-loving, rapidly modernizing country, deeply committed to improving the lives of ordinary people and workers. "Our tourists talked about the successes of Soviet people in fulfilling the five-year plan, about the achievements of Soviet science and culture, about the activities of youth organizations of the USSR, about the organization of everyday life and leisure of youth, about youth's rights and participation in the economy, politics and cultural life," wrote the leader of a 1960 trip to England in his report home.[53] Soviet students told their West European counterparts about the system of education in the Soviet Union, about pay for various categories of workers and white-collar workers, about medical care and possibilities for rest and vacation, about the activities of the young people of the Soviet Union in Siberia and the Far East.[54] In a game of ideological divide and conquer, tourists distinguished between a friendly Western Europe and an unrepentant United States. The Soviet policy of peaceful coexistence was said to be maintained "despite the unidealistic, aggressive actions of American militarists against the Soviet Union."[55]

As if for a play or musical concert, tourists had to prepare for these ideological displays. Soviet guidebooks were one form of preparation. Guidebooks taught travelers how to be tourists—what museums to visit and what sites to see—but they also instructed tourists in the proper ways of understanding and evaluating what they saw and experienced. Pre-trip seminars provided an even more explicit script. In contrast to people traveling to Eastern Europe, who typically met with

---

[50] Interview with Harold Shukman, St. Antony's College, Oxford, June 2003.
[51] RGASPI, f. m-5, op. 1, d. 197, ll. 36–37 (Report to Sputnik, 1964).
[52] *SCR General Trip report*, 1964, 8–9 SCR Archives.
[53] RGASPI, f. m-5, op. 1, d. 94, l. 8 (Trip report, England, 1960).
[54] RGASPI, f. m-5, op. 1, d. 197, l. 32.
[55] RGASPI, f. m-5, op. 1, d. 94, l. 8.

their guide and some local instructors for a quick briefing before departure, tourists to capitalist countries typically met for two to four days of training in Moscow before heading west.[56] Students traveling to Austria in 1960 attended a pre-trip seminar where they learned, for example, about Austrian history, economics, literature, and music. The students were also educated in Soviet politics and history and taken on an excursion to an exhibition about the Soviet economy.[57] The instructions continued when tourists arrived in a foreign country where they were met by the Soviet ambassador or a consular member and taken to the embassy to register their passports, receive further information about the country they were visiting, and hear any "necessary recommendations" about proper "norms of behavior for Soviet tourists."[58] This was meant to insure that even as they were exposed to European culture and beauty, tourists were inoculated against ideological influences and unhealthy enthusiasms.

All of this was an effort to standardize the discourse and behavior of Soviet tourists abroad. If the tourist experience was still troublingly unpredictable, what Soviet citizens said and did should not be. Notably, although much of the rhetoric resembled longtime Soviet discourses of self (apart from the discussion of peaceful coexistence) growing up Soviet was not enough to ensure a proper performance. The need for a tourist script evokes Andrei Yurchak's argument about the increasingly fixed and ideologically clichéd authoritarian language of late socialism. Beginning in the 1960s, according to Yurchak, the "performative dimension" of Soviet discourse, with its "reproduction of conventionalized and ritualized forms," became even more important than the "meanings which might be associated with these forms." "As long as one reproduced the precise forms of language, the correctness of the meanings conveyed was guaranteed."[59] In *Everything Was Forever, Until It Was No More: The Last Soviet Generation,* Yurchak describes the processes through which the "normalized and fixed structures" of authoritative discourse were replicated in Central Committee documents, films, school curriculum, and monuments.[60] Training for tourists to Western Europe effected to do the same. That said, Soviet authorities were not alone in this effort, even if they were more rigid and authoritarian. By the early

[56] RGASPI, f. m-5, op. 1, d. 52, l. 22 (Instructions on formulating documents and sending young tourists abroad); d. 95, l. 97 (Trip report, Italy, 1962); GARF, f. 9520, op. 1, d. 420, l. 11 On pre-trip training, also see Kharkhordin's discussion of the tourist *kollektiv*, Kharkhordin, *The Collective and the Individual*, 109–10.

[57] RGASPI, f. m-5, op. 1, d. 55, l. 12. Beginning in 1977, tourists received the brochure *USSR: 100 Questions and Answers.* Aleksei Popov, "Sovetskie turisty za rubezhom: ideologiia, kommunikatsiia, emotsii (po otchetam rukovoditelei turistskikh grupp)," *Istorichna panorama: nayk. statei,* vol 7. (Chernovci, 2009), 50.

[58] RGASPI, f. m-5, op. 1, d. 94, l. 4; GARF, f. 9612, op. 1, d. 373, ll. 1, 6; f. 9520, op.1, d. 423, l. 13 (Trip report on a non-hard-currency exchange from Uzbekistan to Austria, 1961).

[59] Andrei Yurchak, *Everything Was Forever, Until It Was No More: The Last Soviet Generation* (Princeton 2006), 50–53.

[60] Yurchak, *Everything Was Forever,* 26.

1960s, the US government was also actively encouraging travel to the Soviet Union, and also, if less forcibly, trying to direct what American citizens said about the United States while abroad. "You are about to have one of the most rewarding experiences of your life—first-hand contact with the Soviet people," the United States Information Agency argued in a document it prepared for American tourists traveling to the Soviet Union. "It will be more rewarding if, when you come back, you can feel that you have successfully communicated a realistic picture of America, and have contributed, as far as one private individual can, to a lasting peace between our two countries."[61]

COMRADELY AND CORRECT

Soviet tourists faced the suspicions not only of their West European hosts but also of their Soviet handlers, who were anxious to make sure tourists remained loyal and behaved appropriately. Travelers were kept under close watch, and their behavior monitored by trip leaders who were carefully chosen Komsomol, Trade Union, and Party activists. Group leaders reported back to authorities about how the tourists were received, about people and organizations to be trusted or not trusted, about what West Europeans knew or did not know about the Soviet Union, and about the behavior of their charges. Their testimonies were read by authorities in Intourist, in the Trade Union Excursion Bureau, in the Komsomol, and in various Party organizations, including the Cultural Departments of the Central Committee and the Ministry of Foreign Affairs.

Notably, while reports about travel to Eastern Europe frequently complained about problem behaviors, reports about travel to Western Europe generally praised the behavior of Soviet travelers. "Every member" of a group to England in 1960 was reported to have "understood the goal of the trip, entered into discussions and arguments at meetings, correctly explained our positions."[62] The discipline of a youth Sputnik tour to Italy was said to have been "good," and the relationship between the tourists and their leaders "comradely and correct."[63] In part, this reflects the performative aspects of trip reports; group leaders understandably eager to present their trips as successful and their charges as well-behaved (something explored in greater detail below). However, there is also good reason to believe that most tourists to Western Europe behaved as expected.

Some were anxious about traveling to places so long portrayed as dangerous. These fears were reinforced by Soviet authorities, who may themselves have been uncertain, or who may have recognized that caution usefully discouraged

---

[61] "Communicating with the Soviet People: Suggestions for American Tourists and Students," NARA, USIA Office of Research, RG 43, Box 19, S-23–60.

[62] RGASPI, f. m-5, op. 1, d. 56, l. 7; GARF, f. 9520, op. 1, d. 420, l. 11.

[63] RGASPI, f. m-5, op. 1, d. 95, l. 1 (Trip report, Italy, 1964).

independent activity. Travelers were warned that Western security agencies would be watching their "every move."[64] They were instructed not to walk about by themselves, especially in stores and at night, and not to give anyone their home addresses.[65] Many tourists, understandably and not surprisingly, accepted these instructions. "For unexperienced people, like me, who had never gone abroad," Evgeniia Gutnova recalled, "I accepted this in good faith and not without fear set out on my journey."[66]

Many were surely sincere socialists for whom the character they were being asked to perform was not only familiar but consistent with their own beliefs and understandings of self. Yurchak challenges us to take seriously that for "great numbers" of Soviet citizens in the 1960s and 1970s, "many of the fundamental values, ideals, and realities of socialist life (such as equality, community, selfless-ness, altruism, friendship, ethical relations, safety, education, work, creativity, and concern for the future) were of genuine importance, despite the fact that many of their everyday practices routinely transgressed, reinterpreted, or refused certain norms and rules."[67] This was especially the case, presumably, for the carefully chosen traveler to the capitalist West who, as a member of the elite, was a beneficiary of the Soviet system. In addition, no matter what they might have believed in private and at home, they often felt compelled to represent the USSR positively when abroad. "National pride before foreigners is an immensely powerful emotion," journalist Hedrick Smith wrote about Soviet citizens in the early 1970s. "A magazine editor told me that I was mistaken if I thought Russians had to be coached by officials on what to tell foreigners. Even without prompting, he said, common people exaggerate their standard of living to Westerners visiting their homes and factories. 'It is natural,' he said. 'People feel, 'We're Russians. We must appear well before foreigners.'"[68] Performance anxiety only escalated when Soviet citizens traveled abroad. Gutnova remembers being eager to defend the Soviet Union against slight or embarrassment. Proud of the USSR, yet aware of Western Europe's illustrious cultural heritage, Gutnova worried that she and her fellow Soviet tourists would inadvertently resemble those made fun of in Nikolai Leikin's satirical novel from the turn of the century.[69] Leikin mocked a group of Russians on a tour of Europe as "uncom-fortable in fashions that did not suit them, served dishes that soured their appetites, fluent only in vocabulary words for "hotel room" and "liquor," and in constant distress over cross-cultural gaffes."[70] Indeed, early tourists, like first

---

[64] Gutnova, *Perezhitoe*, 315.
[65] Gutnova, *Perezhitoe*, 316.
[66] Gutnova, *Perezhitoe*, 316.
[67] Yurchak, *Everything Was Forever, Until It Was No More*, 8.
[68] Hedrick Smith, *The Russians* (New York, 1976), 412–13.
[69] Gutnova, *Perezhitoe*, 316.
[70] Louise McReynolds, "The Prerevolutionary Russian Tourist: Commercialization in the Nineteenth Century," in Gorsuch and Koenker, *Turizm*, 17.

time travelers most places, did commit social gaffes. The first Soviet tourists to Italy in 1956 (there to attend the Winter Olympics) garnered lots of attention both for the novelty of their visit and because they ordered spaghetti for breakfast. Later groups learned quickly, becoming in the words of the *New York Times*, "quiet and well-behaved and eager to please."[71]

Tourists also behaved because they were under surveillance. In contrast to domestic tourism, a goal of which was to produce a self activating and autonomous subject, international tourism emphasized discipline over independence. Travelers were kept under close watch by Soviet trip leaders (and by the KGB), whose disciplinary observation helped reinforce appropriate behavior and whose reports determined if tourists would be allowed to travel again.[72] Mutual surveillance, of one tourist by another, also helped ensure obedience; tourists were not supposed to walk alone but always to travel in threesomes while strolling in Western cities.[73] While a month at the Black Sea away from the usual close confines of a communal apartment provided the domestic tourist with opportunities for private behaviors and personal liaisons unavailable or not allowed at home,[74] international travelers, especially those visiting capitalist countries, were more closely scrutinized than they were at home.[75] "While drinking a capitalist Coca-Cola or seeing a bourgeois sex film, the tourist will go through mental agonies wondering whether the group leader or some secret informer within the group will see him doing it," Soviet emigre (and defector) Leonid Vladimirov wrote in London's *Telegraph* in 1966.[76] The tourists praised most highly were those who in the words of one glowing report, "agreed at every step with the leader of the group."[77] When a radio engineer traveling to England in 1956 asked to meet with an English radio worker, the Soviet embassy agreed but insisted that he be accompanied by the group *starosta*. The radio worker resisted this requirement and agreed to be accompanied only after it was made clear that he had no choice. He was not recommended for further travel abroad.[78] Some tourists were not unduly bothered by the scrutiny. Valeria Kunina knew that her group to England was accompanied by representatives of the KGB, indeed they instructed the group what to do and how to behave, but

[71] HU OSA, RFE/RL RI, Soviet Red Archives, 1953–1994, Old Code Subject Files, 300-80-1, Container 1048 (Olympic Fans saw Italy, 1957).

[72] RGASPI, f. m-5, op. 1, d. 197, l. 35.

[73] Kharkhordin, *The Collective and the Individual*, 110.

[74] Anna Rotkirch, "Traveling Maidens and Men with Parallel Lives—Journeys as Private Space During Late Socialism," in *Beyond the Limits: The Concept of Space in Russian History and Culture*, ed. Jeremy Smith, Studia Historica 62 (Helsinki, 1999).

[75] RGASPI, f. m-5, op. 1, d. 55, ll. 16–22 (Trip report, Austria, 1961).

[76] HU OSA RFE/RL RI, Soviet Red Archives, 1953–1994, Old Code Subject Files, 300-80-1, Container 1049.

[77] RGASPI, f. m-5, op. 1, d. 94, l. 10.

[78] GARF, f. 9612, op. 1, d. 373, l. 13.

she was not bothered, nor surprised. She expected it.[79] So too for Natalia P.: "You know, for some reason I really didn't give the matter much thought. I was so disciplined, so . . ."[80] Others reacted differently. A Jewish scientist on a trip to the West recalled lying to the American scholar when asked if there was academic discrimination against Jews in the USSR. He was "afraid . . . that if he told her the truth, somehow the word would get back to Moscow and he would be denied further trips abroad." He told his story to Hedrick Smith having already decided to emigrate to Israel.[81]

Be it because of internal discipline or external, most tourists said what they were supposed to. But not all. Although I have found no evidence of tourists defecting in the 1950s or early 1960s in the archival materials I have had access to,[82] Soviet tourists did sometimes speak and behave in ways that challenged the ideal performance of the Sovietness. In contrast to travel to Eastern Europe for which, as I have described in Chapter Three, authorities were particularly worried about manners and clothing, political preparation was most at issue for travel to the West.[83] Poor answers to political questions prompted trip leaders to ask for more "serious and deep" pre-trip preparation about "the most hard-hitting issues" of Soviet internal politics, the German question, nuclear arms, the international youth movement, and contemporary literature and art.[84] More preparation might have helped guard against indiscretions like that of I.M. Danilin, a radio worker who when asked by an English journalist when the Soviet Union would achieve full communism, responded "that it would be in about twenty years."[85] Also a problem was the tourist who when asked about the current state of language training in the Soviet Union replied that fewer people knew English in the USSR than English people knew Russian because the system of teaching languages in Soviet universities was so poor.[86] More serious was the case of E.V. Mironova, who on a trip to Austria spoke about the purges to the Austrians sitting near her in a restaurant, and of a student who on a trip to the Netherlands publicly shared information about high-school and university-level

---

[79] Interview with Valeria Emmanuilovna Kunina, Moscow, 2004.

[80] Raleigh, *Russia's Sputnik Generation*, 111.

[81] Smith, *The Russians*, 19.

[82] Other travelers did defect of course, most famously Rudolf Nureyev. See David Caute, *The Dancer Defects: The Struggle for Cultural Supremacy during the Cold War* (Oxford, 2003), chp. 17.

[83] This is not to say that clothing was of no concern. Generally of greatest concern (and the references are occasional even here) were trips to France where competing in the arena of culture and fashion might be understood as a sort of politics. Thus the trip leader to France who complained of his Komsomol-aged charges that too "little attention" had been paid when choosing them to their "cultural level," "appearance, [and] clothes." RGASPI, f. m-5, op. 1, d. 174, l. 32 (Trip report, France, 1964).

[84] See, for example, RGASPI, f. m-5, op. 1, d. 160, l. 67 (Trip report, Belgium, 1962); d. 197, l. 22.

[85] RGASPI, f. m-5, op. 1, d. 159, l. 34.

[86] RGASPI, f. m-5, op. 1, d. 197, l. 36.

study of military affairs in the Soviet Union.[87] Sometimes the inadequacies were more embarrassing than they were dangerous. At a lively discussion (in Austria) about the Nazi argument that Germans were the master race, Comrade Bondarchuk blurted out: "How odd, reading our books it's clear isn't it that the master race has always been us, Russians!"[88]

Bondarchuk was reported to be "not a bad Comrade" if not well prepared. Mironova, on the other hand, was said to be drunk. Danilin was reported to be "poorly politically prepared," but also unduly "familiar," acting in an excessively "free and easy" fashion. The supposed causes of bad behavior for these individuals are familiar ones: drunkenness, youthfulness, and a "lack of political preparation." Age in particular was at issue. "Experience has shown" that the young people between the ages of eighteen and twenty do not yet have enough "life experience," one delegate complained at a Moscow conference on international tourism. They "sometimes incorrectly admire life abroad."[89] Komsomol groups could be more diverse than adult groups; these were professionals in training rather than adults at the top of their game. More than two-thirds of the people traveling with the Komsomol to capitalist countries in 1960 were younger than thirty years of age.[90] But here too, the desirability of the trip to Europe, combined with some anxiety on the part of authorities about youthful indiscretions, meant that places theoretically reserved for students were sometimes taken by middle-aged bureaucrats and professionals.[91] Nationality too was sometimes, if more rarely, said to be at fault. A leader of a group of young tourists to France complained about the "uncultured" people in his group from the national republics and questioned whether it was "expedient" to select tourists according to nationality.[92] Evidently, a successful performance depended on the training, discipline, and skill of the "actors," something older, experienced, and (in some cases) Russian tourists were believed most likely to possess.

"THE WORLD APPLAUDS THEM"

It was not only tourists who were performing, but trip leaders. Theirs was a "play within a play,"[93] performed for audiences at home with their reports shaped by their understanding of audience expectation. As such, trip testimonies

---

[87] GARF, f. 9520, op. 1, d. 423, l. 33 (Trip report, Austria, 1961); RGASPI, f. m-5, op.1, d. 160, l. 50 (Trip report, The Netherlands, 1961). This part of the trip report to The Netherlands was underlined by the reader and an exclamation point put next to it.

[88] GARF, f. 9520, op. 1, d. 423, l. 12.

[89] GARF, f. 9520, op. 1, d. 438, l. 185.

[90] RGASPI, f. m-5, op. 1, d. 52, l. 9.

[91] RGASPI, f. m-5, op. 1, d. 56, l. 7.

[92] RGASPI, f. m-5, op. 1, d. 174, l. 33.

[93] Dening, "The theatricality of observing and being observed," 452.

emphasized the political and the performative, secondarily described the educative and cultural, and generally said little about leisure time except when it interfered with more purposeful goals.[94] The emphasis on the serious and scientific has little in common with the intimate, often ironic voice of the twenty-first-century travel writer (or, more notably, with the sometimes romantically touristic tone of Soviet reports about travel to Eastern Europe with their discussions of landscape and architecture). Instead, these reports more closely resemble those of early eighteenth-century European scientific and scholarly travelers, whom, as described by Orvar Löfgren, traveled "for a practical purpose, for commerce or fact-finding . . . for information on local economy and society."[95] The reports were generally (if not exclusively) factual and largely devoid of the personal, be it the feelings of the trip leader or the personal experiences of tourists. In a 1964 synopsis about a trip to France, the trip leader noted in just one sentence that the tourists had free time during their seven days in Cannes, but said nothing about what they did in this time. Much of the account was devoted to descriptions of meetings with young communists as organized by the Soviet Embassy.[96]

The peculiarly Soviet conditions of the relationship between writer and reader influenced the performative nature of these accounts. If group leaders were themselves surveyors, of both their tourists and of the countries they traveled to, they were themselves also kept under observation. The testimonies of trip leaders abroad resembled those of Soviet guides for foreigners visiting the Soviet Union home who, as Michael David-Fox has described for the 1920s and 1930s, faced pressure to report details of conversations and "answers to politically sensitive questions" as a form of "political insurance."[97] Likewise, it was not atypical for reports in the 1950s to describe in careful detail not only the questions that local students asked of their Soviet counterparts, but each politically correct answer.[98] Whether traveling to a fellow socialist country or to capitalist countries, trip leaders would have known that any possibilities for future trips, as well as possibilities for advancement at home, depended on their own behavior and that of their charges while abroad.

This is not to imply, however, that trip reports were negative about the capitalist West or that trip leaders were not delighted to be traveling abroad. On the contrary, West European states were largely portrayed as interesting and attractive countries from which the Soviet Union had things to learn. Trip reports provided information about skills, behaviors, and technologies that the Soviet Union might benefit from, particularly in the arenas of technology,

[94] RGASPI, f. m-5, op, 1, d. 197, l. 22; d. 56, l. 7; GARF, f. 9612, op. 1, d. 373, l. 32.
[95] Orvar Löfgren, *On Holiday: A History of Vacationing* (Berkeley, 2002), 18.
[96] RGASPI, f. m-5, op. 1, d. 174, l. 64.
[97] Michael David-Fox, "The Fellow Travelers Revisited: The 'Cultured West' through Soviet Eyes," *The Journal of Modern History* 75 (June 2003): 313.
[98] See, for example, RGASPI, f. 5-m, op. 1, d. 174, ll. 103–107 (Trip report, France, 1964).

consumption, and service. Accounts commented favorably about European service and cleanliness including a bus driver who wore a neat and clean uniform, and an hotel that had hot water "round-the clock." There was praise for the Scottish hotel rooms with individual "transmitters" through which one could contact the restaurant and order room service.[99] The technologically advanced and consumer-oriented West admired here is familiar from Soviet praise from the 1920s for Taylorism (the American theory of time management which aimed to increase labor productivity), and from the 1930s for the attractiveness of German window decorations and the self-service options at large American department stores like Macy's.[100] It was consistent too, with Khrushchev's open admiration, indeed envy, of capitalist technology. "The Paris airport [Orly] is very well-equipped," Khrushchev reported about his visit to France in 1960, "its runways have excellent concrete surfaces. The West must be given credit, or for it knows how to use concrete better than we do. There were no bumps or rough spots.... Unfortunately things are not like that in our country.... The difference struck you right in the eye, and unfortunately the comparison was not in our favor."[101]

Admiring trip reports were balanced by reassuring ones. Much of the reassurance found in trip leader reports was mimetic: the authoritative language of late socialism circulated from authorities to tourists and trip leaders and then back to authorities in the form of a trip report. Particularly useful to this end, was the enthusiasm West Europeans were said to show for their Soviet visitors. Instead of commenting on the pleasures of Italy or France, accounts often emphasized the pleasures of hearing good things about the Soviet Union: "On the squares and in the museums of Rome, on the embankments and streets of Venice, on trains, in restaurants ... the Italians, finding out that we were Russians, stopped with pleasure, entered into conversation, and ... asked about the Soviet Union, about the life of Soviet people."[102] During our entire trip, "wherever we were, we felt considerably cared for as representatives of the great Soviet people, and sincere admiration for the achievements of our country," a trip leader to Greece and Italy wrote.[103] In part, this rhetoric was that of peaceful coexistence. But it was also used to counteract long-standing anxieties about Russia's inferiority vis-à vis the "West." In this, private trip reports for authorities at home resembled the language of published travelogues in the Soviet press.[104] In a 1958 article entitled "The world applauds them," *Ogonek* published pictures of Soviet performers

[99] GARF, f. 9612, op. 1, d. 373, ll. 4, 27
[100] Gronow, *Caviar with Champagne,* 74–78.
[101] Sergei Khrushchev, ed. *Memoirs of Nikita Khrushchev: Statesman (1953–1964),* vol 3 (University Park, 2007), 196.
[102] RGASPI, f. m-5, op. 1, d. 95, l. 3.
[103] RGASPI, f. m-5, op. 1, d. 95, l. 25.
[104] Marina Balina, "The Literature of Travel," unpublished paper (2003), 10, 12.

together with quotations from international newspapers commending the Soviet visitors.[105]

In part, this effort was aimed at re-imagining the Soviet Union as "European" by describing positively a shared history and culture between Western Europe and the USSR. This was a shared Europeanism that excluded the USA: one group of Soviet tourists to Cyprus were said to have been met with enormous enthusiasm, while no one was especially interested in a group of American tourists visiting there at the same time.[106] Ultimately, however, the goal was to beat Europeans at their own game: to be as cultured as the citizens of the "civilized" West while defending and extending socialism. To this end, trip reports sometimes showed tourists as more knowledgeable about European culture and history than West Europeans themselves. "Before our trip to England we did not think that we would know more than English students about the works of many contemporary English writers and artists, film directors, about the contemporary economic position of their country," one Sputnik guide wrote.[107] But to their pride, Soviet youth displayed "a wider range of interests," more "erudition," deeper knowledge on specialist questions [about British writers and artists] than did English youth themselves.[108] When a local guide in Scotland was unable to answer the questions of Soviet tourists about Scottish geography, history, literature, and art, it was the tourists who provided explanations to the guides about historical monuments and events.[109] In contrast to the tourists' deep knowledge about European culture and history, the Scottish guide was said to be engaged and active only when discussing the cruder "aspects of the 'free world'."[110]

As we have seen, however, not all tourists behaved in such an exemplary way. The sending of relatively untested individuals, and in relatively large numbers, sometimes challenged trip leaders' need to provide positive reports. So too when tourists met hostile audiences who questioned Soviet presentations of self. Although political authorities in the Khrushchev era urged tourist authorities to promote Soviet achievements among a wide range of foreign audiences, the conflict between ideals and experience meant that a trip leader's job was easiest when groups met with friendly locals. Thus the elusion evident in some reports. A trip leader to England in 1956 wrote that one of the most important aspects of the trip had been establishing contact with the "regular" people of England, but in this case, "regular" people meant the employees at the newspaper the *Daily*

---

[105] "Im aplodiruet mir," *Ogonek* 20 (1958): 22. Also see "Communist Bloc Participation at International Film Festivals," USIA Office of Research and Intelligence, 5 December 1960, NARA, RG 306, Box 3, R-82–60, 3.

[106] RGAPSI, f. m-5, op. 1, d. 202, l. 10 (Trip report, Cyprus, 1964).

[107] RGASPI, f. m-5, op. 1, d. 197, l. 31.

[108] RGASPI, f. m-5, op. 1, d. 197, l. 31.

[109] RGASPI, f. m-5, op. 1, d. 94, l. 4.

[110] RGASPI, f. m-5, op. 1, d. 94, l. 6.

Worker and English workers associated with the British–Soviet Friendship Society[111] The doctors, lawyers, and professors who hospitably took care of another group "on every step of their way" were associated with the Belgian Communist Party.[112] Some of this was not only desirable but unavoidable. Friendship societies were frequent sponsors of Soviet tourists and responsible for organizing their itineraries and activities. The [British] Society for Cultural Relations with the USSR, entertained tourists at SCR "garden parties," arranged for them to visit British homes, and introduced them to British colleagues.[113] The advantage of working with friendship societies went beyond the organizational and touristic, however, as it was the demonstratively hospitable locals in friendship societies that were most likely to satisfy Soviet desires not only to perform, but to be applauded.

PERFORMANCES BY LOCALS

A successful performance depends on audience response, performance being by nature an interactive process. As suggested above, many meetings with West Europeans were quite cordial, satisfying Soviet desires for a warm welcome. In her memoirs, Gutnova remembers the people she met in Great Britain taking "a lively interest in our country, system of education in schools and universities, in everyday life and art." "They were almost always friendly, warm, and avoided arguments."[114] The experience of a group of tourists to Great Britain in 1956 who were personally welcomed by the Lord Provost of Glasgow, was typical in the earliest years of travel. The tourists presented the Provost with a Palekh box; he invited them for a cup of coffee followed by a visit to watch a municipal meeting.[115] That Soviet tourists were greeted by the Lord Provost—an honor repeated in many of the towns and cities visited by early Soviet tourists—is a good reminder of how extraordinary these early visits were for West Europeans.

However, Soviet tourism presented an opportunity for political performance by Europeans as well as by their Soviet visitors, and West European agendas were not always the same as Soviet ones. The Soviet Union had tried to influence international opinion prior to the 1950s, but its efforts in the 1920s and early 1930s were primarily directed at individuals assumed to be sympathetic with the Soviet project.[116] Beginning in the mid-1950s, Soviet efforts were newly aimed at a much wider audience of the capitalist public whose opinions were necessarily

[111] GARF, f. 9612, op. 1, d. 373, l. 30.
[112] RGASPI, f. m-5, op. 1, d. 160, ll. 63–67.
[113] Annual General Meeting Trip report, 13 May 1967 in "SCR Events 1960s," SCR Archive.
[114] Gutnova, *Perezhitoe*, 319–20.
[115] GARF, f. 9612, op. 1, d. 373, l. 2.
[116] Michael David-Fox, "From Illusory "Society" to Intellectual "Public": VOKS, International Travel and Party-Intelligentsia Relations in the Interwar Period," *Contemporary European History*

more varied. "It's characteristic that practically no one asked us about [Soviet] cosmonauts even though during the very period of our trip they were returning to Earth and being met in Moscow," complained one trip leader to Italy.[117] Sometimes, the problem was one of ignorance. Trip leaders frequently grumbled that what European locals knew about the USSR was often "outdated." British art and literature students had heard of the 15th-century icon painter Andrei Rublev but not about Soviet cultural figures such as Maxim Gorky, Vladimir Mayakovsky, and Mikhail Sholokhov.[118] West Europeans thought about Siberia as a "place of exile," and were surprised to hear that it was highly industrialized with major cities and universities."[119]

More troublesome were anti-Soviet comments and questions. If Soviet propaganda could be scripted, questions from West Europeans could not: How do you explain the Soviet response to the Hungarian Revolution? What is the current state of relations with Yugoslavia? Can you freely criticize your government in the press? What is the Soviet relationship with China? What you have to do in order to be able to travel to the West? Can I correspond with you or will you be followed for that? Wouldn't you like to stay here?[120] Answers to these questions—as recorded by trip leaders—were admirably agile. When asked about the cult of personality, one group to France is said to have responded: "a smart person always understands that the unmasking of the mistakes of the past is the best guarantee to not repeat these mistakes in the future."[121] More difficult to answer were the frequent questions about living conditions and consumer goods. "Do you have butter in the Soviet Union? Where did you buy that suit?"[122] Answers sometimes stretched the limits of credulity. When asked if Soviet citizens owned personal property, one group replied that "very many people have their own cars, apartments and cooperative housing, dachas, garden plots and so on."[123] If in the Soviet Union, the regime and its citizens understood that Soviet power was based on the promise of future goods and opportunities, the Soviet Union-as-road-trip required the performance of current successes and achievements.

Soviet émigré's were an additional source of conflict. They asked provocative questions about the lack of freedom in the Soviet Union. They approached tourists on the street to talk with them and hand out anti-Soviet materials.[124]

11, no. 1 (2002): 7–32; David-Fox, "Stalinist Westernizer? Aleksandr Arosev's Literary and Political Depictions of Europe," *Slavic Review* 62, 4 (2003): 733–59.

[117] RGASPI, f. m-5, op. 1, d. 95, l. 7.

[118] RGASPI, f. m-5, op. 1, d. 159, l. 32.

[119] RGASPI, f. m-5, op. 1, d. 159, l. 31; d. 197, l. 32.

[120] These types of questions are described in many trip reports. For two examples, see RGASPI, f. 5-m, op. 1, d. 174, ll. 103–107; d. 56, l. 12.

[121] RGASPI, f. 5-m, op. 1, d. 174, l. 106.

[122] RGASP, f. m-5, op. 1, d. 56, l. 12.

[123] RGASPI, f. 5-m, op. 1, d. 174, l. 104.

[124] RGAPSI, f. m-5, op. 1, d. 197, l. 20; RGANI, f. 5, op. 30, d. 320, ll. 12–13 (KGB report to the Central Committee, 1960).

Those working as guides were viewed with particular antipathy. Groups to England were warned about a local guide who spoke very good Russian and not such good English, who gave her tourists English-language journals and other gifts, and who tried to get the tourists to go shopping with her.[125] Some guides—émigré and otherwise—were accused of more nefarious behavior. One Italian-Russian guide was repeatedly reported to be working with the police, a fact discovered when her police identity card fell out of her pocket.[126] She was described as going out for coffee every evening for twenty or thirty minutes, each time meeting and speaking with two people.[127] Other times, tour guides were thought to be fine, but bus drivers were viewed suspiciously. The British bus driver "Jack" was said to know more about the tour program than the guide and could answer any question. According to the Soviet Embassy, "Jack" knew a little Russian but tried not to reveal it, all the better to keep the tourists under close observation.[128] It is not surprising that trip leaders and other Soviet authorities worried about espionage. After all, Soviet guides reported to authorities about foreign tourists.[129] And indeed, British tour guides did report to British authorities about their charges and their trips and presumably other local tour guides did too.

Like Soviet authorities who sometimes sent thirty-five-year-olds on Sputnik trips, and accompanied all trips with leaders and KGB minders, it appears that European authorities also sometimes supervised encounters. Trip leaders objected that meetings with "ordinary" local citizens sometimes appeared staged. Instead of meeting with the young workers one Soviet group had expected, they met with "real gentlemen" wearing ties and smoking pipes.[130] Forty-five-year-old ringers answered the questions one group of British students supposedly found too difficult to answer, while a group of French students was felt to be too well prepared to be believed.[131] Indeed, a 1956 British Foreign Office document recommended that local representatives meeting with Soviet visitors should be prepared in advance to answer questions about the British educational system, about where British students could study Russian, about the Parliamentary system, about housing and family budgets, and about local industries. The goal, in this case, was not to point out problems with the Soviet Union, but to impress visitors with information about the United Kingdom: "It makes a good impression" if local representatives provide handouts with statistical information. University tours, especially if conducted by "a world famous professor" and trips

[125] GARF, f. 9612, op. 1, d. 373, l. 29.

[126] RGASPI, f. m-5, op. 1, d. 95, l. 96.

[127] RGASPI, f. m-5, op. 1, d. 95, l. 4.

[128] RGASPI, f. m-5, op. 1, d. 94, l. 6.

[129] See, as just one example, the report on a group of American tourists in 1957, RGANI, f. 5, op. 30, d. 225, ll. 45–47.

[130] RGASPI, f. m-5, op. 1, d. 56, ll. 19–20 (Trip report, England, 1960).

[131] RGASPI, f. m-5, op. 1, d. 197, l. 44; d. 57, l. 99 (Trip report, France).

to technical marvels, industrial giants, and "very modern" hospitals were on the list of desirable destinations.[132]

Most frustrating to Soviet authorities was the apparent immunity of the Western European press to Soviet rhetorical strategies. Soviet tourists were frequently interviewed by newspaper, radio, and television reporters, and the results, according to Soviet reports, were too often "rubbish." "Sensationalist" news reporting described Russian students as "astonished [by the wonders of Europe]."[133] Trip leaders complained that questions about clothing and popular culture were meant to compare the Soviet Union unfavorably to Western Europe.[134] Unpleasant questions of this type were explained—and probably rightly so in some cases—as deliberately provocative. The European press did try to manipulate what Soviet tourists said for their own purposes, as in a group who were interviewed by the BBC about their positive feelings about their European trip so that the interview could be rebroadcast in Eastern Europe.[135] On the occasion of Khrushchev's trip to United States in 1959, to take another similar, if non-European, example, American officials wrote a confidential list of questions to be put to Khrushchev by "reporters" (aka USIA stringers): "Is your idea of coexistence compatible with jamming of US radio broadcasts, restricting foreign travel in two thirds of your country, preventing the free sale of US publications to the Soviet public, and continuing to refuse exit permits to Soviet citizens desiring to join their relatives in the US? "[136]

PERFORMING ON THE INTERNATIONAL STAGE

In *Performing Justice: Agitation Trials in Early Soviet Russia*, Elizabeth Wood describes how Soviet citizens learned to "act Bolshevik," not, she notes, "in the conscious sense of someone 'acting a part'" but in the more complex sense of learning to adopt "a series of behaviors that one feels are appropriate and correct to the situation."[137] The performative aspect of Soviet life, especially official life as embodied in authoritative language, only increased in late socialism according to Andrei Yurchak. Participating in ritualized acts of discourse and action "reproduced oneself as a 'normal' Soviet person."[138] What happened when the Soviet Union took these performances abroad? They were successful, but not

[132] The National Archives, London, Foreign Office FO 371 122948 (On treatment of Soviet delegations in the UK, 1956).
[133] RGASPI, f. m-5, op. 1, d. 94, l. 10.
[134] GARF, f. 9612, op. 1, d. 373, l. 32.
[135] RGASPI, f. m-5, op. 1, d. 197, l. 21.
[136] "Public affairs aspect of Khrushchev's trip," Memorandum for meeting of 28 August 1959, NARA, RG 59, Box 4, file 3.4.
[137] Elizabeth Wood, *Performing Justice: Agitation Trials in Early Soviet Russia* (Ithaca, 2005), 10–11.
[138] Yurchak, *Everything was Forever*, 25.

always in the way the authorities wanted. In their private reports for authorities at home, some trip leaders acknowledged a misfit between the performative strategies of Soviet tourists—politically focused and unrelentingly serious—and the European market. "The French love it if you speak with humor," one trip leader noted in frustration. "Your joke will show up in the newspaper but everything else that you might have said about . . . friendly relations, about the struggle for peace, about the life and studies of youth, all of this 'propaganda' will not appear in the newspaper."[139]

This observation was an important one. The kinds of ritualized, rhetorical performances that were so automatic for Soviet citizens, often made West European observers suspicious. Although Soviet citizens, as Yurchak argues, understood that form and meaning were separate, they did not immediately conclude from this that Soviet project as a whole was without significance: they recognized the ritualistic qualities of the reproduction of authoritative discourse, but could still feel "an affinity for many of the meanings, possibilities, values, and promises of socialism."[140] Some Western European observers, in contrast, dismissed it all as propaganda, suspicious about touristic behaviors which appeared too obviously choreographed. At issue were conflicting notions of authenticity. Newspapers, like *The Times*, were skeptical about speeches by Soviet visitors, but they enthusiastically covered the otherwise ordinary, and thereby "authentic," touristic behaviors of Soviet tourists in unusual detail as a first glimpse of the otherwise elusive *homo sovieticus*.[141] West European observers, in other words, were most likely to be moved by the very kinds of encounter—a conversation over dinner, a glimpse of Soviet tourists on a shopping spree—that Soviet tourist authorities most worried about. The next chapter turns to these more informal encounters in the urban landscapes, department stores, cafés and bordellos of the capitalist West.

---

[139] RGASPI, f. m-5, op. 1, d. 174, l. 30.
[140] Yurchak, *Everything Was Forever*, 28.
[141] "Class Divisions for Russian Tourists," *The Times* (14 July 1956): 6.

5

Fighting the Cold War on the French Riviera

If Soviet tourism to Western Europe in the Cold War was primarily about politics and performance—the performance of Khrushchev's new policy of peaceful coexistence—it was not only that. It was also about consumption: the consumption of European beauty, cultured urban spaces, leisure experiences, and material items. In *Both Sides of the Ocean: A Russian writer's travels in Italy and the United States*, Victor Nekrasov describes, with deep appreciation, a warm spring evening spent in the small Italian town of San Gimignano. Of this turreted town, Nekrasov writes: "Between the towers you could see the Tuscan skyline and the tiled roofs, brown as the Tuscan soil. I stood by the window and thanked all those unknown town fathers of the seventeenth century for saving this beauty for me and for all of us, this fairy tale, this improbable beauty."[1] Nekrasov was, like most privileged Soviet travelers to Europe, ostensibly on a working vacation. He was also, evidently, on holiday.

It is unsurprising that for tourists, travel to Western Europe was in part about consumption. It is more surprising that this was also true for Soviet authorities. If, as one trip leader wrote, the main purpose of travel to Western Europe was "to destroy existing incorrect notions about the life of our people, and about our country," it was also an opportunity to "familiarize" tourists with "life" else-where.[2] Consider, for example, two Soviet guidebooks written for travelers to Western Europe. Like the politically didactic guidebook described in the previous chapter (*A cruiseship trip around Europe*)[3] these two guidebooks were also published in the early 1960s. In these guides, however, the politically instructive materials are largely absent. In the first, *Voyage around Europe*, tourism to Western Europe is defended as an exchange with countries whose culture is recognized as admirable. *Voyage around Europe* emphasizes the glorious sights of an ancient history: "For the tourist, Rome is above all a city-museum. The streets and squares of the 'eternal city' include a multitude of monuments to the past." The guidebook describes the Vatican as a beautiful architectural site with "one of

---

[1] Victor Nekrasov, *Both Sides of the Ocean: A Russian Travel Writer's Travels in Italy and the United States*, trans. Elias Kulukunis (New York, 1964), 28.
[2] Rossiiskii gosudarstvennyi arkhiv sotsial'no-politicheskoi istorii (hereafter RGASPI), f. m-5, op. 1, d. 56, l. 15 (Trip report, England, 1960).
[3] *Kruiznoe puteshestvie vokrug Evropy na teplokhode "Estoniia,"* (Intourist brochure, 1961), 3.

the richest museums in the world." Paris is depicted as a city where "every walk in the streets is its own excursion into the past."[4] This past includes the revolutionary—the Paris Commune—but also the monarchal, as embodied by the Louvre and the Palace of Versailles. The primary goal of Soviet tourism to Western Europe as imagined in this guidebook is making the Soviet citizen "cultured" through firsthand exposure to Western European culture and history, and by extension integrating the Soviet Union into a civilized West European body politic.

The second guide, also from the early 1960s, differs yet again. This thirteen-page detailed description of cities and sights in England and Scotland resembles, with a few small exceptions, the type of information a capitalist tourist might have read before departure for London or Edinburgh. Urban landscapes, museums, public squares, and palaces are all described without obvious ideological overtones. The Parliament buildings, Buckingham Palace, Westminster Abbey, and the Tower of London are depicted as sites of "great interest" for tourists. The Victoria and Albert Museum, a museum of art and design which celebrates the consumer experience, is warmly described, as is the armory of the Tower of London, with its collection of royal crowns and the "largest diamond in the world." The guide provides information about appropriate amounts to tip (10 percent in restaurants and for taxi drivers, but nothing in the subway, on buses, or at bars), and about the opening hours of stores ("In London most stores located in the West End are open on Thursday nights until seven or eight p.m."). The only indication that this is a Soviet guidebook is the brief reference to Karl Marx and Vladimir Lenin, who are noted to have worked in the reading room of the British Museum, and a short description of the history of communist movements in London.[5] Tourist trips to *this* Western Europe provided opportunities for leisure for a Soviet elite fortunate enough to experience in person places other Soviet citizens could only imagine.

Taken together, these guidebooks from the early 1960s suggest multiple, and sometimes contradictory, roles for tourists to Western Europe: as performers of Soviet superiority, as students of European history and civilization, and as consumers of leisure and material items. How should we understand this diversity? It echoes, in part, the multiple meanings of the "West" in the Russian and Soviet imagination. As Michael David-Fox has argued, Soviet ideology "could not be univocal on the fundamental question of the 'West'" because the West itself was so multivalient; it included "all of European imperialism,

---

[4] *Puteshestvie vokrug Evropy* (Intourist, ca. 1961), 14, 17, 20.

[5] This last guide (1962) is distinguished from the first two in that it was written for trip leaders taking Soviet tourists abroad, but this alone is not enough to explain the difference. Gosudarstvennyi arkhiv Rossiiskoi Federatsii (hereafter GARF), f. 9520, op. 1, d. 503, ll. 181–95 (Information useful in order to become familiar with the countries and cities through which Soviet tourists travel, 1962).

capitalism, society, science, technology, and culture."[6] The multiple Wests of both the Soviet and pre-revolutionary Russian imagination were reiterated in the Wests of the guidebooks: the belligerent capitalist West as enemy; the historical and cultural West as exemplar of civilization; the modern West as advanced consumer paradise.

The Khrushchev-era relationship to an imagined Europe was ambivalent. Ideologically, competition was clearly called for. But what about culture? Or technology? Or consumption? These were arenas of possible affinity rather than enmity, but anxiously so. In the 1961 Party Program, Soviet citizens were imagined as "absorbing and developing all the best that has been created by world culture."[7] But how to do this, and remain socialist? If the Khrushchev regime was to distinguish itself from its Stalinist predecessor through its attention to the consumptive needs of the Soviet population, rapid progress toward these goals depended on emulating capitalist successes. The Seven-Year Plan, adopted in 1959, pledged improvements in the quantity and variety of consumer goods. Shoes, children's goods, television sets, electric irons, and women's spring coats were all to be improved.[8] The 1961 Party Program went further, promising that the 1960s would usher in the era of communism—meaning mass political activism, international respect, and the fulfillment of dreams of abundance for all.[9] "The mood of the people and the productivity of their labor to a large extent depend on living conditions and good service," Khrushchev insisted at the Twenty-Second Party Congress in 1961.[10]

Soviet success meant "outstripping the more advanced capitalist countries in their standard of living," beating them at their own game so to speak.[11] How then to distinguish between socialist consumption and capitalist consumerism? Khrushchev was eager, as György Péteri has felicitously put it, to "provide a workable way toward an *alternative* modernity," with "distinctly *socialist* characteristics."[12] Khrushchev struggled to define the difference between socialist

---

[6] Michael David-Fox, "Stalinist Westernizer? Aleksandr Arosev's Literary and Political Depictions of Europe," *Slavic Review* 62, no. 4 (Winter 2003): 758–59.

[7] *Programma Kommunisticheskoi partii Sovetskogo Soiuza priniata XXII s"ezdom KPSS* (Moscow, 1962), 278–79.

[8] Susan E. Reid, "Who Will Beat Whom? Soviet Popular Reception of the American National Exhibition in Moscow, 1959," *Kritika: Explorations in Russian and Eurasian History* 9, no. 4 (Fall 2008): 864; K. Skovoroda, *Planovoye khozyiastvo* no. 2 (February 1960): 43–53/ *Current Digest of the Soviet Press* [hereafter *CDSP*] 12 (April 20, 1960): 7.

[9] See the discussion, for example, in Rósa Magnúsdóttir, "Be Careful in America, Premier Khrushchev! Soviet perceptions of peaceful coexistence with the United States in 1959," *Cahiers du Monde Russe*, 47/1–2 (January-June 2006): 117–21.

[10] Nikita Khrushchev, "Report of the Central Committee of the 22nd Congress of the Communist Party of the Soviet Union," in *Documents of the 22nd Congress of the CPSU*, vol 1, available at http://www.archive.org/details/DocumentsOfThe22ndCongressOfTheCpsuVolIi, 120.

[11] Khrushchev, "Report of the Central Committee of the 22nd Congress," 115.

[12] György Péteri, "The Occident Within—or the Drive for Exceptionalism," *Kritika: Explorations in Russian and Eurasian History* 9, no. 4 (Fall 2008): 937, 934.

consumption and capitalist consumerism in his speech to the Twenty-Second Party Congress. "Personal ownership by the toiler of a large number of things," is "not at variance with the principles of communist construction as long as it keeps within reasonable bounds and does not become an end itself."[13] In capitalist consumerism, in contrast, "the concept 'mine' is a supreme principle" and "the prosperity of some is possible only at the expense and ruin of others."[14] Alexei Yurchak has explicated the distinction as one between the positive, enriching traits of internationalism and the negative, undermining qualities of cosmopolitanism.[15] Appreciation for "aesthetic beauty, technological achievement, and the genius of the working people who created [bourgeois luxuries]"[16] was to be encouraged; indeed, the ideal Soviet citizen now had to have knowledge of the world, and even a certain kind of *savoir faire,* of which cultured behavior and leisure were a part. The enthusiasm of the black marketeer for a foreign clothing and culture was, on the other hand, emblematic of cosmopolitanism. The distinction, I will argue, is almost entirely one of intention: appreciation versus enthusiasm, affinity versus intimacy.

The relationship between Soviet tourism and consumption was not only an official one, however. This chapter explores the consumer experience of Soviet tourists to Europe. It briefly describes tourists' journeys by plane, train, and cruiseship, their arrival in a foreign country, and the most common itineraries, but focuses on the Soviet "tourist gaze" (including the café and the soda fountain) and a discussion of shopping and souvenirs.[17] Soviet tourists, like tourists everywhere, consumed images, experiences, and material items when they traveled. Some of these were purchased with money, others were "collected" through looking, watching, touching, feeling. The sources for this experiential journey necessarily differ from those in previous chapters. Trip reports about travel to Western Europe, as explained previously, emphasize the political, the performative, and the routinized. For this reason, this chapter more than any other relies on travel writing, memoirs, and interviews to provide a window into experience and feeling: pleasurable walks along city streets, glimpses into glittering shop windows, emotions of wonder and dismay, feelings of pride and embarrassment.

---

[13] Khrushchev, "Report of the Central Committee of the 22nd Congress," 131–32.

[14] Khrushchev, "Report of the Central Committee of the 22nd Congress," 132.

[15] Andrei Yurchak, *Everything Was Forever, Until It Was No More: The Last Soviet Generation* (Princeton, 2006), 163.

[16] Yurchak, *Everything was Forever,* 169–75.

[17] On the concept of the tourist gaze see, John Urry, *The Tourist Gaze* (London, 2002, second edition), 3.

IMAGINING THE WEST

Although Soviet tourists *experienced* the West for the first time, they were not without prior knowledge: ideological, political, and cultural. Contact between peoples should not be imagined as "socio-cultural wholes" suddenly brought into relationship, James Clifford has argued, but as "systems already constituted relationally, entering new relations through historical processes of displacement."[18] Soviet travel practices were, as Ellen Strain observes about travel practices everywhere, "mediated by expectation, societally shaped viewing practices, and a dense process of culturally situated interpretation."[19] To that end, before we set off on our journey, I pause first for a discussion of the "West" as imagined, an imagining that shaped both the experience of travel to Western Europe and the meaning of that experience. Previously existing relationships and imaginings influenced Soviet goals—both official and individual—for tourism to the capitalist West. Transnational experiences in turn influenced what it meant to be Soviet.

That Russia's tangled relationship with Western Europe was central to its political, cultural, and economic identity is, as David-Fox argues, a "truism:" "Russian articulations of proximity and distance from Europe were central to the self presentations of rulers, on the one hand, and to the dissemination of norms of civilization for elite society and the rest of the people in need of 'Enlightenment,' on the other."[20] Tourists in late Imperial Russia persistently preferred a trip to Europe, despite commercial promotion of domestic tourist sites and spas (and despite Dostoevsky's fierce repudiation of travel to Western Europe as evidence of Russia's "servile worship" of Western Europe).[21] After the revolution, diplomatic and cultural elites in the 1920s and 1930s combined knowledge, fondness, and admiration of the West with scorn and hostility.[22] For the writer and committed communist, Isaac Babel, the West in 1920 was an "intoxicating enemy." Upon meeting an American airman shot down by the Red Army, Babel wrote: "Our cause is strong. Ah, but all at once—the smell of Europe, its cafés, civilization, power, ancient culture, so many thoughts, I watch him, can't take my eyes off him."[23] Until the late 1930s, when fear of the foreign definitively outweighed earlier willingness to learn from a "civilized," and modernized West,

---

[18] James Clifford, *Routes: Travel and Translation in the Late Twentieth Century* (Cambridge, 1997), 7.

[19] Ellen Strain, *Public Places, Private Journeys: Ethnography, Entertainment, and the Tourist Gaze* (New Jersey, 2003), 4.

[20] David-Fox, "Stalinist Westernizer," 733.

[21] Susan Layton, "The Divisive Modern Russian Tourist Abroad: Representations of Self and Other in the Early Reform Era," *Slavic Review* 68, no. 4 (Winter 2009), 853, fn. 31; 865.

[22] David-Fox, "Stalinist Westernizer," 733–59.

[23] As cited in Jonathan Brent, *Inside the Stalin Archives* (New York, 2008), 177.

the Soviet relationship to the West was hesitant and ambiguous, but not unrepentantly hostile. Soviet educators openly admired the educational institutions and legislative efforts of Western experts and educators.[24] Knowledge of the West was not only the purview of the political elite. Soviet armchair tourists could read travelogues, stories about foreign destinations, and tales of expeditions both domestic and foreign in the pages of the Russian *National Geographic* magazine, *Vokrug sveta*.[25] Even ordinary Soviet citizens needed to know about and learn from the scientific and cultural achievements of the West, as well as about its failures.

The transfer of information and influence was not supposed to be one way. Left-leaning intellectuals, sympathetic journalists, and members of the working class from around the world were invited to see the wonders of the Soviet Union firsthand. VOKS, which was founded in 1924, managed "societies of friends" of the Soviet Union, coordinated information and propaganda activities abroad, welcomed foreign intellectuals, and arranged scientific and cultural exchanges. Intourist, founded in 1929, received travelers and tourists (mostly working-class delegations and left-leaning intellectuals) from capitalist countries aiming through travel and informal diplomacy to positively affect Western views of the Soviet Union. Importantly, however, it was almost entirely intellectuals and diplomats, medical experts, and white collar professionals such as engineers and educators, who actively participated in the "circulation of knowledge"[26] across borders. Very few ordinary Soviet citizens met these visitors—the numbers of visitors remained small and their activities and contacts were closely managed. Even fewer Soviet citizens, only very carefully screened members of the diplomatic and intellectual classes, traveled abroad themselves. Many Bolshevik authorities in the 1920s, although not all, doubted the ability of Soviet citizens to experience the West without capitulating to it or compromising Soviet interests.[27]

That said, the West was available for view in other ways. Fashion enthusiasts were avid consumers of the flapper styles available for review in the Soviet magazine *Mody sezona* [Fashions of the Season]. Moviegoers watched Charlie Chaplin and Harold Lloyd cavort on the silver screen and welcomed Mary

[24] See the discussion in Catriona Kelly, "'The Little Citizens of a Big Country': Childhood and International Relations in the Soviet Union," *Trondheim Studies on East European Cultures and Societies*, no. 8 (March 2002).

[25] The magazine was founded in 1861, stopped publication for 10 years, and began again in 1927.

[26] On the "circulation of knowledge," see Susan Gross Solomon, "Circulation of Knowledge and the Russian Locale in "Special Issue: Circulation of Knowledge and the Human Sciences in Russia," *Kritika: Explorations in Russian and Eurasian History* 9, no. 1 (Winter 2008): 9–26.

[27] See the archival materials on prohibiting travel in Katerina Clark and Evgeny Dobrenko, *Soviet Culture and Power: A History in Documents, 1917–53* (New Haven, 2007), 7–22.

Pickford and Douglas Fairbanks to Moscow in 1926.[28] Members of the intelligentsia "lived with the images of European street corners, cafés, and palaces" they had gained through reading European literary classics.[29] "For an infinitely long time," remembered art historian Mikhail German, "as if reading a cozy fairy tale, I read one of the most charming novels in the world—*The Pickwick Papers*, an amazing book, where there already exists Dickens in his entirety, his England, his unique unhurried humor, the divinely shy sentimentality."[30] Still, for many Soviet citizens, far from the centers of power, interaction with, or even knowledge of, foreign cultures remained unlikely. It was mainly urbanites, especially in the big cities of Moscow and Leningrad, for whom the West remained available for view, consideration, and consumption.

In the 1930s, neither contact with, nor information about, the West disappeared entirely, even as it was ever more closely controlled. Some knowledge about the outside world—positive as well as negative—remained available to ordinary people. Stalinist authorities aimed to create a Soviet commercial culture that would rival Western standards, contradicting an earlier generation of Bolshevik asceticism and egalitarianism with their promotion of homegrown luxuries such as caviar and champagne, but also of American consumer goods such as ketchup, cornflakes, and jazz music. In the mid-1930s, a few Soviet delegations traveled to capitalist countries, this time to learn about consumer culture (everything from paper plates to window decorations) as well as about technology.[31]

It would not be until the late 1930s—the Great Purges—that fear of "infection" from the foreign would definitively outweigh the comparative advantages of international contacts, and the USSR turn firmly inwards. While Intourist continued to welcome foreign tourists, and their hard currency, the number of visitors declined and additional controls were put on their contact with Soviet citizens. In 1937, there were approximately 13,000 foreign tourists, in 1938, only 5000, and between 1939 and the declaration of war and June 1941, fewer than 3000.[32] The regime reinforced Soviet patriotic identity by promoting misinformation and demonizing the Western other. If Soviet citizens still "knew" the West as presented in Dickens, theirs was now a view of Dickens shaped by a Stalinist perspective. When a group of British students visited the Soviet Union in May 1951, they complained about the "extremely distorted" view of contemporary British life they encountered among their Soviet

---

[28] Anne E. Gorsuch, *Youth in Revolutionary Russia: Enthusiasts, Bohemians, Delinquents* (Bloomington, 2000), chp. 6.

[29] Eleonory Gilburd, "Books and Borders: Sergei Obratzov and Soviet Travels to London in the 1950s," in *Turizm: The Russian and East European Tourist under Capitalism and Socialism*, ed. Anne E. Gorsuch and Diane P. Koenker (Ithaca, 2006), 228.

[30] Mikhail German as cited in Gilburd, "Books and Borders," 239.

[31] Jukka Gronow, *Caviar with Champagne: Common Luxury and the Ideals of the Good Life in Stalin's Russia* (Oxford, 2003).

[32] *Sovetskoe zazerkal'e: Inostrannyi turizm v SSSR v 1930–80-e gody* (Moscow, 2007), 8, 22–3, 67–77.

colleagues: "It was difficult to convince them that the work of Dickens and Galsworthy gives little indication of the present-day life of our country. Some students even cited the Eatonswill elections in *The Pickwick Papers* as an example of British elections. The students seemed incredulous at anything strange to them. Our formal meeting at [the] Moscow University Club . . . was punctuated with [disbelieving] laughter."[33]

And yet, even then, at the height of Soviet xenophobia, Party ideologues condemned "foreignism" but still took a "secret and extreme pleasure" in Western products."[34] For more ordinary people too, the West was not entirely beyond reach, especially during the war. Exposure to the Allied West during the war was a source both of information and of material items for postwar citizens. After the war, the Soviet regime itself released American and West European "trophy" films captured by the Red Army for public view.[35] The *frontoviki* returning from Central European and German cities brought home jazz records (the Glenn Miller Orchestra and Benny Goodman), Western clothes, and, as Juliane Fürst has documented, "glimpses of an entirely different world, which seemed bright and vivacious."[36] Teenage children of the postwar period experimented most openly with "Western" styles. In his memoirs, jazz musician Andrei Kozlov describes the many youth in this period who were fascinated by Western music and style. The *stiliagi* (stylish ones) are the best-known.[37] But in the early 1950s there was also the *statnik* who embraced everything American ("music, clothing, shoes, hairstyles, headgear, even cosmetics"), the *italiano* who sought out Italian fashions (or made his own based on Italian models), and the *demokrat* (or *sovparshiv*), who admired items from the socialist countries of Eastern Europe.[38] These young people frequented used clothing stores where they hoped through constant trolling to snag clothing sold by foreigners living in the Soviet Union. Indeed, the Soviet desire for foreign goods provided such a good source of income for some embassies and foreign correspondents, that the clothing trade was declared illegal in 1956 when it became evident, as described by Irving R. Levine, that "personnel of certain embassies [had begun] to take advantage of the commercial . . . opportunities. It . . . is said that they shipped in crates of dresses and, without even going through the

---

[33] "British students visit the Soviet Union," in box entitled: "Visits to the USSR, handbooks and reports, 1930s–1960s," [British] Society for Cultural Relations with the USSR Archive (hereafter SCR Archive).

[34] Catriona Kelly, *Refining Russia: Advice Literature, Polite Culture, and Gender from Catherine to Yeltsin* (Oxford, 2001), 232.

[35] Juliane Fürst, "The Importance of being stylish: Youth, culture, and identity in late Stalinism," in *Late Stalinist Russia: Society between reconstruction and reinvention*, ed. Juliane Fürst (London, 2006), 213.

[36] Fürst, "The Importance of being stylish," 216.

[37] Mark Edele, "Strange Young Men in Stalin's Moscow: The Birth and Life of the Stiliagi, 1945–53," *Jahrbücher für Geschichte Osteuropas* 50 (2002): 37–61.

[38] Aleksei Kozlov, *Kozel na sakse* (Moscow, 1998), 82–83.

:nse of rumpling them to lend them the appearance of having been worn, trucked the goods directly from railroad station to Commission Store."[39]

Still, the official attitude toward the West remained one of hostility. In 1947, Andrei Zhdanov famously introduced a campaign against "kowtowing" and "servility before the West." Russocentrism—introduced in the 1930s as an alternative to proletarian internationalism—strongly increased.[40] "Writers and journalists who praised anything foreign did so at their risk," Robert English explains, "while scholars who tried to publish abroad or even correspond with foreign colleagues were in peril.... The international isolation of Soviet intellectual life was virtually complete."[41] The Stalinist travel narrative, as described in Chapter One, constantly reaffirmed the superiority of the Soviet Union.[42]

After Stalin's death, the borders were re-opened, if tentatively, to cross-cultural movement and exchange. The degree of opening varied, as did the impact. For intellectuals living in Moscow or Leningrad, the change was immense. In 1960, close to 300,000 tourists from capitalist countries visited the Soviet Union, most of whom visited the Soviet Union's two major cities.[43] In his memoir, Mikhail German describes encounters with the West (through language, culture, material items, personal encounter, and travel) as *the* defining experience of the Thaw. In 1954, German met his first foreigners, Swedish sailors in Leningrad: "Foreigners! The blue-gold Swedish flag. A sensation. A dream, impossible!" Reeling under the impact, German committed himself to learning both English and French, the latter through studying Soviet textbooks which taught foreign grammar through references to the Lenin mausoleum. He listened to the BBC and Voice of America. He learned about "European culture" by reading Ilya Ehrenberg's book *People, Years, Life.* He enjoyed the fruits of his colleagues' first early forays abroad, including two records by Yves Montand brought home from Paris.[44]

For others, further from the centers of power, the impact was less dramatic and the conclusions drawn less certain. Natalia P. studied English at a special foreign language school in the closed city of Saratov (the very existence of a special English school in a closed city being a good example of the contradictions of the Khrushchev era). When interviewed about her childhood and adolescence in the late 1950s and 1960s, Natalia remembered that while she "adored Britain" it was

---

[39] Irving R. Levine, *Main Street, U.S.S.R.* (New York, 1959), 337.

[40] On Russocentrist etatism, see David Brandenberger, *National Bolshevism: Stalinist Mass Culture and the Formation of Modern Russian National Identity, 1931–1956* (Cambridge, 2002).

[41] Robert D. English, *Russia and the Idea of the West: Gorbachev, Intellectuals, and the End of the Cold War* (New York, 2000), 47.

[42] For a similar Polish Cold War travel narrative see Katarzyna Muawska-Muthesius, "The Cold War Traveller's Gaze: Jan Lenica's 1954 Sketchbook of London," in *Under Eastern Eyes: A Comparative Introduction to East European Travel Writing on Europe,* ed. Wendy Bracewell and Alex Drace-Francis (Budapest, 2008), 330–31.

[43] *Sovetskoe zazerkal'e,* 94.

[44] Mikhail German, *Slozhnoe proshedshe: Passé composé* (St. Petersburg, 2000), 161, 233–34, 262, 264–65.

"very hard to obtain any information that wasn't distorted."[45] "[W]hen I was in school the West was something far away, abstract. Something that was unreal, let's put it that way, because after all, Saratov was a closed city and there were practically no contacts to speak of."[46] Aleksandr Konstantinov, a 1967 graduate of the same high school in Saratov, remembers a wider exposure, but his associations—as he remembers it now—are also more ambiguous than those of German:

We formed our ideas of the West mostly from caricatures in newspapers. The American was always depicted as Uncle Sam, with a striped flag and with striped pants. Moreover, there was also the English lion. I don't recall how they depicted the French, but the three always were drawn together. Regarding what I really thought, I probably had some sort of prejudice. It's hard for me to recall. I probably believed that there were people there who, generally speaking, weren't interested in our country's well-being. After all, the pressure on us was strong. . . . On the other hand, there was interest and curiosity. Mother attended the first American exhibition in Moscow. Of course, it made a huge impression on her. . . . from what I remember, she told us about the system of grants, about American kitchens, American cars, and the general style – lighthearted, cheerful, open.[47]

Some Soviet citizens fell in love with what they imagined the West to be. Others were hesitant, confused, even hostile.[48] Even if they admired an imagined West, however, this does not necessarily mean that they were anti-Soviet.[49] Some felt a defiant Soviet patriotism when confronted with Western, especially American, products and propaganda. As one young woman remembered about Western radio broadcasts: "When I heard Voice of America, I knew that what they said about Russia was true, absolutely true, but it still made me mad. . . . there was something insulting about hearing it from outsiders. It was as if the foreigners were laughing at us. It did not make me angry so much at our system as at Voice of America."[50]

Importantly, if the United States was the target of enmity as well as envy, Western Europe was often imagined as a different West than the United States, a safer form of capitalist West whose dangers were mitigated by the legacy of European culture and history. The distinction was an old one between the history, beauty, and civilized urban culture of Europe and the superficial glamour

---

[45] Donald J. Raleigh, ed. and trans., *Russia's Sputnik Generation: Soviet Baby Boomers Talk about Their Lives* (Bloomington, 2006), 98–99.

[46] Raleigh, *Russia's Sputnik Generation,* 112.

[47] Raleigh, *Russia's Sputnik Generation,* 35–36.

[48] See, for example, the discussion of Soviet viewers' negative response to foreign art in Eleonory Gilburd, "Picasso in Thaw Culture," *Cahiers du Monde Russe* 47, nos. 1–2 (January-June 2006): 65–108, and Susan E. Reid, "In the Name of the People: The Manège Affair Revisisted," *Kritika: Explorations in Russian and Eurasian History* 6, no. 4 (Fall 2005): 673–716.

[49] Yurchak, *Everything was Forever,* 202–206.

[50] Hedrick Smith, *The Russians* (New York, 1976), 412–13.

of American style, fashion, and commodities.[51] As we will see, however, travelers to London, Paris, and Rome found that even civilized Europe was not immune from cosmopolitan decadence. "From those first hours my book knowledge of Paris melted in the burning hot flow of reality," Mikhail German remembered about his 1965 trip to France.[52] The Western Europe experienced by Soviet tourists was that of the safe historical past, but also of a more dangerous contemporary capitalism.

GETTING THERE

Consumption as a form of Cold War competition began upon leaving home. "I liked the flight," gushed Evgeniia Gutnova about her trip to Great Britain. "The Aeroflot plane astonished me: clean, a delicious breakfast (we took off early in the morning), a marvelous cloudy landscape visible from the window."[53] Aeroflot would have been delighted by Gutnova's assessment: a typical early Aeroflot advertisement showed a man and a woman relaxing in evident pleasure and comfort on a roomy plane.[54] The Soviet Union began a regular air service to a few foreign countries in 1956 (including reciprocal service between Aeroflot and Ariana Afghan Airlines!) with numbers increasing every year.[55] Soviet air travel, like air travel most places, was closely linked to modernity and to Cold War competition over who could best ensure access to the "good life." In a series of stamps from the late 1950s, it was Tupolev planes that were shown super-imposed on the globe rather than the more usual hammer and sickle.[56] One showed a Soviet jet flying around the world, beginning in Moscow and passing over Beijing, Delhi, Paris, and New York.[57] The in-flight experience was sup-posed to be a comfortable one. On flights from Paris to Moscow, travelers were provided with "little eating tables [and] napkins wrapped in cellophane." They were also proudly presented with a piece of paper showing their route and listing the cities they were flying over: "Amsterdam, 17:21; Copenhagen, 18:13; Riga,

---

[51] Anxiety about American influences postwar was not particular to the Soviet Union. Europeans too worried about American cultural penetration and domination. On fear of American glamour see Stephen Gundle, "Hollywood Glamour and Mass Consumption in Postwar Italy," in *Histories of Leisure*, ed. Rudy Koshar (Oxford, 2002).

[52] German, *Slozhnoe proshedshee*, 430.

[53] Evgeniia Vladimirovna Gutnova, *Perezhitoe* (Moscow, 2001), 316.

[54] *Ogonek* 3 (1953), back page; *Ogonek* 25 (1959), back page.

[55] "On Commercial Cooperation and Reciprocal Service between USSR Aeroflot and Afghan Airline," *Izvestia* (2 November 1956), 4/*CDSP* 8, no. 44 (12 December 1956): 22. The Soviet and British governments agreed to begin regular air services between Moscow and London in 1957; a year later Soviet newspapers complained that there were still no planes flying. "The British have the Floor," *Sovetskaia Rossia* (1 August 1958)/*CDSP* 10, no. 42 (26 November 1958): 16.

[56] H. E. Harris, ed. *Statesman Deluxe Stamp Album*, 1968 (no page).

[57] http://www.stamprussia.com/index.html.

19:03; landing Moscow, 20:02."[58] Not all travelers were as pleased as Gutnova by their experience on Aeroflot, however. German recalled his trip to Paris on a Soviet "Tu-104"—"about which the newspapers had marveled"—as so frightening that "for every one of the twelve days in France I thought about the return trip with horror."[59] For German, it was the "transparent, stunningly clean" Parisian airport with its shop windows full of "unbelievably wonderful products," its "soft sofas," and its lack of "lines, crowds, and uproar," that first told him that he had arrived someplace different.[60]

Soviet authorities appreciated the importance of the optics of arrival: a 1960 article in *Izvestiia* crowed about the opening of a modern, new airport for international flights (Sheremetevo), but notably, the description of the amenities was set in the future tense: "The roof of the station will be transformed into a platform for those seeing travelers off. It will provide a wonderful view of picturesque surroundings. A summer café located in a birch grove will open its doors hospitably."[61] The importance of international air travel was, as this suggests, more symbolic than actual. Despite the attractive full-page advertisements in Soviet magazines, the majority of Soviet tourists voyaged not by air, but by train—something true not only of Soviet citizens but of most intra-European travelers in the postwar period.[62] Like air travel, the new international destinations available to Soviet citizens via train were deployed as both physical evidence of peaceful coexistence and of Soviet "modernity." The announcement in *Izvestiia* of the opening of "direct, uninterrupted rail connection" from Moscow to Paris beginning May 29, 1960, emphasized international connections and technological achievement: "It will leave Moscow daily along with the Moscow–Berlin train. The trip will take about fifty-four hours. The speed will be 56.5 km per hour."[63] For most travelers, however, consumer reality did not match the rhetoric. Fifty-four hours on a train was often far from a pleasure, and the trips were often longer: a group traveling from home from Italy to Leningrad had to make five train transfers (Mestre, Venice, Vienna, Warsaw, and Moscow).[64]

---

[58] Alexander Werth, *Russia under Khrushchev* (Westport, 1961) 43.

[59] German, *Slozhnoe proshedshee*, 427.

[60] German, *Slozhnoe proshedshee*, 427–29.

[61] "Sheremetyevo is an International Airport," *Izvestia* (15 May 1960), 6/*CDSP* 12, no. 20 (15 June 1960): 42.

[62] It was the railway that had first made mass tourism possible in the late nineteenth century. Jill Steward, "Tourism in Late Imperial Austria: The Development of Tourist Cultures and Their Associated Images of Place," in Baranowski and Furlough, *Being Elsewhere*, 109.

[63] Nesterenko, "Moscow to Paris without Transfer," *Izvestia* (26 March 1960)/*CDSP* 12, no. 13 (27 April 1960): 31, 44. Even more "modern" was the possibility of traveling by car. A few fortunate members of the Moscow Auto Club spent a summer holiday driving around France in their own cars (eight Volgas and a Chaika), but this was very rare. Open Society Archive, Budapest (hereafter HU OSA), Records of Radio Free Europe/Radio Liberty Research Institute (hereafter RFE/RL RI) Soviet Red Archives, 1953–1994, Old Code Subject Files, 300-80-1, Container 1048 (Four car crash of Soviets, 1962).

[64] GARF, f. 9520, f. 1, op. 1, d. 618, l. 16 (Complaints about inadequacies in services provided for Soviet citizens travelling abroad).

Then, as now, cruiseships were one answer to the dilemma of how to make the voyage as pleasurable as the destination. "The food and service were impeccable," reported the satisfied trip leader of a group of tourists who traveled to Great Britain in 1956 on the *Molotov*.[65] In the transit time between brief stops (eight hours in Copenhagen, fifteen hours in Athens, two and a half days in England), Soviet passengers on board ships such as the *Victory, Molotov* or *Kalinin* could buy souvenirs at small kiosks or have their hair done in the ship's beauty parlor. They could partake in chess tournaments, table tennis, evenings of dance, music, and film.[66] These leisure activities were available for everyone, although tourists with more money or better connections traveled more luxuriously. On the *Victory*, tourists were placed into five classes of cabins: twenty-two deluxe cabins, thirty-two first-class rooms, 121 second-class rooms, 194 "tourist-class" rooms, twenty-six third-class rooms. There were also three classes of restaurants.[67] "If anybody still thinks that Russia has produced a classless society," the American John Gunther concluded after his trip on a Soviet cruiseship, "he should travel on the *Victory*."[68]

Agitation and propaganda were meant to remind travelers that they sailed as Soviet citizens. Reading rooms were stocked with Soviet newspapers. Ship radios regularly announced information about events at home and provided descriptions about the political and economic character of each country to be visited.[69] There were other, less rewarding, ways in which the cruiseship experience resembled other Soviet vacation experiences with problems common to most Soviet holiday bases, be they floating or land-based. There were complaints that the food on board was not diverse enough, that the restaurants were not open long enough, and that the shops were not well stocked.[70] The cabins were very small, perhaps because some of these ships were retooled German merchant vessels taken as a form of postwar reparation. The ships had very little deck space and no deckchairs.[71] Indeed, the original name of the *Victory* was the *Adolf*

---

[65] GARF, f. 9612, op. 1, d. 373, l. 1 (Trip report, Great Britain, 1956); GARF, f. 9520, op. 1, d. 420, ll. 6–7 (Trip report, European cruise, 1961).

[66] "Red Voyage: Russian Passenger Ship Sprang Many Surprises on English Travelers," *The Times* (13 June 1961): 14.

[67] GARF, f. 9520, op. 1, d. 420, l. 6. See also l. 13 (Trip report, Baltic cruises, 1961); d. 370, l. 17 (Trip report, international travel, 1960).

[68] John Gunther, "Russia's Riviera," *Harper's Magazine* (October 1957): 29. The ideal of comfortable conditions on board ship was not unique to the postwar period. A 1936 directive from the party control organization insisted that all ships (domestic and international), should have clean and comfortable conditions including linen on the dining-room tables, a barbershop, fresh newspapers, a book kiosk, and so on. The inspiration for the directive was that so many of the steamships failed in these and other respects. Diane P. Koenker, "The Proletarian Tourist in the 1930s: Between Mass Excursion and Mass Escape," in Gorsuch and Koenker, *Turizm*, 131.

[69] GARF, f. 9520, op. 1, d. 420, l. 7.

[70] GARF, f. 9520, op. 1, d. 1008, ll. 150–52 (Trip report, European cruise, 1966).

[71] Gunther, "Russia's Riviera," 29.

Hitler. The taps in the bathrooms still read "auf" and "zu."[72] As of yet, a socialist consumptive experience could not compete with a capitalist one.

BEING THERE

Tourists today, even group travelers, are accustomed to carefully considering ahead of time the smallest details of every trip from the location of the hotel to the comfort of the tourist coach. Soviet tourists, in contrast, had no control over either lodging or itinerary, both of which were largely determined by local agencies and organizations. Upon arrival, tourists were processed (sometimes at great length) by customs and immigration, during which time trip leaders discussed the proposed excursion program with representatives of local tourist firms.[73] Then, after a visit to the local Soviet Embassy or Consulate, tourists were escorted to their lodgings. Some tourists were pleased about their accommodations; one group of young people was reported by their trip leader to have lived in the "best motels," traveled in comfortable buses and in the "deluxe" compartment on the train, and eaten good food.[74] Other tourists were less happy. Soviet tourists usually stayed in small hotels and in bed and breakfasts, often not the highest class of accommodation.[75] While students may have been happy with simple accommodations, higher ranking people may have been used to, or at least have hoped for, better conditions. They would have also known that West European travelers to the Soviet Union were put up in the best available lodging. When Harold Shukman traveled to Moscow in the spring of 1954, he and his group of twenty British students stayed in the Metropole in Moscow, where Shukman had a piano in his room.[76] In contrast, a British guide admitted to his group that only Russian tourists were put in a certain "very poor" hotel in South Kensington near the Soviet Embassy, where the rooms were cold and the

---

[72] German, *Slozhnoe proshedshee*, 263; Laurens van der Post, *Journey into Russia* (London, 1964), 145.

[73] GARF, f. 9520, op. 1, d. 420, l. 8. Tourists traveling by train or air from Moscow to Western Europe were met at the first point of entry to Western Europe. A group heading to England in 1960 were met in West Berlin by a representative of the tourism bureau of the English National Union of Students and by three young people from the West Berlin Union of Students. The British representative then accompanied the group from Berlin to London. RGASPI, f. m-5, op. 1, d. 94, l. 4 (Trip report, England, 1960); RGASPI, f. m-5, op. 1, d. 56, l. 1 (Trip report, Scotland, 1960).

[74] RGASPI, f. m-5, op. 1, d. 94, l. 6.

[75] Interview with Gerald Smith, Oxford, June 2003; German, *Slozhnoe proshedshee*, 429.

[76] Interview with Harold Shukman, St. Antony's College, Oxford, June 2003. Travel to the Soviet Union could be a good financial deal for West Europeans. British subjects could take a holiday on the Black Sea for 2 pounds 10 shillings a day (about seven dollars), or a sea cruise from London to Leningrad for thirty-three pounds (about ninety-two dollars), both less expensive than a trip to France. HU OSA, RFE/RL RI, Soviet Red Archives, 1953–1994, Old Code Subject Files, 300-80-1, Container 1048 (Russia opens door, 1960).

breakfasts very bad.[77] Travelers to Belgium were warned ahead of time that they should be prepared for the poor living conditions: one group was not provided with any towels throughout their trip, and except for one good shower in Oostduinkerke, they were unable to wash.[78] At issue was the economics of tourism in the USSR versus in capitalist Europe. Intourist was a government agency enabled to use state funds to impress foreign tourists. Soviet travelers, on the other hand, paid their fees via Intourist to West European private agencies and organizations, who booked accommodations accordingly.

Fortunately, Soviet tourists spent very little time in their hotel rooms. They explored major historical and cultural sites; met and were sometimes entertained by foreign colleagues, dignitaries, and journalists; toured factories or other work-sites; and snuck in a little time to shop. The experience of a group of tourists on a two week long trip to France (six days in Paris followed by seven days in Cannes followed by three days in Paris) was representative with its mixture of touristic excursions, meetings with interested local people, and excursions to factories. The group strolled along the banks of the Seine, gawked at the Eiffel Tower and the Museum of Contemporary Art, and toured Versailles. They spent a day at the Simca automobile factory. One evening they met with a group of students at a youth center in Paris, where they had a conversation, according to the trip report, about art and the Soviet poet Evgenii Evtushenko.[79]

Tourists had little free time. On one ten-day trip to Great Britain, the only scheduled free time was part of a morning on the seventh day, which the group used for going to the shops.[80] A group of Armenian tourists to Great Britain were so busy that they had just fifty minutes to see the British Museum, forty minutes in the National Gallery in London, and twenty minutes to see Oxford.[81] Passengers on cruiseships were particularly short of time, so short that trip leaders sometimes complained, especially when the lack of time got in the way of educational and political activities. The leader of a 1966 tour to Europe on the ship *Taras Shevchenko* grumbled that with only six hours in Stockholm the trip onshore was "not worth it." The tourists saw little of interest and the only people they could converse with were the waitresses in restaurants.[82] The rushed, and sometimes claustrophobic, experience of Soviet tourists was not particular to Cold War sightseeing, of course; it is common to the group travel experience almost everywhere. But it was exaggerated when independent activity was so frowned upon.[83]

[77] RGASPI, f. m-5, op. 1, d. 159, l. 33 (Trip report, England, 1962).
[78] RGASPI, f. m-5, op. 1, d. 160, ll. 67–8 (Trip report, Belgium, 1962).
[79] RGASPI, f. m-5, op. 1, d. 174, l. 60 (Trip report, France, 1964).
[80] GARF, f. 9612, op. 1, d. 373, l. 27 (Trip report, England, 1956).
[81] GARF, f. 9612, op. 1, d. 478, l. 54 (Trip report, Great Britain).
[82] GARF, f. 9520, op. 1, d. 1008, ll. 146–48 (Trip report, European cruise).
[83] German, *Slozhnoe proshedshee*, 432–33.

Figure 15 Soviet tourists in the Louvre, 1957. RIA Novosti.

Itineraries were set by local organizations such as the Swiss Friendship Society, the British Educational Interchange Council, and travel agencies like Thomas Cook and Sons.[84] The itineraries varied depending on who was responsible, although almost every Soviet tourist group to England visited the British Museum, watched the changing of the guard at Buckingham Palace, visited Poets' Corner in Westminster Abbey, and marveled at the height of St. Paul's Cathedral. If they ventured outside of London, they typically went to Edinburgh and Glasgow, and stopped briefly in Birmingham, Manchester, Stratford-upon-Avon, and Oxford. Tourists to France saw the equivalent sites in Paris

---

[84] GARF, f. 9520, op. 1, d. 423, l. 8 (Trip report, Switzerland, 1961); RGASPI, f. m-5, op. 1, d. 94, l. 7; d. 56, l. 5; d. 57, l. 87 (Trip report, France, 1960).

Figure 16 Soviet tourists visit Karl Marx's tomb at Highgate Cemetery, London, 1963. RIA Novosti.

and typically spent some time in the South of France, in Nice and Marseilles. Every tour group visited the grave of Karl Marx in London or laid flowers at the wall of the communards in the Père-Lachaise Cemetery in Paris.[85]

Tourist-guests of Friendship Societies enjoyed additional arrangements. The [British] Society for Cultural Relations with the USSR frequently hosted Soviet travelers. If in 1956, it was rare and very notable for the SCR to sponsor Soviet tourists, it quickly became common with approximately 7000 Soviet tourists passing through London via the auspices of the SCR from June 1960 through the end of July 1961 alone.[86] The purpose of the SCR, as stated in 1924, was to recruit members from the British intelligentsia on Soviet behalf. In 1956, "in light of the developments in the USSR since the Twentieth Party Congress" the SCR claimed that it now had "no commitment to a particular political line."[87] It remained devoted, however, to "promot[ing] understanding between the British and Soviet peoples."[88] The British government was suspicious about the leftist

[85] RGASPI, f. m-5, op. 1, d. 197, l. 1; d. 174, l. 100 (Trip report, France. 1964).

[86] These numbers were bolstered by the inclusion of London as a port of call on Soviet cruises around Europe. *SCR General Report*, 1960–1961, 2. SCR Archive.

[87] *SCR General Report*, 1956–1957, 3. SCR Archive.

[88] *SCR General Report*, 1956–1957, 4. SCR Archive. The SCR was supposed to recruit members from the British intelligentsia while the British-Soviet Friendship Society and the Anglo-Soviet Friendship Committee effected to attract supporters from the working class. Aiko Watanabe,

leanings of the SCR and other friendship societies; before 1956, the policy was to refuse admission to foreigners invited by friendship societies. After 1956, they decided to permit these invitations, reluctant to threaten the "marked improvement in Anglo-Soviet relations."[89] The SCR worked to introduce Soviet tourists to their British colleagues.[90] Members of a group from the All-Russian Theatrical Society were received by the Deputy Lord Mayor of Birmingham, visited the Shakespeare collection at the public library, and met colleagues at the Alexandra Theatre, where they attended a reading of Dylan Thomas' *Under Milk Wood*.[91] The 700 Soviet tourists who visited London in December 1964 on the maiden voyage of the Soviet cruiseship the *Ivan Franko* were welcomed by the SCR, who arranged on their behalf visits to Parliament with sympathetic legislators.[92]

The arrangements made by local groups, friendship societies and otherwise, were mostly, if not always, satisfactory. The leader of a group of Armenian youth complained that they had no opportunity to meet with French people and spent too much time looking at historical monuments including churches, "in which they had absolutely no interest; it very quickly bored us."[93] K. Riaizova, who accompanied a group of Komsomol members and physical culture workers to England, protested that the organizers of her trip were too anxious to acquaint them with the "English way of life," forcing them to spend a lot of time on "private farms" and giving them no time at all with young workers in factories and enterprises in London.[94] Riaizova suspected that they were purposely being kept away from factories so that they would not learn about the real and troubling conditions of the British working class.[95] It is difficult from reports such as these to distinguish the opinions of tourists from the voice of the trip leader concerned to satisfy reader expectations at home. Were tourists really disappointed, as another trip leader reported, that they had to "waste" time at Speakers' Corner in Hyde Park or at the famous market in Petticoat Lane? Would they really have preferred, as the trip leader argued, to have gone to meetings or visited factories?[96] In some cases clearly not; one group of tourists assertively disagreed with their trip leader, demanding more free time in London in place of yet another visit to an electrical plant.[97] In other cases, however, Soviet

"Cultural drives by the periphery: Britain's experiences," www.history.ac.uk/ihr/Focus/cold/articles/watanabe.html; "Obshestva anglo-sovetskoi druzhby," http://psi.ece.jhu.edu/>kaplan/IRUSS/BUK/GBARC/pdfs/peace/eng59-3.pdf.

[89] The National Archives, London, Foreign Office, FO 371 129025 (Communist Front Organizations, 1957).

[90] Annual General Meeting Report, 13 May 1967 in "SCR Events 1960s," SCR Archive.

[91] *SCR General Report*, 1964, 8–9. SCR Archive.

[92] *SCR General Report*, 1964, 8–9, SCR Archive

[93] RGASPI, f. m-5, op.1, d. 57, l. 98.

[94] RGASPI, f. m-5, op. 1, d. 56, l. 18 (Trip report, England, 1960).

[95] RGASPI, f. m-5, op. 1, d. 56, l. 19.

[96] GARF, f. 9612, op. 1, d. 373, l. 27.

[97] GARF, f. 9612, op. 1, d. 478, l. 25 (Trip report, England, 1961).

tourists surely did want visit factories. Pragmatically speaking, travelers were expected to report back to their work collectives on what they saw. Touring factories also allowed tourists to be on a more equal status with their hosts, at least during part of their trip. Finally, these were Soviet people for some of whom work did matter, and comparisons were interesting.

THE BEAUTIFUL LIFE ABROAD

In Victor Nekrasov's account of his travels in Italy, he argues that one of the most pleasurable aspects of travel was "the unexpected: a chance meeting, a new acquaintance, a sudden argument, a question that takes you by surprise."[98] "Yes, I'm definitely against notebooks," he concludes, "against inspection tours and planned visits, and I'm against timetables."[99] Nekrasov had to work hard to find free moments, however. In his position as delegate, and erstwhile tourist, to the Congress of the European Society of Writers in Florence, Nekrasov was busy with meetings, appearances on television, conferences, and roundtable discussions, in addition to "receptions, luncheons and dinners." These "proved impossible to avoid," he complained, "despite the fact that they are not the ideal means of getting to know a country."[100]

What kind of "knowing" did the Soviet regime hope that its travelers would bring home? Not the kind of intimate, unregulated knowing that Nekrasov desired. Desirable instead were tributes to Europe's history, beauty, and civilized urban culture, combined with reminders that home was best. Nekrasov's *Both Sides of the Ocean* satisfied this expectation with its evocations of the romantic, historical Italy of the Soviet imagination (even as it violated other expectations with its more intimate, unapproved, images of popular pleasures.) Nekrasov waxed rhapsodic about the beauties of the Tuscan landscape: "A sunny spring day, wondrously clear. The road weaves in and out among the hills, through patches of forest, to silvery olive groves. Now it breaks free into a valley, and before you the line at the horizon opens out with such beauty and such delicacy that you hold your breath. I have never seen such a horizon anywhere." This road, he writes, is more beautiful than any he has seen before: "I have seen many beautiful roads in the world: the Georgian-Military Road to Lake Ritsa, the serpentine windings in the Crimea, the roads of Saxony, of Schwartzwald [sic], of Southern Bohemia, and Slovakia. But none of them can compare with the road from Siena to San Gimignano."[101]

---

[98] Nekrasov, *Both Sides*, 5.
[99] Nekrasov, *Both Sides*, 7.
[100] Nekrasov, *Both Sides*, 23–4.
[101] Nekrasov, *Both Sides*, 26–27. Note that the Georgian Military Road actually goes nowhere near Lake Ritsa.

And yet, while more beautiful than any road he has ever seen, it is "somehow familiar." "Yes, of course," he recalls. "I've seen it all before. In the Uffizi. In the Palazzo Pitti. In Siena itself." The Tuscan landscape and San Gimignano are a living museum to the Renaissance. Nekrasov's ode to Italy's ancient beauty reflects the Soviet passion for the Renaissance as the aesthetic ideal. The Renaissance, Eleonory Gilburd has argued, is what Soviet viewers meant when they thought "about beauty and pleasure, about an art that enraptures."[102] Together with the Russian classics, education in the USSR emphasized knowledge of the "Great Masterpieces" of European art. After the war, Soviet scholarship laid special claim to the heritage of the Renaissance, insisting that it was the Soviet victory that "had saved European civilization from barbarity."[103] Nekrasov's literary portrait of Italy's landscape is consistent with this adoration of an historical Europe. Awe and longtime familiarity combine in his description of the Ponte Vecchio in Florence: "It's an ancient bridge, hundreds of years old. It is the most picturesque bridge in the world, a bridge and a street at the same time.... There must be a million pictures and postcards of it, pictures taken in all shades of daylight and from every angle. I took pictures of it, too, but I've been sketching it ever since I was a child. A famous bridge."[104] Nekrasov's insertion of himself as having sketched this bridge ever since he was a child underscores his own upbringing as a citizen of Europe.

The beautiful life abroad was also located in Europe's contemporary urban landscape, its city squares, its parks, and especially its cafés. When film director Andrei Konchalovskii stepped off the train on his arrival in Rome, he was struck by the lively Italian street scene that greeted him: "The square was full of people, illuminated, glowing, with music playing!"[105] Polish travel writer, Ryszard Kapuściński, whose opportunities for leisure and consumption at home would have been the envy of his Soviet neighbors, was likewise entranced by the Italian cafés and bars he saw on his trip to Rome in 1956: "I did not notice the architecture, the statues, the monuments; I was fascinated only by the cafés and bars. There were tables everywhere on the sidewalks, and people sat at them, drinking and talking, or simply looking at the streets and the passerby. Behind tall, narrow counters barmen poured drinks, mixed cocktails, brewed coffee. Waiters bustled about, delivering glasses and cups with a magician's agility and bravura."[106] Nekrasov too sang the praises of the "sweet" Italian *trattoria* with its life of casual contemplation and observation: "If all the *trattorias, osterias,* and bars in Italy were closed for some reason... where would a poor [Italian] fellow go to find out the latest news; to have a glass of wine; to play

---

[102] Gilburd, "Picasso in Thaw Culture," 79.
[103] Gilburd, "Picasso in Thaw Culture," 78.
[104] Nekrasov, *Both Sides*, 13.
[105] Andrei Konchalovskii, *Nizkie istiny* (Moscow, 1998), 112.
[106] Ryszard Kapuściński, "The Open World: A legendary travel writer's first trip abroad," *The New Yorker* (5 February 2007): 60.

dominoes; to meet pretty Lucia; or Carlo and Alberto, whom he has absolutely got to see for some reason; or just to sit in a corner and think about something that he can't think about at home?"[107]

In addition to being a place of leisure, community, and simple pleasure, the café was a site of romance. In his travel account, "Paris days and nights," V. Safonov describes himself strolling the streets of the Latin Quarter and the hills of Montmartre, where he stumbles at last onto a small café and longingly watches a "gentlemen admirer" kiss a girl with no attention to the lively party around him.[108] Of course, touristic imaginings of the café and of kissing couples were not cultural symbols for Soviet tourists only. In John Urry's analysis, *The Tourist Gaze*, he makes mention of this same "sign" of Frenchness for the North American and European traveler: "When tourists see two people kissing in Paris what they capture in the gaze is 'timeless romantic Paris'."[109] For Soviet authorities, this "timelessness" was part of what made the romantic café so attractive and appropriate; in its historicity the café resembled Italian musicians and the beauties of San Gimignano. The romantic was an apolitical, and thus permissible, aspect of a "civilized" European culture that the Soviet Union under Khrushchev comfortably imagined itself a part of. Thus the contradiction of an otherwise belligerently pro-Soviet article about a cruise trip around Europe that paused to describe in rosy terms a Parisian police officer who stopped traffic while a boy and girl kissed in a crosswalk.[110]

Even as Nekrasov describes Italian café life in loving detail, however, he does not yet belong there. This lack of belonging is evident in how he, and other Soviet travel writers, portray their relationship to the café, and to the European street scene more generally. They do not describe themselves as sitting in a café, but as voyeurs, sometimes envious ones, of local habits. They are appreciating a life of leisure that belongs to others while themselves passing on. An image published in *Vokrug sveta* of a man and a woman kissing passionately while standing on the back platform of a Parisian bus, was evocative and romantic, but also voyeuristic.[111] The side of the tourist bus window is visible in the shot, the lovers clinging to the back of a city bus at some distance away. This is what you can see in Paris, the photo suggests admiringly, not at home. The voyeuristic style is true not only of Soviet travel accounts, of course; many travel accounts describe the encounter with the foreign as one of distance not integration. In the Soviet instance, however, a sense of passing by the café rather than sitting in it, also reflects reality; with so little hard currency to spend, the cost of a cup of coffee in a café meant less money available for other purchases. A sense of distance was also

[107] Nekrasov, *Both Sides,* 62.
[108] V. Safonov, "Parizhskie dni i vechera," *Vokrug sveta* (4 April 1958), 25. In 1960, France had some 200,000 cafés. "Mon Dieu! A *crise* in France's cafés?" *The Globe and Mail* (26 May 2009): B4.
[109] Urry, *The Tourist Gaze,* 3.
[110] Iurii Arbat, "Evropeiskie kartinki," *Krokodil* 26 (20 September 1959), 11.
[111] Safonov, "Parizhskie dni i vechera," 25.

reinforced in the Soviet case due to the almost insurmountable combination of imagined political superiority and cultural inferiority evident in the Soviet relationship to Western Europe.

SODA FOUNTAINS AND SEX

If Soviet tourists—carefully chosen ones—could travel to Paris in order to educate themselves about European culture and history, they were not "to stare at Paris... and sigh with longing," as one 1964 Soviet trip leader to France warned.[112] Affinity was fine, desire was not. In an article entitled "Not on the tourist path," Alexei Adzhubei (a frequent international traveler, editor of *Izvestia,* and son-in-law of Khrushchev), reminded both travelers and armchair tourists what they should know about the "real" Italy: "If you use the services of one of the many firms servicing travelers, you might conclude that Italians actually live as written about in travel books or as described by guides: happy, carefree, and always in the magnificent, far away past." In truth, Italian history was built on "sweat and blood" and the areas away from the wealthy streets of Rome are narrow and dirty.[113] Adzhubei's article is illustrative of the ambivalence of the Khrushchev-era relationship with Western Europe. On the one hand, much like earlier articles from the Stalinist press, Adzhubei emphasizes the dirty underbelly lying beneath capitalist glitter. On the other, Adzhubei's article is written for an audience now presumed to be familiar with the international tourist experience. The article begins by stating in confident terms what every citizen of the newly internationalist Khrushchev era is expected to understand: "Italy attracts tourists from all corners of the earth," including the USSR.[114]

If Europe's beautiful landscapes or timeless cafés were examples of an acceptable and historically rooted internationalism, other aspects of capitalist consumer culture were threateningly cosmopolitan. In contrast to the civilized life of the café, British students who "gathered at soda fountains, and their windows and tables, lazily talking to each other and indifferently watching passersby," were described as emblematic of bourgeois degeneracy.[115] "Young boys and girls" hanging out at the soda fountains were the opposite of the aesthetic beauty found in the Parisian and Italian café, representing instead an uncomfortable and unconformist androgyny, their hairstyles and clothes rendering them "indistinguishable" one from the other.[116] In contrast to the café, the leisure culture of the

---

[112] RGASPI, f. m-5, op. 1, d. 174, l. 33 (Trip report, France, 1964).
[113] A. Adzhubei, "Ne po turistskomy marshrutu," *Ogonek* 7 (1958): 4.
[114] Adzhubei, "Ne po turistskomy marshrutu."
[115] RGASPI, f. m-5, op. 1, d. 197, l. 5.
[116] RGASPI, f. m-5, op. 1, d. 197, l. 5.

soda fountain was not timeless; it was specifically rooted in contemporary capitalist consumer culture. The leisure life of West European youth was not something that could be safely watched at a distance and brought home via a photograph. Problematically, however, it was just this leisure culture, not that of the café, that was already present in the Soviet Union in the subversive dress and lifestyles of Soviet youth. Newspapers and magazines at home condemned the "disgustingly" boyish haircuts of young women who lost their femininity along with their decency in their enthusiasm for the contemporary music and fashion of Western Europe and North America.[117] Soviet authorities were anxious to prevent further exposure to decadent forms of dress and dance.[118] When one local English organization tried to organize an evening of dance for Soviet youth with their English peers, the trip leader quickly intervened. He stood up and gave a short speech in which he spoke about "the goal of our trip, about the Komsomol, about the struggle of the Soviet people for peace." He succeeded in getting the dances stopped. "In future [gatherings], the English did not try to show us the twist and shake, but tried to invite people with more life experience to meetings who were told ahead of time that the gathering would consist of a serious discussion."[119]

If the soda fountain was cosmopolitan other to the internationalist pleasure of the café, sex served the same vis-à-vis romance. Sex and tourism have long been closely associated, ranging from the explicit (the sexual tourism of Thailand and the red-light districts of Amsterdam), to the implicit (the scantily clad women used to advertise seaside resorts). What about Soviet tourism? In the Soviet Union, sex outside of marriage was condemned as harmful for individual and for society, distracting people from productive activity on behalf of the Soviet project.[120] For the most part, within the USSR little was done to forcibly enforce these sexual standards. Domestic travel provided a well-known opportunity for extramarital affairs, with wives and husbands often traveling separately on their weeks of trade union facilitated travel to the Crimea and to the Baltics. But what to do about travelers to the capitalist West? Here desire for intimacy with the Western other was made manifest, and dangerously so. Tourists who traveled in pursuit of sexual adventure in the capitalist West did so in explicit opposition to Soviet norms and instructions. Homosexuality and venereal diseases were said in one report to have been brought home via "the widespread exchange of tourists, long trips abroad, [and] acquaintance with the perverted morals of bourgeois

---

[117] Robin Havelaar, "Dandies and Harlots: Gender and Youth Deviance in Soviet Jazz Discourse, 1954–1964," unpublished paper, UBC, April 2009, 10.

[118] Juliane Fürst, "The arrival of spring? Changes and continuities in Soviet youth culture and policy between Stalin and Khrushchev," in *The Dilemmas of De-Stalinization: Negotiating cultural and social change in the Khrushchev era*, ed. Polly Jones (London, 2006), 134–53.

[119] RGASPI, f. m-5, op. 1, d. 197, l. 6.

[120] Deborah Field, *Private Life and Communist Morality in Khrushchev's Russia* (New York, 2007), 52–54.

countries."[121] Honeymoon travel abroad was discouraged for fear that newly-weds would spend too much time alone in their hotel rooms.[122] As late as 1980, Aleksandr Konstantinov remembered being told in a briefing received before a trip to Italy, that if he even ended up "in a train compartment with a person of the opposite sex, [he] immediately had to register a protest."[123]

Evidence is scant, but anecdotal information suggests that although it was prohibited, sex was a welcome form of leisure activity for some Soviet travelers abroad.[124] The popular Soviet comedic film, *The Diamond Arm* [Brilliantovaia ruka], includes tongue-in-cheek scenes about sexual tourism, one of a Soviet tourist being enticed by a Turkish prostitute and another of an illicit encounter with a foreign call-girl.[125] (In real life too, a lack of experience sometimes led to the comedic. A group of Soviet men seeking a striptease while in France ended up mistakenly and confusingly in a venue for male erotic dance.[126]) In *Russia under Khrushchev*, Alexander Werth describes an encounter in the early 1960s with a Soviet foreign trade official who described a trip to Europe as a journey from bordello to bordello. At first, the experience appears unpleasant: prostitution is described as a sign of capitalist degeneracy. "I was in Paris, and then in Marseille, from where I sailed on the Soviet ship," the official relayed. "French women are terribly immoral. Prostitutes everywhere. Marseille full of bordellos. And we were taken on a trip to Pompeii. And then, for a tip to the guide, we were shown... Oh dear, to think that people did *that* sort of thing 2,000 years ago! Then we called at Piraeus; also heaps of bordellos; they do a lot of business, especially thanks to the American naval base there. It's what they call Free World Solidarity, I suppose." Up to this point, the description is as expected. We are led to question both argument and disdain, however, given what the official then says about his last port of call in Odessa: "The first night a comrade of mine and I were having dinner at the hotel, and there were two girls who latched onto us. Mine was a pretty good-looking *devushka*. I asked her if I could see her home, and she said I could. It was good fun, and I stayed till two in the morning. 'Time you went home,' she said, 'and the tariff is seventy-five rubles.' I was really furious. 'The tariff, what tariff? You lousy bitch, you're not behaving like a Soviet citizen. I would have given you 100 rubles, perhaps 200—but, since it's the 'tariff,' here's seventy-five, and not a kopek more.'.... Terrible city Odessa... must be that Greek and Turkish influence."[127] That Soviet tourists, like many

---

[121] As cited in Field, *Private Life*, 56.

[122] Alexei Popov, "Tenevye storony zarubzhnogo (Byezdnogo) turizma v Sovetskom Soiuze (1960–1980-e gg.)" *Kultura narodov Prichernomoria* no. 152 (Simferopol 2009): 151–55.

[123] Raleigh, *Russia's Sputnik Generation*, 45.

[124] There is not much archival evidence about sex. For an exception, see RGASPI, f. m-5, op. 1, d. 197, l. 34 (Report to Sputnik, 1964).

[125] *Brilliantovaia ruka* [The Diamond Arm]. Director: Leonid Gaidar. USSR, 1968.

[126] Interview with Valeria Emmanuilovna Kunina, Moscow, 2004.

[127] Alexander Werth, *Russia under Khrushchev* (New York, 1962), 87–88.

Figure 17 Decadent Europe, 1948, by Danish cartoonist Herluf Bidstrup, as reprinted in *Risunki* (Moscow, 1969).

tourists, were interested in the illicit encouraged some West European travel organizations to include the semi-scandalous in their itineraries. Tourists could be strongly warned, and punishment inflicted, but tourist groups were, to some degree, at the mercy of local guides. It is not clear that they minded. When Mikhail German's tourist group was taken by their French guides to see the variety show at the Moulin Rouge, his Soviet trip leader "watched the show with an expression of poorly concealed lust combined with panicked fear. He waited for it to get worse, and it did. In one of the acts a lady undressed completely, leaving only a triangle of sequins." When the tourists used their "final [French] francs" to rent binoculars, the trip leader "became as still as a corpse" but did not stop them.[128]

FOREIGN TRINKETS

When one trip leader complained in 1962 that too many tourists travel "only for a trip abroad" as opposed to for more socialist-minded reasons, it is likely that he had shopping in mind.[129] Every trip, even those with the most purposeful of agendas, included some time for shopping. It was the trip leader herself of one excursion to Italy who took her tourists to stores and markets in Florence (and the group *starosta* who wrote a report complaining about the leader's excessive focus on shopping).[130] Even the secret police shopped. A KGB officer who accompanied Soviet dissident Vladimir Bukovskii on his forced exile from the Soviet Union in 1973 looked down with pleasure at Switzerland while flying overhead: "Everybody here has his own house and his own plot. It's good when there's an 'abroad' in the world, and returning home from some service assignment, you can bring the wife some foreign trinkets. Isn't that the highest blessing?"[131]

---

[128] German, *Slozhnoe proshedshee*, 442–43. A Soviet joke about sex and tourism went as follows: "Советский турист (Т) заблудился в Сан-Франциско и под вечер забрел в квартал розовых фонарей. К нему обращается сутенер (С):
C : What do you want?
Т : Сорри, май инглиш соу бед. Ай вонт…
C : A girl?
Т : Ай вонт…
C : A boy?
Т : Ай вонт…
Долго смотрит в словарик и наконец выговаривает:
Т : Ай вонт совиет консул.
C : О-о-о, it's possible. But very expensive…"
(With thanks to Alexey Golubev, Petrozavodsk State University.)

[129] RGASPI, f. M-5, op. 1, d. 202, l. 16 (Character report, Cyprus, 1962).

[130] GARF, f. 9520, op. 1, d. 729, l. 24 (Trip report, Italy, 1964).

[131] Vladimir Bukovsky, *To Build a Castle: My Life as a Dissenter*, trans. Michael Scammell (London, 1978), 345.

What did Soviet tourists buy? "We were gripped," Mikhail German remembers, "by an unspeakable longing for the beautiful foreign life—for clothing above all."[132] Levinson-Lessing came home from Belgium and Holland with "white cuffs extending from the arms of his fashionable gray jacket, his cheeks shaved with new thoroughness and a fresh European gloss, and with unprecedentedly elegant glasses perched on his nose."[133] Tourist Antonovskaia bought a red blouse on a shopping excursion in Britain (and having decided that she did not like it, ran to the store in order to exchange it on the next morning).[134] Others bought practical items difficult to find at home such as the automobile headlight purchased by a traveler to Scandinavia.[135] Travelers purchased fashion magazines, sheer nylon stockings, sweaters, perfumes, records, and transistor radios. Soviet shortages were not the only, or even principal, reason for these requests; many Soviet citizens placed a premium on goods from foreign countries.[136] In the mid-1950s, imported goods were most often from China, but following the worsening of Sino-Soviet relations in the late 1950s, imports of clothing and goods were increasingly from Eastern European countries: shoes from Czechoslovakia, knitted wear from Yugoslavia. These items were of good quality and relatively inexpensive. The most desirable, however, were goods from capitalist countries, which were considered to be of the best quality and most fashionable.[137]

Even for those able to travel, however, much of this longing went unrequited. When Mikhail German was instructed by Soviet authorities that he should not buy "lots of things" on his trip to Paris, he laughed: "On what money?!"[138] If in the Soviet Union, it was the scarcity of goods that prevented purchases, in Western Europe everything was available but at hard-currency prices out of reach for most Soviet tourists. The amount of hard currency each tourist could receive from Intourist varied, sometimes year by year, but it was never very much. "The most humiliating aspect [of trips abroad]," according to Gutnova, was having so little hard currency. "There wasn't enough to leave a tip . . . to take city transport, or to buy a few small souvenirs."[139] Safra Mikhailovna remembers running through stores on her 1964 trip to Finland looking for the least

---

[132] German, *Slozhnoe proshedshee*, 265.

[133] German, *Slozhnoe proshedshee*, 282.

[134] GARF, f. 9612, op. 1, d. 373, l. 5.

[135] GARF, f. 9520, op. 1, d. 420, l. 18.

[136] Irving R. Levine described, for example, "a certain set of Russian women" who "preferred inferior coats of artificial fur, made in the USA., to the genuine product made in Russia." Irving R. Levine, *Main Street, U.S.S.R.* (New York, 1959), 343.

[137] See the entry on "import" in N. Lebina, *Entsiklopediia banal'nostei. Sovetskaia povsednevnost': kontury, simvoly, znaki* (St. Petersburg, 2006), 171–73.

[138] German, *Slozhnoe proshedshee*, 426; On Soviet visitors being price-conscious see The National Archives, London, Foreign Office, FO 371 166264 (UK-Soviet Cultural Exchange, 1961).

[139] Gutnova, *Perezhitoe*, 324,

expensive version of coveted items.[140] Andrei Konchalovskii received only about twenty dollars in his 1962 trip to Italy. He hoped to make a little bit more by selling the two bottles of vodka he had stuck in his suitcase, or even more desperately, the camera he had brought along as a participant in the Venice Film Festival. In the end, he acquired thirty dollars more through the "impudent and *po sovetskoi* habit" of asking a friend for money.[141]

Some part of the small amount of money a tourist had was usually spent on souvenirs. The souvenir was material evidence of a hard-won voyage to imaginary lands, an object not "of need or use value," but of nostalgia. "We do not need or desire souvenirs of events that are repeatable," Susan Stewart writes. "Rather we need and desire souvenirs of events that are reportable, events whose materiality has escaped us, events that thereby exist only through the invention of narrative."[142] German remembers having to make a choice between spending what little hard currency he had on an ephemeral treat in a café or on a small souvenir to bring home: "On the first evening my traveling companions, not listening to my warning that coffee was expensive, in their greed and ignorance drank coffee at a café and wasted three times more money than I—in my arrogance—did on a beautiful goblet."[143] Tourists without much money to spend but eager to buy a little something for themselves as well as for friends, often resorted to the inexpensive and typically touristic. Nekrasov purchased reproductions of art on "some kind of break-proof and scratch-proof plastic" to take home from his trip to Italy. "You could stand there all day picking them out," he wrote. "It's both a pleasant and an agonizing job, when you don't have that much money, and you want to buy everything you see."[144] A difference between the Soviet tourist's relationship to the souvenir, and that of the European or North American tourist, was what happened to the souvenir upon returning home. As described by Stewart, most souvenirs end up in the attic or the cellar, "destined to be forgotten," emblems of "the death of memory."[145] For the Soviet tourist, however, for whom a trip to Western Europe was impossibly difficult to achieve and unlikely to be repeated, the material memory of a trip abroad was proudly displayed. In his memoir published in 2000, German admits that the inexpensive Parisian goblet bought on his first trip to Paris in 1965 sits even now on his writing desk.[146]

---

[140] Interview with Safra Raisa Mikhailovna (27 July 2009), courtesy of Alexei Golubev, Archive of the Oral History Centre of Petrozavodsk State University.

[141] Konchalovskii, *Nizkie istiny*, 111, 117.

[142] Susan Stewart, *On Longing: Narratives of the Miniature, the Gigantic, the Souvenir, the Collection* (Durham, 1993), 135.

[143] German, *Slozhnoe proshedshee*, 433.

[144] Nekrasov, *Both Sides*, 86.

[145] Stewart, *On Longing*, 150–51.

[146] German, *Slozhnoe proshedshee*, 433. See, similarly, the discussion of Svetlana Boym's aunt's commode in Svetlana Boym, *Common Places: Mythologies of Everyday Life in Russia* (Harvard, 1994), 150–57.

The eagerness to bring something home is common to the tourist experience everywhere. But the lack of hard currency meant that despite the plethora of goods, the effort required "to get" (*dostat*) just the right thing sometimes resembled shopping at home, where, as German explains, the striving for goods was a type of "national sport."[147] In the Soviet Union, "even the march to a grocery store was an adventure, the shopper becoming a conquistador, hoping for success and prepared for defeat." The shopper often returned "worn out and bloodstained."[148] In Western Europe, in contrast, shopping was a consumptive experience, but also a leisure experience. Memoirs and travel accounts about the West European shop and street scene are bursting with tourists' expansive and unaccustomed enjoyment of cheerful service, liveliness, light, and color. On Evgeniia Gutnova's first evening abroad, she walked with a group of colleagues along London's "famous shopping artery," Oxford Street. It was evening but "all the stores were open, the windows sparkled." Not used to such "abundance," their heads "went round and round."[149] "Three things dazzled me in particular," the Polish travel writer Ryszard Kapuściński recalled about his first trip abroad to Italy in 1956. "First, that the stores were brimming with merchandise, the goods weighing down shelves and counters, spilling out in colorful streams onto sidewalks, streets, and squares. Second, that the sales ladies did not sit, but stood looking at the entrance; it was strange that they stood in silence, rather than sitting and talking to one another. The third shock was that they answered the questions you asked them. They responded in complete sentences and then added, *Grazie!*"[150]

How did Soviet authorities respond to the compulsion to shop? Within limits, the experience of the European street and store was to be encouraged. Susan Reid has described the didactic efforts of the Khrushchev era to promote a consistently "contemporary"—meaning modernist and functional—style in fashion and home decorating, a new kind of decor for which travel to Western Europe could be instructive.[151] But if shopping was acceptable as an educative leisure experience, it was not acceptable as a Soviet-style consumptive experience, the desperation of which could be embarrassing. In their pre-trip instructions, tourists to Paris in 1965 were not forbidden to shop, but were told not to "stare in windows" and not to "buy lots of things."[152] A group of tourists from Armenia were criticized by their trip leader for misbehaving while shopping in

---

[147] German, *Slozhnoe proshedshee*, 420–21. On the importance of the word meaning "to get" (*dostat*) for the *Homo Sovieticus*, see Dale Pesmen, *Russian and Soul: An Exploration* (Ithaca, 2000), 134.

[148] German, *Slozhnoe proshedshee*, 420–21.

[149] Gutnova, *Perezhitoe*, 317.

[150] Kapuściński, "The Open World," 60.

[151] Susan Reid, "Cold War in the Kitchen: Gender and the De-Stalinization of Consumer Taste in the Soviet Union under Khrushchev," *Slavic Review* 61, no. 2 (Summer 2002): 211–52.

[152] See the list of instructions given Soviet tourists to Western Europe in German, *Slozhnoe proshedshee*, 426.

Stockholm: they "fussed about the counter, repeatedly tried on items for personal wear, and made a lot of noise in the shops."[153] Trip leaders were anxious that the Soviet Union not be embarrassed by the consumptive desires of their tourists, longings which made visible the lack of consumer items at home. One group of tourists accepted a gift of leather gloves from a British tannery until they learned that a local newspaper journalist had written them up as a lucky group of Russians who would not have to queue for gloves that winter. They then felt compelled to return the gloves, claiming that the work was inferior to Soviet products.[154] Indeed, it is true that the British did sometimes try to take advantage of Soviet tourists for political and commercial gain. The department store Marks & Spencer's offered another group of Soviet tourists a round of free shopping at their store, telling them that when foreign visitors shopped in their store for the first time, they were invited to take what they liked for free. The presence of photographers and the persistence of the store manager led the Soviet trip leaders to refuse, understanding that Marks & Spencer's was playing to capitalist conceptions of an impoverished Soviet Union for the sake of advertising.[155] Some Soviet citizens surely regretted the principled response of their trip leaders: on other trips, tourists appear to have eagerly accepted gifts including tennis rackets, scarves, brushes, lipstick, and fashion magazines.[156] Harold Shukman, who worked briefly as a British guide and translator for Soviet tourists in the 1950s, remembers a Soviet group who while visiting Birmingham asked to have some time off to wander about on their own without being accompanied. They started off empty-handed but returned with suitcases full of purchases. Shukman's understanding was that they had gone to Marks & Spencer's, but they were unwilling to speak of what they had bought and insisted that the suitcases were their own.[157]

RETURNING HOME

Travelers brought home new ideas, new material goods, and a newly improved social status. For some Soviet tourists, however the "experiencing of

---

[153] GARF, f. 9520, op. 1, d. 420, l. 16.

[154] Interview with Gerald Smith. See the archival trip report of this incident in RGASPI, f. m-5, op. 1, d. 197, l. 21.

[155] RGASPI, f. m-5, op. 1, d. 197, l. 47. On the famous case of Nina Ponomareva, the Olympic discus champion, whose contentious arrest for shoplifting five hats from a store on London's Oxford Street almost led to the Bolshoi ballet cancelling its performance at the Royal Opera House, see David Caute, *The Dancer Defects: The Struggle for Cultural Supremacy during the Cold War* (Oxford, 2003), 472–74.

[156] GARF, f. 9612, op. 1, d. 373, ll. 6, 47.

[157] Interview with Harold Shukman.

otherness"[158]—the ability to leave—mattered more than the otherness itself. Personally experiencing places that others could "know" only through reading about them, provided privileged Soviet tourists with valuable social and cultural capital, which they then acted out for audiences at home. The Russian playwrights Victor Rozov and Alexander Shtein spoke to a meeting of the All-Russian Theatrical Society about their impressions of the London theater and the Edinburgh Festival and about their personal meetings with playwrights and actors.[159] Traveler Dmitri Eagen'evich put together a film about his 1956 travels around Europe by cruiseship which he showed at various clubs in Moscow. "This extraordinary film," *Ogonek* gushed, reveals a "significant trip of Soviet people through European countries, their thrilling meetings with local people, their arrival in every port and city, the places of beauty and significance which the Soviet tourists saw."[160] Not all reports were by elites. If in 1956 the Vice-President of the Soviet Academy of Sciences spoke at the Geographic Society meetings about his trip "Around Europe on the Ship 'Victory',"[161] in 1961, the Novosibirsk trade union formed a study circle called "On the map of the world" at which those who had gone abroad spoke about their experiences to others.[162]

In his 1961 travelogue, Nekrasov put the question of privilege front and center. He took on the role of intelligent, honest, wry observer only slightly advantaged by virtue of good fortune, from his compatriots left at home. He began his account with a story about the status that the rare trip to Western Europe provided for the traveler.

'So you went to Italy again?'
  'Yes.'
'How did you like it?'
  'Well . . . I got terribly tired . . . Anyway, two weeks is such a short time. . . .'
'Yes, that's true . . . But still . . .'
  'Well, how can I tell you . . . ? Naturally I found it interesting.'
'What do you mean it naturally you found it interesting?'
  'Well . . . for the usual reasons. We did so much running around in those two weeks – actually, to be exact, we had 13 days – there was so much to talk to people about, so much to see, that it will take me about six months to figure it all out.'
'Mm. Yes. . . . of course.'

---

[158] Greg Dening, "The theatricality of observing and being observed: Eighteenth-century Europe 'discovers' the ? century 'Pacific'," in *Implicit Understandings: Observing, Reporting, and Reflecting on the Encounters between Europeans and Other Peoples in the Early Modern Era*, ed. Stewart B. Schwartz (Cambridge, 1994), 453.

[159] *SCR General Report*, 1960–1961, 3. SCR Archive.

[160] Iu. Polevaia, "Kinootchet o puteshestvii," *Ogonek* 38 (September 1956): 25.

[161] GARF, f. 9520, op. 1, d. 317, l. 17 (On the fulfillment of plans for travel abroad, Leningrad Oblast, 1956).

[162] GARF, f. 9520, op. 1, d. 468, l. 75 (TEU meeting on foreign travel, 1961). This was also a routine part of domestic "proletarian tourism," a way to multiply the number of people able to learn from travel.

He was silent after that. I could see his dissatisfaction in the way he looked at me. It was the same look that I must have given, 10 years earlier, to one of our famous writers who is always sent to any kind of Congress. As he hung up the telephone, I heard him snarling: 'Now I'm in for it! I have to go to Paris again.'

He saw how surprised I was and he explained it to me: 'if you only knew how tiresome I find all of these trips – Paris, Stockholm, Geneva. You run around like a squirrel on a treadmill. You can't do any work, and you don't get any rest either.'

I was surprised and indignant, even personally offended.

And now I felt this man looking at me in the same way: 'The poor thing got so tired, you see. Two weeks was just not long enough for him. He had too many impressions, he saw too much, and now he just can't digest it all.'

I felt him thinking all this and I felt uncomfortable."[163]

Despite his sympathy for those left behind, Nekrasov was not immune from the self-satisfied hauteur of the returning traveler. He expressed discomfort with the difference travel to the West provided, even as he swooned with delight at the wonders of the trip itself. He inserted information into his account to signal his experience and sophistication. When describing his trip from Moscow (via Paris) to Rome's Fiumicino Airport "glittering with light and glass" Nekrasov inserted in parentheses: "I can't decide which is better, the new Orly in Paris or Fiumicino."[164] Still, Nekrasov had the good manners to recognize his pretensions and the impact they had on those at home:

"I was telling [a friend from Kiev] about something or other, and I happen to let him slip that one evening I just didn't feel like going to the Palazzo Vecchio. I'd been there every day, you see, morning and evening.

'Well, what are we coming to?' He said, and there wasn't a trace of sympathy in his voice. 'And, for that matter, didn't you get bored with Florence itself? Morning and evening, night and day?'

I began to feel uncomfortable."[165]

Travel accounts were one means of exhibiting privilege. Objects were another, items purchased abroad gaining great symbolic value beyond their original use value by virtue of their exclusivity when they crossed the border. Clothing—the smart new jacket or silk blouse purchased in Paris or Oslo and proudly worn at home—was an especially visible marker of the elusive internationalism afforded the traveler. Clothes bought abroad were quickly recognizable by their style and by their fabric, the patterns and colors on Soviet mass-produced clothing being less diverse. Returning tourists also shared their photographs with office mates, the rarity and value of which suggested by the initials carefully written on the

[163] Nekrasov, *Both Sides of the Ocean*, 3.
[164] Nekrasov, *Both Sides of the* Ocean, 11–12.
[165] Nekrasov, *Both Sides of the Ocean*, 14–15.

back by viewers as the photos were passed around.[166] Souvenirs and small gifts, such as European chocolates, were highly valued gifts, conferring status on the recipient as well as the giver. T.I. remembered a family friend bringing her back a jacket from Germany which he visited in his capacity as a military officer: "It was not a very good-looking jacket, I did not like it, but it was something at least." "Some kids," on the other hand, "had wealthier parents like my friend L. P's parents. Her dad went to France. He was a party boss in our city, so he would bring her perfume and some good clothes."[167] The gift of perfume, records and magazines, stories and photos enabled giver and receiver to render visible their higher status—elite status in the Soviet Union being reinforced through the consumption of mass material culture abroad.

All of this made those without access to travel deeply envious. When Mikhail German ran into a colleague who had wrangled his way onto a Komsomol trip to France, he found it hard to concentrate on what he was being told about the trip, too busy wondering "why not me?"[168] The "us" versus "them" in this was not the Soviet Union versus the West, but privileged Soviet citizens versus those left at home. Social, educational, gender, and financial differences deliberately mini-mized in other areas of Soviet life were made explicit through the application process, experience, and recitation of travel abroad. "People were divided into 'exiters' (*vyezdnykh*) those who went often, and 'non-exiters' (*nevyezdnykh*), those for whom it was difficult to leave," Gutnova observes.[169]

Those left at home sometimes responded with an ironic worldliness, position-ing themselves as more sophisticated than those who had traveled. In their 1956 satirical poem, "Around and About (A Guide for Tourists Wishing to Write Travelers' Diaries)," Vladimir Mass and Mikhail Chervinskii mocked the clichéd travelers' tale, criticizing banal travel accounts to Europe for "pil[ing] up cliché on cliché" in the "usual, standard and long approved style:"

> We met, I recall . . . (on the walks of Hyde Park,
> On the quai at Le Havre, on the square of St. Mark)
> A man wearing . . . (glasses, a hat, a beret).
> At first he was naturally somber and dour;
> When he learned who we were, he decided to stay
> And cried . . . ("*Guten Tag!*" "*Buona sera!*" "*Bonjour!*"),
> And tears of emotion welled forth from his eye.
> We badges exchanged as we bade him good-by.

---

[166] As was true, for example, of the travel photographs shown to the author by Valeria Emmanuilovna Kunina, Moscow, 2004.

[167] Interview of T.I., Vancouver, 2004.

[168] German, 283–84. On the envy and resentment aimed at Soviet citizens who traveled abroad, also see Nordica Nettleton, "Driving Towards Communist Consumerism: AvtoVAZ," *Cahiers du Monde Russe*, 47/1–2 (January–June 2006): 142–3.

[169] Gutnova, *Perezhitoe*, 315.

And then after that wherever we'd walk,
All the people came up to us simply to talk.[170]

Mass and Chervinskii's target is the press for publishing these cautious tales that stuck to tried and true representations of warm Soviet encounters with the West, but also the "persons already too well known to fame" who abuse their right to travel by saying nothing new, plagiarizing one from the other. The implication is even though Mass and Chervinskii cannot travel, their understanding of Europe is the more sophisticated.

Authorities also used satire to deflate the self-satisfied superiority of returning tourists. A short story from *Iunost'* [Youth] entitled "Galloping around Europe," begins with a description of a group of young women chattering excitedly about an upcoming party thrown to celebrate the return from Europe of a young man named Victor. "He promises to tell us lots of interesting things!" one exclaims. At the party, Victor is shown to be dressed more stylishly than anyone else. Initially, everyone is enraptured by how he looks and what he says. This enthusiasm is quickly deflated. It turns out that Victor knows less about Europe than the people gathered to hear his stories. He calls the poet Robert Loretti "Robert Spaghetti". He tells the group that his favorite site in Rome was the Eiffel Tower. When asked if records available in Europe were better than those available in the Soviet Union, he describes with enthusiasm his purchase of a record by Stan Kenton. The piece leaves unsaid, but understood, that those truly in the know would not consider a record by a big-band orchestra, most famous in the late 1940s and early 1950s, to be a significant purchase. It is clear that a trip to Europe was wasted on Victor, who at the end of the article is shown to be a last-minute replacement for another tourist. The article warns Soviet citizens to avoid undiscriminating enthusiasm for the decadent, illusionary Europe of fashion and fun, even as they are encouraged to dream of travel for the more purposeful pursuits of performance and education.[171] Status, it suggests, should not come from the consumption of Western popular culture, but from the informed consumption of European history and civilization be that through travel abroad or education at home.[172]

"I DIDN'T BELIEVE MY EYES"

Permitting Soviet citizens to travel abroad was part of the Khrushchev regime's "high-risk strategy"[173] of opening up the Soviet Union to contact and exchange

---

[170] Vladimir Mass and Mikhail Chervinsky, "Around and About (A Guide For Tourists Wishing To Write Travelers' Diaries)," in *The Year of Protest: An Anthology of Soviet Literary Materials*, ed. Hugh McLean and Walter N. Vickery (New York, 1961), 115–18.

[171] Ark. Arkanov, "Galopom po Evropam," *Iunost'* 8 (August 1963): 109–10.

[172] Arkanov, "Galopom po Evropam," 109–10.

[173] Reid, "Who Will Beat Whom?" 862.

with foreign countries and cultures. As Susan Reid has argued about the state's decision to allow the United States to exhibit American consumer goods and domestic products at the American National Exhibition, the Khrushchev regime believed the "benefits important enough to justify the risks," confident "that the USSR was well placed to repulse the threats."[174] Confidence in Soviet achievements, the desire for international prestige, and commitment to the policy of peaceful coexistence made travel for high-ranking Soviet citizens appear worth the risk. Was it? What was the impact, for individuals, of permitting Soviet tourists, albeit carefully selected ones, to experience the capitalist West firsthand?

For Andrei Konchalovskii, traveling to a West European elsewhere permanently upset the didactic meanings assigned by authorities to both home and abroad. He felt a "blow," a "shock," upon first seeing the bustling city squares and cafés of Rome in his 1962 trip to Italy. It was "my first realization that there were different standards of living," Konchalovskii remembers. "We spent the entire evening sitting in the trattoria. . . . We drank wine for three dollars. I will never forget the feeling of ease, happiness, light, music, holiday. All of my subsequent ideological vacillations and anti-patriotic actions started with this."[175] As he "watched young people, students, happy, bronzed, sitting on the banks," he wondered "why is it not like this at home?"[176] "I returned to Moscow scorched by the West," Konchalovskii concludes.[177]

Not all travelers believed what they saw in West European shop windows. Some, Caroline Humphrey observes, read the West as a "kind of mirage or trick." The Soviet "experience of deception [in which goods were advertised as available but were not] was both interiorized and globalized, as though that was the way things were in the world in general," she argues. Humphrey draws from the experiences of Vladimir Bukovskii and Vladimir Voinovich who were deported from the Soviet Union in 1976 and 1980 respectively. Both men believed that the amazing number and quality of items displayed in shop windows "must be for show (*napokaz*) like in a Soviet shop window, and of course no-one will buy them. That is why there are no queues and such huge quantities of goods lie around unsold."[178] Some tourists in the Khrushchev era surely also doubted the reality of what they saw, experiencing the West as a form of exhibitionary propaganda. In this they resembled those Soviet citizens who

---

[174] Reid, "Who Will Beat Whom?" 862.

[175] Konchalovskii, *Nizkie istiny*, 112.

[176] Konchalovskii, *Nizkie istiny*, 116.

[177] Konchalovskii, *Nizkie istiny*, 120. According to A. A. Kriuchkov, shop windows in particular, were "a very effective means of propaganda for the 'Western way of life.' Soviet tourists, falling from a country of universal deficit into a society of 'consumer abundance,' not infrequently experienced a distinctive cultural shock and found it necessary to take a new look at their relationship to 'the Soviet way of life.'"A.A. Kriuchkov, *Istoriia mezhdunarodnogo i otechestvennogo turizma* (Moscow, 1999), 69.

[178] Humphrey, *The Unmaking of Soviet Life*, 54–55. Also see Yale Richmond, *Cultural Exchange and the Cold War: Raising the Iron Curtain* (University Park, 2003), 180–81.

expressed "doubts about the objectivity" of the consumptive displays at the American National Exhibition in Moscow in 1959.[179] That said, my evidence suggests that for most travelers in the 1950s and 1960s, virtual tourism differed from being there in person; the immersionary impact of experiencing shop windows in multiple cities and countries, talking with local residents, and sometimes having dinner in private homes challenged expectations in ways that exhibitions at home might not have. "I didn't believe my eyes," Konchalovskii writes with a reference to his experiences in Italy.[180] In Konchalovskii's case, in contrast to Bukovskii and Voinovich, the phrase conveyed wonder, not disbelief.

Konchalovskii's description of himself in "shock" might reflect in part when he wrote his memoir. Many post-Soviet memoirs, if freed from the most obvious of Soviet controls, are still highly politicized as members of the intelligentsia use their memoirs to distinguish themselves post facto from Soviet socialism, deploying personal history to describe their language as separate from "the language of power."[181] That Konchalovskii's memoir was a product of when it was written does not mean, however, that the *frisson* of excitement and awareness he describes was imagined entirely after the fact. Other memoirists describe the same excitement, even if their larger conclusions sometimes differ. For Mikhail German, "authentic"[182] Paris was different than he imagined, still wondrous, but also disappointing. More precisely, it was not Paris that was disappointing, but the failure of expectations, the loss of fantasy that the encounter with Paris provoked. German is rhapsodic about his experiences in contemporary Paris, but at the same time nostalgic about an imaginary Paris he had experienced through literature and art: "Storybook Paris died. It was the exchange of an imaginary, conceptual, living-only-in-one's soul Paris for the indisputable reality of a one and only, genuine, city—a process which, at bottom, was wistful."[183] At issue was not disappointment in a specific difference between the imagined and real, but the loss of a fantasy of other which was had been so constitutive of German's Soviet self. In this way, German, like Konchalovskii, was irrevocably (if differently) changed by his travel to Western Europe as that which he thought he knew was upset.

For Evgeniia Gutnova, however, a trip to Western Europe was less transformative. In her memoirs, she describes herself as unsurprised by what she experienced in the capitalist West, even as she enjoyed its pleasures. So too for Valeria Kunina, a dedicated communist who in an interview about her travel to England and Italy said she was delighted to travel abroad but was not surprised nor transformed by what she saw of West European living standards, knowing before

---

179 Susan Reid, "Who will beat whom?" 893.
180 Konchalovskii, *Nizkie istiny*, 216.
181 Patrick Seriot as cited in Yurchak, *Everything Was Forever*, 6.
182 German, *Slozhnoe proshedshee*, 434.
183 German, *Slozhnoe proshedshee*, 434. Also see 440–41.

she left that it was "a different world."[184] Gutnova put it differently, if to the same end. She emphasized similarities, describing people on the streets of London as "just like us, only a little bit more elegantly dressed."[185] The similarities suggested friendly relations between equals rather than the profound inferiority and disillusionment of Konchalovskii's memoirs. Gutnova returned home "refreshed" from the new impressions she received from her travel abroad, but not fundamentally altered.[186] For her, travel abroad was "an occasion for celebration" not resistance or even uncertainty.[187] Gutnova's experience suggests that enjoying the West did not necessitate a rejection of the Soviet self.

How do we understand the diversity of experiences and interpretations? In part, the diversity reflects human diversity. Even as experiences abroad were politically and culturally mediated, individualized reactions persisted. Mikhail Gorbachev and Boris Yeltsin had very different responses, to take two well-known examples, to their first experiences in Western countries. "When Gorbachev saw for himself Western countries with their higher standards of living . . . ," Archie Brown observes, "he could have given up both on the idea of socialism and his admiration for Lenin, but he did not. For Boris Yeltsin it was enough to see an American supermarket for the first time to be converted to a belief in capitalism."[188]

For the Khrushchev era in particular, however, I would argue that Gutnova's reflections may best capture the attitude of many tourists traveling abroad. A trip to the West and the purchase of Western material items more often reaffirmed the traveler's privileged status within a positively viewed system than it generated resistance to this system. Privileged tourist-consumers were, after all, drawn from groups most likely to be supportive of the regime. In this, the Soviet tourist in the Khrushchev era differed from East European citizens of late socialism for whom, as described by Katherine Verdery, "acquiring consumption goods and objects conferred an identity that set one off from socialism."[189] For many privileged Soviet travelers in the 1950s and early 1960s, it was possible for them to admire, purchase, and envy Western consumer goods, and still believe in the future of Soviet socialism. Khrushchev had promised that Soviet citizens would soon have what capitalist ones did but without the excess and exploitation; he insisted that consumptive pleasures need not be capitalist. The possibility of Soviet tourism abroad appeared to be evidence of this. This, combined with pride in the

[184] Interview with Valeria Emmanuilovna Kunina, Moscow, 2004. So too for Safra Raisa Mikhailovna, who described herself as unchanged in her attitude toward Soviet reality following a 1964 trip to Finland. Interview with Safra Raisa Mikhailovna (27 July 2009).

[185] Gutnova, *Perezhitoe*, 317.

[186] Gutnova, *Perezhitoe*, 322.

[187] Gutnova, *Perezhitoe*, 323.

[188] Archie Brown, "Gorbachev, Lenin, and the Break with Leninism," *Demokratizatsiya*, 15, no 2 (Spring 2007): 238.

[189] Katherine Verdery, *The Transition from Socialism: Anthropology and Eastern Europe* (Cambridge, 1992), 25–26.

achievements and vitality of the USSR, an enthusiasm bolstered by the achievements of Sputnik I, the world's first artificial satellite, and Yuri Gagarin, led many to feel enthusiastic about Soviet accomplishments, hopeful that the Soviet Union would indeed "catch up and overtake" the capitalist West.[190] This would change as the failures of Soviet socialism came to outweigh its promises, but for some people in the Khrushchev era it was possible to believe that the USSR was, or would soon be, better than its competitors. In 1956, after all, Soviet tourists complained about British eggs and tinned ham, comparing them unfavorably to "first class" food aboard the Soviet cruise ship *Molotov*.[191]

---

[190] In a 1960 survey, 73.2. percent reported that their living standards had improved due to higher wages, more goods, better food, and improved housing conditions. In another survey, 96.8 percent felt that mankind could prevent nuclear war. B. A. Grushin, *Chetyre zhizni Rossii v zerkale obshchestvennogo mneniia. Epokha Khrushcheva* (Moscow, 2001), 84, 125–26; "Introduction," Donald J. Raleigh, *Russia's Sputnik Generation*, 16–19, and interviews throughout especially 72–73, 85, 132, 167, 231, 235; Werth, *Russia under Khrushchev*, 52, 74–75, 133; Reid, "Who Will Beat Whom?" 883–90; Vladislav Zubok, *Zhivago's Children: The Last Russian Intelligentsia* (Cambridge, 2009), chp. 4.

[191] GARF, f. 9612, op. 1, d. 373, l. 28 (Trip report, England, 1956).

6

Film Tourism: From Iron Curtain
to Silver Screen

In 1957, the Soviet newspaper *Komsomolskaia pravda* railed against the Holly-wood film *Silk Stockings* for its "cheap, vulgar" portrayal of Soviet tourists to Paris. Not only poorly dressed, they were purported to know nothing even about "ordinary silk stockings."[1] Notably, *Komsomolskaia pravda* did not question the idea of Soviet citizens traveling to Paris, nor that they should be dressed in a contemporary and elegant manner while there. Instead, the newspaper objected to the Hollywood portrayal of Soviet citizens as uneducated about universally accepted norms of Western culture. In contrast, Soviet films of the same era portrayed their citizens as contemporary in style, and Soviet cities as desirable destinations for tourists both domestic and international. In the 1965 movie *A Foreign Woman* [Inostranka],[2] a pre-revolutionary citizen of Russia living in France returns as a tourist to her native city of Odessa. Scenes of beautiful, sunny Odessa replete with parks, nice cars, and shops—all accompanied by a soundtrack of soft jazz—are meant to suggest to the viewer that between Odessa and Paris, there was not much difference.

This chapter explores the place of Soviet film in negotiating the armchair traveler's understandings of the "West," and of Soviet identity in relationship to this imagined West.[3] I am especially interested in portrayals of travel and tourism, some domestic, others international. If selected Soviet citizens were newly permitted to travel to places previously out of bounds, for most people the capitalist West remained inaccessible. It was no longer behind an impenetrable iron curtain, however. Film was a means of safely introducing Soviet citizens to their newly expanded universe. It was a form of virtual travel both pleasurable and purposeful, helping viewers distinguish good influences from bad. Many of these dangerous influences were familiar ones: the foreigner as spy, decadent

---

[1] S. Vladimirov, "Fabrication on the screen," *Komsomolskaia pravda* (24 August 1957), 3/ *Current Digest of the Soviet Press* (hereafter *CDSP*) 9 (1957), 18.
[2] *Inostranka* [A Foreign Woman]. Directors: Aleksandr Seryj and Konstantin Zhuk. USSR, 1965.
[3] On the relationship between tourism, film, and the "map—real and imaginary—of Sovietness" in the 1920s and 1930s, see Emma Widdis, *Visions of a New Land: Soviet Film from the Revolution to the Second World War* (New Haven, 2003), especially chps. 4 and 5.

capitalist, and seductress.[4] But Khrushchev-era distinctions between internationalism and cosmopolitanism were sometimes new ones. In the films to be discussed, Americans are shown as redeemable and Moscow is promoted as a city of cultural sophistication rather than industrial achievement. Cinematographic portrayals of travel and tourism—including travel by Soviet citizens and by foreigners—sometimes reveal a blurring of old Stalinist binaries between "us" and "them." In contrast to scholarship such as that of Walter Hixson, who argues in *Parting the Curtain: Propaganda, Culture, and the Cold War* that it was American "cultural infiltration" that led to the eventual collapse of communism by teaching Soviet citizens about Western alternatives, I take a less triumphalist approach, emphasizing the importance of Soviet agency over Western, specifically, American cultural penetration.[5] Soviet citizens did not learn about jazz only via illicit listening to radio broadcasts or from watching foreign movies: soft jazz served as the soundtrack to popular homegrown Soviet films. It was not only that "Western" differences could be tolerated, but that some of these differences were made acceptably, and even officially, Soviet.

FILM AND TOURISM

One of the attractions of the movie-going experience is being engulfed in the action on screen—a snowstorm, a dark alley, a jazz club in Paris—images that make the viewer feel as if they are "living within this great breathing, palpable place."[6] The all-encompassing nature of film which is rooted in its visual and auditory qualities, its scale, and in the illusion of movement, help convince the viewer not only that what she is seeing might, someday or somewhere, be experienced, but that she is in fact experiencing it.[7] Going to the movies, as this suggests, is itself a kind of tourism. Fundamental to the epistemologies of both film and tourism is the centrality of movement and the capacity to influence the imagination through sight and sound. Also fundamental to both is an ambiguous relation to the "authentic."[8] Both film and travel partake in what

---

[4] On Thaw films that display an "anxious distrust" of foreigners, see Julian Graffy, "Scant Sign of Thaw: Fear and Anxiety in the Representation of Foreigners in the Soviet Films of the Khrushchev Years," in Stephen Hutchings, ed. *Russia and its Other(s) on Film* (Houndmills, 2008), 27–46.

[5] Walter L. Hixson, *Parting the Curtain: Propaganda, Culture and the Cold War, 1945–1961* (New York, 1997, 1998).

[6] David Denby, "Big Pictures: Hollywood looks for a future," *The New Yorker* (8 January 2006): 60.

[7] Peter Ruppert, "Tracing Utopia, Film, Spectatorship and Desire" *Utopian Studies* 7, no. 2 (1996), 145. On the convergence of cinematic vision and international travel, see Stephen Hutchings, "Introduction," in *Russia and its Other(s) on Film*, 8–9.

[8] The authenticity, or not, of the tourist experience has been a matter of long scholarly debate. The most prominent defender of tourism as a search for authenticity is Dean MacCannell, *The Tourist: A New Theory of the Leisure Class* (1976; reprint Berkeley, 1999). John Urry has questioned the possibility of authenticity, emphasizing instead the constructed nature of the tourist gaze in *The*

Ellen Strain has called "the illusion of demediation," an illusion that "offers the false promise of communion with authenticity."[9]

The Bolsheviks were alert to the transformative potential of blending illusion and reality. In director Dziga Vertov's 1926 film, *A Sixth of the World* [Shestaia chast' mira], the immersive powers of film enabled Soviet armchair viewers to travel across Soviet territory in a series of (staged) expeditions aimed to help them imagine the unmapped territories of the Soviet Union as Soviet space.[10] Combining the seemingly truth telling aspects of a visual encounter with the imaginary aspects of storytelling is not unique to Soviet cinema, of course. More particular to the Soviet Union was the effort to make people believe that the fantastical was authentic, or would be someday. In the 1954 movie *The Reserve* [Zapasnoi igrok],[11] the images of luxury tourism aboard a Soviet cruise ship are impossibly utopian. A beautiful restaurant on board is decorated with Greek-style columns, there are flowers on the tables, and the helpful waiters wear clean white jackets. Denying the economic realities and severe shortages of the early 1950s, the film shows female Soviet tourists lounging on a Black Sea beach in well-fitting swimsuits and fashionable hats, an impossibility when many Soviet citizens still wore their underwear for a dip in the sea.

Tourism and film can both be fantasy breakers as well as makers. The films of the Thaw were aimed in part at challenging the fantasy world of socialist realism, even as they arguably sought to build new fantasies. As part of the post-Stalin turn, cultural producers in the Khrushchev era argued against the "varnished and prettified" image of reality shown in socialist realist films.[12] Admittedly, this was far from a straightforward process; there were many continuities with the past.[13] And commentators observed that newer Soviet films still did not always rise above the stereotypical even if these stereotypes were sometimes new ones. An article in *Izvestiia* derided the "commonplaces" of the 1960 Soviet film *Roman*

Tourist Gaze: Leisure and Travel in Contemporary Societies (London, 1990). More recent work questions this dichotomy. See Rudy Koshar, *German Travel Cultures* (Oxford, 2000) and Ellen Strain, *Public Places, Private Journeys: Ethnography, Entertainment, and the Tourist Gaze* (New Brunswick, 2003), 2–6 and throughout.

  [9] Strain, *Public Places*, 4.
  [10] Widdis, *Visions of a New Land*, 108, 3.
  [11] *Zapasnoi Igrok* [The Reserve]. Director: Semen Timoshenko. USSR, 1954.
  [12] Hopf, *Social Construction of International Politics*, 72.
  [13] Alexander Prokhorov, "Inherited Discourse: Stalinist Tropes in Thaw Culture," Ph.D., University of Pittsburgh, 2002, http://etd.library.pitt.edu/ETD/available/etd-07242002-135513/; Graffy, "Scant Sign of Thaw," 27–43. On Thaw cinema more generally see Josephine Woll, *Real Images: Soviet Cinema and the Thaw* (London, 2000). On Soviet attitudes towards the West as expressed in post-revolutionary and Stalinist films see Oleg Kovalov, "Zvezda nad step'iu. Amerika v zerkale sovetskogo kino," *Iskusstvo kino* 10 (2003), www.kinoart.ru/magazine/10-2003/review/Kovalov0310. On representations of the West, with particular attention to the Brezhnev era, see Sergei Dobrynin, "The Silver Curtain: Representations of the West in the Soviet Cold War Films," *History Compass* 7, no. 3 (April 2009), www3.interscience.wiley.com/cgi-bin/fulltext/122314400/HTMLSTART.

and Francesca [Roman i Francheska], even as these commonplaces were now about Italy: "The screen takes the viewer to Italy, where the action of 'Roman and Francesca' takes place. The streets of a large city, the priest in black cassock and wide-brimmed hat, the nun in the clothes of her order, the crowd of 'common people' listening to a street singer—are these not the same old images that arise in everyone's mind, the same 'tested' color that we have already met in travel diaries?"[14]

After Khrushchev's 1956 speech at the Twentieth Party Congress denouncing the cult of Stalin, Soviet cinema increasingly experienced more autonomy in subject matter and form; films offered various and sometimes contradictory opinions about contemporary questions, exploring the uncertain boundaries of appropriate expressions of difference in a post-Stalin world. This is not to say that Soviet cinema did not still respond to "specific, identifiable, social imperatives."[15] The regime controlled the financing and circulation of movies and films that went beyond the accepted parameters of debate, were censured and removed from circulation. In some areas, however, of which positive images of capitalist culture were one, social imperatives shifted away from earlier Cold War rigidities in which the capitalist West was unhesitatingly portrayed as an alien and dangerous other. Mikhail Romm—the director of the Thaw film *Nine Days of One Year* [Deviat' dnei odnogo goda] which opened up the secret world of Soviet physics for Soviet filmgoers—argued that opening up the secret world of the West was also necessary: "We have lost the habit of considering that something also exists in the West. And this in Russia, the country of the world where more foreign literature is translated that anywhere else. One of the strong points of Russian intellectuals was precisely the fact that they read all of world literature, that they stood at the top in knowledge of world culture. This, too, is one of our traditions."[16] New kinds of films contributed to cinema's popularity, as did Khrushchev-era policies of encouraging movie-going by producing more movies, building more theaters, and lowering ticket prices.[17]

There is a difference, of course, between watching a film about travel and the actual experience of traveling. Insulted by American mockery of Soviet style, the newspaper *Komsomolskaia pravda* railed against the Hollywood film *Silk Stockings,* but when Khrushchev traveled to the 1955 Geneva summit, he was indeed embarrassed by his lack of appropriate attire, in this case an unfashionable "baggy

---

[14] N. Ignatieva, "Along the Beaten Path," *Izvestiia* (11 April 1961)/*CDSP* 13:15 (10 May 1961), 40.

[15] John Haynes, "Reconstruction or Reproduction? Mothers and the Great Soviet Family in Cinema after Stalin," in *Women in the Khrushchev Era*, ed. Melanie Ilič, Susan E. Reid and Lynne Attwood (London, 2004), 115.

[16] Mikhail Romm, "Traditions and Innovations" in Priscilla Johnson, *Khrushchev and the Arts: The Politics of Soviet Culture, 1962–1964* (Cambridge, 1965), 101.

[17] M. R. Zezina, "S tochki zreniia istorii kinozala,' in *Istoriia strany, Istoriia kino*, ed. S.S. Sekirinskogo (Moscow, 2004), 400–401. Soviet citizens went, on average, to the movies at least twice a month. Josephine Woll, *The Cranes are Flying* (London, 2003), 109.

pale-mauve" summer suit with "flapping trousers."[18] It is in experiences such as these that the corporeal experience of travel—the physical sensations associated with the body moving through space and being itself subject to the gaze of the host community—differ from the visual experience of celluloid tourism. When watching a film about the West, socialist audiences did not necessarily experience their clothing as out of fashion. Being there in person, on the other hand, offered the possibility for knowledge and excitement, but also for humiliation and exile. "After a while, I became aware that people were looking at me," Polish travel writer, Ryszard Kapuściński recalled about his first trip abroad to Italy in the late 1950s.

I had on a new suit, an Italian shirt white as snow, and a very fashionable polka-dotted tie [all purchased on arrival with the help of a friendly Italian journalist], but there must have been something in my appearance, in my way of sitting and moving, that gave me away. I sensed that I stuck out, and although I should have been happy, sitting there beneath the miraculous skies of Rome, I began to feel awkward and uncomfortable. I had changed my suit, but I could not conceal whatever lay beneath it. Here I was in the wide, wonderful world, and it was only serving to remind me how alien I felt.[19]

It was easier in film than in real life to imagine one's communist self as equivalent to that of people in the capitalist West; by domesticating capitalist culture, Soviet films removed any unpleasantness but also the danger of uncomfortable firsthand comparisons and the attendant risk of disillusionment to which they sometimes led.

PEACEFUL COEXISTENCE

The Soviet pavilion at the 1958 Brussels World's Fair emphasized Soviet industrial and economic achievements as well as artistic, intellectual, and athletic endeavors. Nothing could substitute for firsthand knowledge, however, and visitors to the pavilion were encouraged to take more than just a virtual tour of the USSR. On the second floor, just before the exit, was an Intourist booth, which invited people to "make a closer study of the world's first socialist country, its science, engineering, history and culture, and come to know its industrious, gifted people."[20] The 1960 film *Russian Souvenir* [Russkii suvenir][21] reveals what happened (or should have happened) when tourists from the capitalist West took up Intourist's invitation to visit the USSR. *Russian Souvenir* reflects the

---

[18] Editor's notes, *Khrushchev Remembers*, trans. and ed. Strobe Talbott (Boston, 1970), 392.

[19] Ryszard Kapuściński, "The Open World: A legendary travel writer's first trip abroad," *The New Yorker* (5 February 2007): 60.

[20] "Pavilion of the U.S.S.R. A Guide," National Archives and Records Administration (hereafter NARA), RG 43, Box 5, BEG 401.

[21] *Russkii suvenir* [Russian Souvenir]. Director: Grigorii Aleksandrov. USSR, 1960.

international politics of the Khrushchev era, in which newly friendly relations between East and West were possible, even if the socialist Soviet Union still remained superior. The film begins with the emergency landing of a plane of stereotypically wealthy Western tourists, including a British Bible scholar, an Italian Countess, and an American millionaire. Originally headed to Moscow, the travelers end up instead in the middle of Siberia. The film follows their efforts to get to Moscow, a premise which allows *Russian Souvenir* to display the natural resources and industrial achievements of the Soviet Union, and to show the gradual transformation of the tourists from prejudiced and uninformed to friendly and admiring.

Upon landing in Siberia, the tourists expect the worst, their images of Siberia informed by its Tsarist and Stalinist history as a site of prison camps. They are also shown to question the story of Soviet modernization. Throughout the film their expectations are repeatedly overthrown. When the group seeks shelter from the snow in an old prison, they expect to find scenes of horror but find instead a group of young people singing Western songs (if politically appropriate ones, namely "Old Man River") at what turns out to be a popular holiday spot. The new Khrushchev-era Siberia has thrown off its past: it is no longer a place of exile and imprisonment, but of energetic industrial activity, vast natural resources, and pioneering spirit. On their travels through Siberia back to Moscow, the travelers are shown enormous diamonds, visit larger-than-life sites of enormous industrial activity, and witness a rocket launching. The difference between the socialist East and the capitalist West is made explicit in a dream-like sequence in which the American millionaire imagines turning a small Siberian village into an American Las Vegas with dancing girls, nightclubs, champagne, and loud jazz music, while a Russian woman dreams of building a sanatorium, a theater, and a House of Culture. Soviet viewers of *Russian Souvenir* are reminded thereby of Khrushchev-era promises of a better life, a life so attractive that foreigners too will be drawn to it. In this, *Russian Souvenir* resembles writer Boris Polevoi's contemporaneous description of Siberia in a conversation with visiting journalist Alexander Werth: "The mineral wealth in East and Northeast Siberia is something quite fantastic... There's quite a gold and diamond rush there at present; I shouldn't be surprised if thousands of young Americans wanted to join in this rush!... The winters are tough, but it isn't a horrible country, as some still imagine. It's the most beautiful country in the world."[22]

The trope of Western decadence versus Soviet industry and Soviet attention to the needs of everyday people is familiar; *Russian Souvenir* might in this sense be seen as a cinematographic version of the Brussels World's Fair. What distinguishes the film from the Brussels' exhibition of Soviet superiority is the accompanying story of personal encounter, in which citizens of the socialist East and

---

[22] Alexander Werth, *Russia under Khrushchev* (Westport, 1961), 236.

tourists from the capitalist West are allowed to meet, discuss, and even fall in love. In every case, it is the Westerner who changes, influenced by the truth of Soviet superiority: unlike Cold War exposés, however, even disagreements are shown to be friendly and Soviet superiority is of a benign kind. When the tourists first set across the steppes in the direction of Moscow, the Countess struggles through the snow in her high heels. A Soviet woman steps up to take charge, giving the Italian her own warmer, more practical, shoes, and carrying her across a rustic bridge while wearing the Italian's high heels. While the tourists are revealed to be ignorant and coddled, they are not dangerous. Citizens of both the socialist East and capitalist West are shown to be looking for happiness and love, and an end to war. The movie ends with two marriages between Russians and their Western visitors, political antagonism overcome by personal attraction. The "Russian souvenir" these tourists take home is their changed attitude to the Soviet Union.

ORDINARY MOSCOW

Russian Souvenir portrays Western travelers experiencing an "authentic" USSR as represented by the virtues of a larger than life Siberia. Effective tourist excursions were supposed to offset the usual, more hostile, capitalist perspective. The anti-Soviet perspective of the typical capitalist visitor was satirized in a 1959 cartoon that shows a Western tourist—identifiable by his Hawaiian shirt and black beret—photographing three large posters of "old" Moscow held up by Western impresarios.[23] The staged scenes include a dilapidated wooden house, a horse and carriage, and two crudely dressed peasants carrying a samovar and a balalai-ka. Behind these staged images, the "real" Moscow is visible with multi-story apartment buildings, a parking lot full of cars, and a store window with manne-quins dressed in contemporary styles. Entitled "An objective view," the cartoon mocks the ideological blinders of Western tourists while it smugly reassures Soviet citizens that socialism will provide for their every consumer desire.

The popular 1963 hit *I walk around Moscow* [Ia shagaiu po Moskve][24] purported to get beyond the false façade of Western propaganda. It was a cinematographic version of the *Krokodil* cartoon, aiming to show both Soviet citizens and the film's large international audience the "real-life" Moscow behind the staged scenes of Western propaganda, complete with the very apartment buildings, cars, and well-dressed citizens of the *Krokodil* cartoon. There are multiple perspectives from which the armchair tourist can "walk around" Mos-cow in the film. He or she might see Moscow through the eyes of Volodia, an earnest young Siberian visiting Moscow for a day. Alternatively, the viewer might

[23] "Ob'ektivnyi vzglad," *Krokodil* 22 (August 10, 1959): backpage.
[24] *Ia shagaiu po Moskve* [I walk around Moscow]. Director: Georgii Daneliia. USSR, 1963.

Figure 18 Hello from Moscow. *Krokodil* (August 1959), back page.

identify with the carefree young Muscovite, Kolia, a construction worker who meets Volodia by chance on the metro, and becomes his informal tour guide. Whether tourist or tour guide, the theme of the journey is evident from the opening images which begin with a scene of arrival at a Moscow airport. Arrival in Moscow is at first slow and quiet, but the movie quickly speeds up with scenes of a bustling capital: cars and buses, crowds of people rushing to and fro, a busy Moscow Metro. In this, *I walk around Moscow* resembles earlier cinematographic tributes to Moscow such as the 1938 film by Aleksandr Medvedkin, *New Moscow* [Novaia Moskva], in which a young man from a rural village and his grand-mother travel to a dynamic Moscow with its fast moving trolleybuses and pedestrians, massive construction scenes, and planes flying overhead.[25] (In *Russian Souvenir*, Moscow is also shown to be larger than life, with its grand boulevards packed with cars, double-decker bridges, and skyscraper hotels.) While symbols of industrial and technological modernity were not particular to the Khrushchev era, in *I walk around Moscow* these older expressions of identity, which emphasized Soviet capacity for industrial production, are joined with newer images which emphasize possibilities for individual consumption, the attractive modernity of the contemporary urban landscape, and foreign tourism. All of this is shown as ordinary. "Nothing controversial, let alone subversive, shadows *I walk around Moscow*," Josephine Woll argues in her history of Khrushchev-era film.[26] It is just this ordinariness of the international that is significant. What makes regular Moscow a good place to live (and a good place to visit) has changed from the Stalinist utopias of the socialist realist film which, in the words of Richard Taylor, were "hermetically sealed against the outside world."[27]

Ordinary Moscow is visible in the everyday setting of *I walk around Moscow*. Film is an especially valuable source for exploring the normalization of the previously excluded, both for what it foregrounds, and for what we can see in background shots of street scenes, apartment interiors, and fashions, all of which helped display and construct a new Soviet normal. Here, consumption—specifi-cally the provision of adequate items to consume—is part of what defines Khrushchev-era Moscow as a modern, internationally-competitive city.[28] When Kolia and Volodia go for a stroll through GUM, the enormous Tsarist-

---

[25] As described in Widdis, *Visions of a New Land*, 176–82.

[26] Woll, *Real Images*, 159. Woll describes *I walk around Moscow* as a safe and uncontroversial "replacement" for another film about youth, *Illich's Gate*. Woll, *Real Images*, 142, 159–60.

[27] Richard Taylor, "'But Eastward, Look, the Land is Brighter': Toward a Topography of Utopia in the Stalinist Musical," in *The Landscape of Stalinism: The Art and Ideology of Soviet Space*, ed. Evgeny Dobrenko and Eric Naiman (Seattle, 2003).

[28] On the Thaw as a period of "fierce [technologically driven] competition between the superpowers for possession of the future," see David Crowley and Susan E. Reid, "Style and Socialism: Modernity and Material Culture in Post-War Eastern Europe," in *Style and Socialism: Modernity and Material Culture in Post-War Eastern Europe*, ed. Susan E. Reid and David Crowley (Oxford: 2000), 9.

era shopping arcade re-opened under Khrushchev, the screen audience hears in the background repeated announcements of all of the things that one can buy, including cameras, televisions, and gardening equipment. Housing needs are also taken care of. Kolia's family lives in a spacious single-family apartment in central Moscow furnished with both a television and piano. In *Russian Souvenir* there are similar scenes, including images of a family moving from an older, rundown house to a clean, new apartment with a smart kitchen and a prominently displayed telephone, all emblematic of the Khrushchev-era housing campaigns. But notably in *I walk around Moscow*, some of what is available to experience and consume is "Western." The sounds of English trumpet loudly on a neighborhood street as a young man learns a new language with the aid of lessons on a record player (the voice on the record slowly intoning "nation/national/international"). A Muscovite buys an English orchestral performance of Tchaikovsky rather than a Russian one. A group dances to a jazz band. There are limits—the jazz is big-band style rather than the edgier jazz popular elsewhere in the late 1950s—but other international influences that were previously decried as cosmopolitan are now made acceptable by being shown as ordinary.

It is not only that Western cultural products are now available in post-Stalin Moscow, but that what it means to be modern and civilized is now based on a Western, specifically European, model. Moscow is promoted as prosperous, sophisticated, and dynamic, no longer through scenes of industrial achievement and agricultural production, but through images of clean neighborhood cafés, of women dressed in smart summer dresses, and of beautiful parks lit up at night. This evokes Khrushchev-era tourist accounts about Western Europe that often emphasized the civilized and carefree beauty of the European urban landscape, its attractive city squares, parks, cafés, and shops. In *Both Sides of the Ocean*, Victor Nekrasov sang the praises of the "sweet" Italian *trattoria* with its life of casual contemplation and observation.[29] The typical Soviet café, according to Nekrasov, was altogether different: "Oh, if it were only like [the Italian café] at the *Abkhazia* in Kiev! [In Italy] you go in and you don't smell the rank, meaty odors of the kitchen, and the waitress doesn't snap at you like a she-wolf and tell you, 'Wait a minute, it won't kill you. There are many of you and only one of me!' The tablecloths are all clean, and the waitresses don't squabble over forks and knives, and there are no plush curtains with tassels, and no angry, haughty doorman . . . Oh, how good it would be!"[30] The sunny, romantic, and dynamic Moscow portrayed in *I walk around Moscow* is the opposite of Kiev's Café Abkhazia. The filmic Moscow resembles Nekrasov's Italy, or indeed, Soviet cinematographic images of Europe as pictured, for example, in a 1960 Soviet

[29] Victor Nekrasov, *Both Sides of the Ocean: A Russian Writer's Travels in Italy and the United States*, trans. Elias Kulukunis (New York, 1964), 62.

[30] Nekrasov, *Both Sides*, 62–63.

short documentary film about Soviet tourists to Sweden.[31] Both Moscow and Stockholm are shown to be beautiful, well-provisioned capitals with friendly citizens. Both have pretty parks, full shop windows, and streets full of cars. The correct soundtrack for both cities, as suggested by these films, is a light jazz accompaniment.

Moscow, like Stockholm, is also a tourist destination. In the postwar Western world, the provision of tourism for one's own citizens plus the impressive hosting of foreign others, was an acknowledged symbol of "modernization."[32] So too in the Soviet Union of the 1960s, as we have seen. In *I walk around Moscow,* tourism to Moscow is shown to have become so commonplace—as suggested by an image of tour buses lined up outside Red Square—that Kolia feels free to gently make fun of it. In one scene, the two young protagonists observe a tired tour guide standing with a group of Central Asian tourists in front of St. Basil's Cathedral. Kolia interrupts the tour guide's lecture to point to the nearby GUM arcade, saying *sotto voce*: "And here is GUM, an example of pseudo-Russian architecture of the late 19th century." It is not only Soviet citizens who travel to Moscow. There is a lengthy scene of an encounter between an English-speaking Japanese tourist traveling through Moscow who stops his taxi to ask the boys for directions. Although they barely understand each other's language, the relations are friendly and non-threatening. The boys are bemused, unsurprised, and hop in the taxi to help the tourist find his way. The connection between the film and tourism was made explicit with the publication of a 1966 travel guide to Moscow that took its title—*I walk around Moscow*— from the movie.[33] The message of both book and movie was that, despite the appeal of the Western, home remains the best, in part because the Moscow of the movie now included much of what made the West appear so attractive.

A WINDOW TO THE WEST

If the first two films promoted Moscow and Siberia as enviable destinations for international and domestic travelers, the third film under discussion, *My Younger Brother* [Moi mladshii brat], explored the Baltics.[34] As described in Chapter Two, the Baltic Republics—newly a part of the Soviet Union—were a popular

---

[31] *Sametki o putesheshvie v Svettsiiu.* Tallinnfilm, 1960, Eesti Filmiarhiiv (EFA), 1427.

[32] See, for example, Karen Dubinsky, "'Everybody Likes Canadians: Canadians, Americans, and the Post-World War II Travel Boom,'" in *Being Elsewhere: Tourism, Consumer Culture, and Identity in Modern Europe and North America,* ed. Shelley Baranowski and Ellen Furlough (Ann Arbor, 2001).

[33] Em. Dvinskii, *Ia shagaiu po Moskve. Putevoditel' dlia turistov* as described in Diane P. Koenker, "Historical Tourism: Revolution as a Tourist Attraction," presented at the conference "Historical Memory and Society in the Russian Empire and Soviet Union (1860–1939)," St. Petersburg, June 2007.

[34] *Moi mladshii brat* [My Younger Brother]. Director: Alexander Zarkhi, USSR, 1962.

destination for Soviet tourists, as they satisfied a longing both for the "away" in a general sense and for the West in particular.[35] The 1962 movie My Younger Brother follows a group of four teenage friends who leave behind stifling Moscow for the attractions of Estonia. Although a less popular film than *I walk around Moscow* (and in many critics' opinions, both then and now, also less effective), *My Younger Brother* is important for this chapter as a journey film that again uses travel as a way to explore new ideological and geographical boundaries, and their limits, during the Thaw. Three male protagonists—Dima, Alik, and Iurka— together with a girl—Galia—set off to Estonia as a way to escape the confines of a planned life; they yearn for adventure, a journey into unknown, and an escape from the certainties of adulthood. Their trip is decidedly not a typical planned Soviet tourist excursion: the script plays with Russian verbs of motion to indicate various kinds of "traveling"—with a single, firm destination in mind or, as in this case, without. When they are asked on the train why they are not joining other youth traveling to contribute their labor to the socialist cause in Siberia, the young protagonist Dima responds: "Everybody is going east; we are going west."

In Tallinn, elements of Estonia's "Western" culture and history are openly admired, especially the timeless beauties of the Old Town. Dima and his friends enjoy the beauty of a Bach organ prelude heard emanating from a nearby church, and experience the powerful emotions of first love while strolling the romantic cobbled streets of Tallinn's Old Town. *My Younger Brother* is more cautious, however, about the appeal of contemporary Western culture. The restaurant at the Hotel Tallinn is clean and attractive, but is also shown to be full of wealthy, vaguely menacing men. The loud jazz soundtrack is used to signal danger, not sophistication. Galia is condemned as a "Brigitte Bardot" when she abandons Dima to dance flirtatiously with an older man.

This ambiguity is consistent with other tourism efforts. It differs, however, from the book upon which the movie was based, Vasilii Aksenov's *A Ticket to the Stars*. The book was more openly admiring of Estonia's carefree lifestyle as influenced by contemporary Western culture: in it the newsstands are enviably said to contain magazines with pictures of Laurence Olivier and Sophia Loren; the protagonists visit a chic café where they drink Cognac under a magical ceiling studded with stars.[36] In contrast, when transforming the novel into a film, Aksenov and the film's director, Aleksandr Zarkhi, were told that the movie should not resemble the book too closely or it would not be accepted.[37] Instead,

---

[35] On the valorizing of "away-ness" in Thaw era film, see Petre Petrov, "The Freeze of Historicity in Thaw Cinema," in *KinoKultura*, 8 (April 2005) www.kinokultura.com/articles.apr05-petrov. html.

[36] Vasilii Aksenov, *A Ticket to the Stars* (New York, 1963), 61, 65, 83.

[37] Woll, *Real Images*, 155. On the differences between the book and the movie see Julian Graffy, "Film adaptations of Aksenov: The Young Prose and the Cinema of the Thaw," in *Russian and Soviet Film Adaptations of Literature, 1900–2001: screening the word*, ed. Stephen Hutchings and Anat Vertitski (London, 2004), 108–13.

the only truly acceptable exotic, the movie seems to suggest, are the Estonians themselves, who are shown in the movie (but not in the book) dressed in traditional clothing and dancing folk dances. The authorities apparently understood that there was something more dangerous about *seeing* contemporary Western culture than reading about it, given the powerfully immersionary aspects of celluloid tourism. While novels can leave out the controversial, film is not as easily sanitized, requiring background shots and visual context, and approaching in this way something closer to the actual experience of travel.

The film and the book do conclude similarly. In both, Dima and his friends settle on a new, Soviet path which leads them to give up their idle lifestyle. Under the influence of a group of older and more settled local men they take up employment in a fishing collective and learn the value of hard work. "Wasn't I capable of anything more daring than rock 'n' roll, the Charleston, calypso, and the smell of coffee and brandy and the taste of lemon slices covered with sugar?" Dima asks himself in *Ticket to the Stars*.[38] In the film, too, the vitality of youth is shown to be attractive, but young people are only truly Soviet when they work hard, listen to their elders, and show the potential to grow up. In this, both the film and book resemble other well-known "youth novels" from the period, in which young people are transformed by a trip to the periphery.[39] In Anatolii Kuznetsov's 1957 novella *The Journey*, and Sergei Antonov's novel *Alyona*, decadent youth from Moscow are transformed into satisfied socialist citizens through their work on behalf of the Soviet Union in the Virgin lands and in Siberia.[40] If in *My Younger Brother*, the destination is Estonia rather than Siberia, the message of transformation is perhaps all the stronger given Estonia's ambiguous imagining as the Soviet Union's "West." Soviet youth represented the hopeful future of a Soviet Union moving out of Stalinism; young people were open, restless, invigorating. But like the Soviet Union as a whole in this period of great transition, they were seen to teeter between positive possibility and dangerous deviance.[41] They could threaten post-Stalinist recovery by traveling too hard in the wrong direction. Indeed, in real life, it was Estonian youth who were encouraged to make a pilgrimage from the periphery to the center, not the other way around. In a 1960 travel account published in *Sovetskaia Estoniia*, a group of Estonian tourists to modern Moscow are described as marveling over elevators that whisked them from the ground floor to the twenty-fourth floor of the university for a view over the city, and noting in wonder that the student

---

[38] Aksenov, *A Ticket to the Stars*, 132.

[39] Katerina Clark, *The Soviet Novel*, 226–31.

[40] Anatolii Kuznetsov, *The Journey*, trans. William E. Butler (New York, 1984); Sergei Antonov, *Alyona*, trans. Helen Altschuler (Moscow, 1960).

[41] The film *Illich's gate* [Zastava Il'icha] (1961) is a particularly well-known example of Khrushchev-era debates about the role of the younger generation. Patricia Johnson and L. Ladedz, ed., *Khrushchev and the Arts; the Politics of Soviet Culture, 1962–1962* (Cambridge, 1965), 147–86.

population of Moscow's University was larger than the entire population of the Estonian city, and university center, of Tartu.[42]

WESTERN CIGARETTES AND HAWAIIAN SHIRTS

While *My Younger Brother* shows the good and bad of capitalist culture, the 1961 film *Foreigners* [Inostrantsy][43] focuses on the truly unacceptable. A short film, part of a "Comedy Almanac" of five short films directed by Eduard Zmoiro, *Foreigners* uses social satire to condemn the desires of young people interested in capitalist consumer culture, especially that illegally purchased from Western tourists. The opening credits of the film are projected against a background of material items typically associated with tourism in the West: a SAS (Scandinavian Airline System) brochure, suitcase labels, postcards relating to foreign travel, Western cigarettes, and a Hawaiian shirt. The movie begins with a shot of a young man sprawled in an unkempt bed. He arises to the lively sounds of the song "Rock around the Clock," dances about the room in his underwear, and pauses only to swig a quick drink. After struggling into a pair of tight jeans, he heads out the door. We next see him at a hotel for foreign tourists, where it becomes evident that he is a black marketeer when he surreptitiously checks out the people walking by and eventually approaches a man carrying an Air France bag. The rest of the movie focuses on the relationship between the young man and the tourist, named "Frank," whom the black marketeer tries to both befriend and exploit. What the viewer quickly learns, but the black marketeer does not know, is that "Frank" is a Russian journalist writing an exposé about black marketeers. The young man and his friends are portrayed as foolish imitators of capitalist culture. In one scene, young men and women laze about in a stupor murmuring the words "Pepsi-Cola," a soft drink famously first introduced to Soviet citizens at the American Exhibition of 1959. A girl asks "Frank" to do her hair in the latest style, with absurd results—including multiple ponytails sticking every-which-way. The marketeers learn that "Frank" is not all he seems only when they surreptitiously look through his suitcase and find out with surprise that the labels in his clothing are Soviet. The final shot of the film is of a newspaper article condemning the black marketeer and his friends.[44]

In his passion for foreign clothing—though not in his naive idiocy—the protagonist of *Foreigners* resembled real-life Soviet jazz musician and clothing aficionado, Aleksei Kozlov. In his 1998 memoir, Kozlov recalls how for him all clothing was divided into two categories: "*firmennoe*, that is produced abroad and

---

[42] *Sovetskaia Estoniia* 157 (3 July 1960), 2.

[43] *Inostrantsy Kinofel'eton.* Part of *Sovershenno ser'ez Komediinyi al'manakh* 1 [Completely Serious. Comedy Almanac 1]. Director: Eduard Zmoiro. USSR, 1961.

[44] Julian Graffy provides a detailed explication of this film in "Scant Sign of Thaw," 38–42.

without fail having the label of some [foreign] company, and ours, Soviet-sewn, which we designated of course "*sovparshiv*" (Soviet party clothes)".[45] Kozlov trolled resale shops in hopes of coming across clothing left for sale by foreign embassy personnel. He also, more riskily, approached foreigners on the street to see if they would sell him their clothes.[46] Stylish youth like Kozlov—a group which included the *stiliagi* but also other groups of fashion-conscious and "idle" youth involved in speculation in foreign goods—were the target of the movie *Foreigners* and of Komsomol and Communist Party press campaigns.[47] In a 1960 article in *Literaturnaia gazeta*, Vasilii Aksenov fretted about these idle young Russians in terms very like those of *Foreigners*. Their life, Aksenov wrote, "consists of the hotels, buzzing with an unfamiliar and hence interesting life; the windshields of cars bearing stickers showing the flags of foreign countries; the chords of jazz behind the plate-glass windows of restaurants."[48]

Aksenov was not entirely unsympathetic, as his novel *A Ticket to the Stars* suggests. He argued that youth were drawn to the wrong kinds of bourgeois culture because the official youth culture offered them was so "stultifying."[49] While he condemned the unconsidered appropriation of popular culture and capitalist goods for personal gain, Aksenov wrote admiringly about the subtle integration of a universally accepted high culture. He praised Hemingway and Remarque, Picasso and Matisse. He described Louis Armstrong, Bing Crosby, and Benny Goodman as "wonderful."[50] *Foreigners* appears, at first glance, less discriminating. The young speculators are made to appear as ridiculous deviationists without redeeming qualities, and no blame is attached to Soviet institutions. While the viewer is advised to avoid the vulgarity of those aspiring to outlandish Western fashion, however, he is also advised to avoid the now passé dress of the obviously working class. Soviet authorities in the Khrushchev era hoped to counteract fantasies of personal consumption and pleasure associated with the West, but they also encouraged, as Susan Reid has put it, a "contemporary," and "measured use of fashion."[51] Thus the journalist "Frank" appears cultured and intelligent in his handsomely cut suit and good haircut, suggesting that the most appropriate attire for the Soviet man of the 1950s and 1960s was

---

[45] Aleksei Kozlov, *Kozel na sakse* (Moscow, 1998), 82.

[46] Kozlov, *Kozel na sakse*, 82.

[47] Juliane Fürst, "The arrival of spring? Changes and continuities in Soviet youth culture and policy between Stalin and Khrushchev," *The Dilemmas of Stalinization: Negotiating cultural and social change in the Khrushchev era*, ed. Polly Jones (London, 2006), 134–53; Yurchak, *Everything Was Forever*, 170–75; Sheila Fitzpatrick, "Social Parasites: How tramps, idle youth, and busy entrepreneurs impeded the Soviet march to communism," *Cahiers du Monde Russe* 47, nos. 1–2 (January–June 2006): 401–403.

[48] Vasilii Aksenov, "A Case is Heard: Princes with the Spirit of Beggars," *Literaturnaia gazeta* (17 September 1060)/*CDSP* 12:36 (10 May 1960): 13.

[49] Aksenov, "A Case is Heard: Princes with the Spirit of Beggars," 13–14.

[50] Aksenov, "A Case is Heard: Princes with the Spirit of Beggars," 13–14.

[51] Reid, "Cold War in the Kitchen," 239.

refined and modestly Western-influenced, if Soviet-made.[52] Indeed, it is "Frank" who speaks good English—a now admirable trait of the "cultured" Soviet person—and the young marketeer who is unable to recognize that his English is not native. If the movie condemns the uninformed aping of capitalist commercial culture, it, like Aksenov, offers a Khrushchev-era alternative.

THE EXOTIC, DISTANT CARIBBEAN SEA

Viewers of *Foreigners* were supposed to leave the theater disgusted by the foolish greed of black marketeers. But the snappy music and glimpse of Western styles may, for some, have had the opposite effect. The challenges of using film as a medium for instructing viewers how to distinguish between cosmopolitanism and internationalism are especially evident in the 1964 joint Soviet-Cuban production *I Am Cuba* [Ia Kuba/Soy Cuba].[53] *I Am Cuba* is not in any obvious way about tourism; the film celebrates the Cuban revolution through its idealized and hugely expressive images of the legacy of colonialism and American domination, the tragedy of the peasants, the struggle of students and workers, and the final battles in the Sierra Maestra Mountains. But the touristic experience is central to the film in two ways. The gaze of the camera is like the gaze of the tourist: the viewer sees the island as if from an airplane, swims with the camera in underwater shots, plunges through the sugarcane fields with Cuban workers, forges her way across crowded streets. The camera, like the tourist, also revels in Cuba's palm trees and expansive beaches. Contradictorily, however, and here we find the second aspect of the touristic, it is images of the tropical appeal of Cuba, and specifically the decadent world of Batista-era American tourism, that are used to bludgeon the past and condemn the excesses of colonialism.

Of all of the films discussed thus far, *I Am Cuba* is the most explicitly anti-Western. There is little here of the acceptably internationalist influence seen in *I walk around Moscow*. The "West" is entirely that of American culture, spectacle, and sex. In one of the film's most renowned scenes, the camera descends in a long traveling shot from an opening rooftop image of sensuous bikini-clad women competing in a beauty contest to a scene of privileged guests sipping cocktails and taking photographs, to conclude with the camera diving into a swimming pool. All of it is accompanied by swinging pop music. In another scene, wealthy American businessmen-tourists exploit Cuban women, the American patrons (shown in exaggerated form with awkward Southern accents) dancing with

---

[52] Western fashions were gradually introduced to the Soviet public in the late 1950s. See Reid, "Cold War in the Kitchen," 237–40; Larissa Zakharova, "Fabriquer le bon goût: La Maison des modèles de Leningrad à l'époque de Hruščev," *Cahiers du Monde Russe* 47, nos. 1–2 (January-June 2006): 195–225.

[53] *Soy Cuba* [I Am Cuba]. Director: Mikhail Kalatozov. USSR, 1964.

unwilling black prostitutes in a nightclub. "All gentlemen are created equal," one American businessman drawls, "This is a democracy. Let's draw lots for the girls."

These images of the decadent eroticism of the tourist experience in colonial Cuba are undeniably anti-American. At the same time, they are undeniably attractive even when contrasted with scenes of poor villages, naked children, and revolutionary enthusiasm. In an interview, the Soviet co-author of the script, poet Evgenii Evtushenko discussed his genuine enthusiasm for the Cuban revolution, but also admitted how much he himself frequented Cuban nightclubs and drank Cuban cocktails while writing the script.[54] As the authors of a booklet accompanying Milestone Film and Video's re-issue of *I Am Cuba* observe: "the film explores (perhaps a bit too enthusiastically for the prescribed purposes of the film) the seductive, decadent (and marvelously photogenic) world of Batista's Cuba."[55] This did not go unnoticed by Soviet authorities. According to the film's cinematographer, Sergei Urusevskii, the film was panned in Moscow because it portrayed scenes of American life in Cuba which authorities did not want shown on Soviet screens.[56] The Cuban revolution was, as described by Petr Vail and Aleksandr Genis in their book about the Soviet 1960s, "a striking event for the Soviet person of the 1960s, a powerful, creative social revolution combined with an exotic, distant [Caribbean] sea."[57] Soviet authorities were pointedly more comfortable with the revolutionary than with the exotic.

CULTURED NOT CAPITALIST

Easier to monitor than real tourism, yet visually captivating, films about travel provided a mechanism by which Soviet citizens at home could safely visit a domesticated elsewhere without leaving home. In contrast to the conventions of many 21st-century travel narratives, these Soviet films about travel did not relish the exotic, but domesticated acceptable differences and demonized dangerous ones. Traveling via film rather than in person circumscribed opportunities to go off the beaten path. The Soviet-imagined "West(s)," as portrayed in the films described here, were not meant to be sites for developing individualism but for learning and affirming officially approved values about which kinds of Western culture were acceptable. In this, Soviet films stood in pointed, and deliberate, contrast to Hollywood productions, with their dangerously seductive

---

[54] Interview with Evgenii Evtushenko conducted by Professor Jerry W. Carlson, City University Television/CUNY-TV, 2004 in *O Mamute Siberiano* [The Siberian Mammoth]. Director: Vicente Ferraz. Brazil, 2005 available in *I Am Cuba: The Ultimate Edition* (Milestone Film and Video).

[55] Dennis Dordos and Amy Heller, "I Am Cuba: The True Story," booklet included in *I Am Cuba: The Ultimate Edition* (Milestone Film and Video).

[56] As interviewed in a documentary film on the making of *O Mamute Siberiano*.

[57] Petr Vail and Aleksandr Genis, *60-e. Mir Sovetskogo cheloveka* (Moscow, 1998), 55.

representations of the glamorous life.[58] These efforts were not always successful. As we have seen, the immersionary aspects of film meant that viewers saw and heard elements of capitalist culture that were attractive and intriguing even as they were being condemned as decadent. But at their core these films were reinforcing a limited kind of tourism in which virtual travel confirmed the superiorities of home.

The nature of a Khrushchev-era "home" was different than that which followed, however. These films also suggest that the Soviet Union was not impenetrable, nor did it wish to be. Its citizens were believed to be confident enough about the Soviet Union's own virtues to be allowed to mix with the foreign if still mostly at home rather than abroad. As portrayed in the films described here, the educated and internationally-aware Soviet citizen, was supposed to be cultured (but not capitalist), youthful and adventuresome (but not immature), romantic (but not sexy), a consumer (but not a black marketeer), and confidently open to new ideas and foreign cultures (but still a Soviet patriot). These films were helping construct a new kind of post-Stalinist Soviet viewer.

The peculiarities of the Khrushchev era are underscored if one compares the films discussed above with the 1967 Brezhnev-era movie *July Rain* [Iul'skii dozhd'].[59] In *July Rain*, Muscovites get glimpses of the outside world, but these glimpses are no longer presented optimistically. Khrushchev's famous phrase "peaceful coexistence" is used cynically to describe relations between two individuals. Some Western imports have become so commonplace that young people have become blasé: they read French novels and dance to jazz music but none of it with great enthusiasm. Instead, the movie emphasizes the persistent distance between the Soviet Union and the capitalist West. One characteristic scene shows elegantly dressed foreign dignitaries emerging from fancy cars on one side of the street while watched from the other side of the street by the ordinary, and distinctly inelegant, citizens of Moscow. *July Rain* represents Brezhnev-era pessimism about the possibility of the Soviet Union becoming truly "international." In contrast, Soviet films about tourism in the Thaw combine cautious optimism about permitting a now Sovietized "difference" with profound anxiety about the threats too much of this might pose: an uneasy combination which, I argue, is characteristic of the Khrushchev era.

---

[58] See the discussion in Rudy Koshar, "Seeing, Traveling, and Consuming," in *Histories of leisure*, ed. Rudy Koshar (Oxford, 2002), 15.

[59] *Iul'skii dozhd'* [July Rain]. Director: Marlen Khutsiev. USSR, 1967. A different, tongue-in-check view of the West, and specifically of travel to the West, can be found in the 1968 comedy *Brilliantovaia ruka* [The Diamond Arm]. Director: Leonid Gaidar. USSR. 1968.

Epilogue

> I wondered what one might experience upon crossing the border. What would one feel? What would one think? Would it be a moment of great emotion, agitation, tension? What was it like, on the other side? It would, of course, be ... different. But what did 'different' mean? What did the other side look like? Did it resemble anything I knew? Was it inconceivable, unimaginable? My greatest desire, which gave me no peace, which tormented and tantalized me, was actually quite modest: I wanted only one thing—to cross the border. To cross that and then to come right back – that would be entirely sufficient, would satisfy my inexplicable yet acute hunger.[1]
>
> Polish travel writer Ryszard Kapuściński remembering his feelings in 1956

The 1950s established patterns for Soviet international tourism, many of which lasted, largely unaltered, until the fall of the Soviet Union. Some of these patterns were positive ones. International tourism continued to increase after Khrushchev. In 1974, approximately two million people traveled abroad, a number that more than doubled by 1985 to four and a half million.[2] Other continuities reflected bureaucratic inertia and persistent anxiety. Permission to travel abroad always required personal or political connections, including the presentation of small gifts—coffee or cognac—to those making decisions. Groups of twenty to forty tourists continued to consist largely of the intelligentsia and other ruling elites, with a smattering of representatives from the working class. International travelers were prepared before departure with ever updated versions of the brochure, *USSR: 100 Questions and Answers*, which provided sample answers to questions such as "Do people in the USSR practice free love?" and "Why do Soviet

---

[1] Ryszard Kapuściński, "The Open World: A legendary travel writer's first trip abroad," *The New Yorker* (February 5, 2007): 58.

[2] The exact numbers vary, but are roughly commensurate. Randolph M. Siverson, Alexander J. Groth, and Marc Blumberg, "Soviet Tourism and Détente," *Studies in Comparative Communism* 13, no. 4 (Winter 1980): 364; *Turist*, no. 10 (1975): 29; V.I. Azar, Otdykh trudiashchikhsia SSSR (Moscow, 1972), 41; G.P. Dolzhenko, *Istoriia turizma v dorevoliutsionnoi Rossii i SSSR* (Rostov, 1988), 154. The ratio of travelers-to-population was still small in contrast to other European countries, but growing, with a more than sixty-fold gain in the number of people who traveled abroad in 1977 as compared to 1958. Siverson et al., "Soviet Tourism" 365.

televisions weigh 40 kg and Japanese televisions only 11?"[3] (Vladimir Vysotsky entitled a 1974 poem, "Instructions before a trip abroad" in which he wrote: "He gave me a brochure to read, as an injunction not to think of behaving abroad as stupidly as we do at home."[4]) Throughout the course of Soviet travel abroad, tourist groups were accompanied by party and trade union monitors and typically included four to six people considered especially well prepared to answer difficult ideological questions.[5]

Eastern Europe remained the prime destination, with other socialist countries—Cuba and Mongolia in particular—attracting rising numbers of visitors.[6] Trips continued to combine pleasure and purpose, even as the destinations sometimes differed. Soviet tourists traveling to Europe in 1978 on the cruiseship *Karelia* heard a reading, in its entirety, of Brezhnev's book about the Virgin Lands.[7] Vacationers to Vietnam visited the Museum to the Revolution in Hanoi and the Museum of the Crimes of American Imperialism, in addition to attending evenings of song and dance. So too in Cuba, where trips included visits to Lenin Park and sugar-cane factories. Travelers to Morocco described the friendly greetings they received on arrival.[8] As Soviet travel abroad become more common, however, contact between tourists and locals sometimes became more routine. "The usual form of contact [between tourist and local in Finland] was in a store, negotiating the sale of vodka," remembered Sergei Arkavin about his 1990 excursion.[9] As earlier, trip leaders could not control every encounter. When Irina Kuropeteva traveled to Finland in late May 1986, she learned new information as of yet unavailable in the Soviet Union about the Chernobyl nuclear disaster a month earlier.[10]

---

[3] Interviews with Eduard Eduardovich Belkovskii (4 July 2009) and Mikhail Leonidovich Gol'denberg (23 July 2009) courtesy of Alexei Golubev, Archive of the Oral History Centre, Petrozavodsk State University; Aleksei Popov, "Sovetskie turisty za rubezhom: ideologiia, kommunikatsiia, emotsii (po otchetam rukovoditelei turistskikh grupp)," *Istorichna panorama: nayk. statei*, vol 7 (Chernovci, 2009), 50–53; Donald J. Raleigh, ed. and trans., *Russia's Sputnik Generation: Soviet Baby Boomers Talk about Their Lives* (Bloomington, 2006), 44, 52. For a 1980 version of parts of the booklet, see www.situation.ru/app/rs/lib/ussr100/ussr100_content.htm.

[4] Vladimir Vysotsky, "Instruksiia pered poezdkoi zarubezh," www.kulichki.com/vv/.

[5] Popov, "Sovetskie turisty za rubezhom."

[6] By the mid-1960s, Soviet tourists were visiting Iceland, Iran, Morocco, Tunisia, and other African countries including a twenty-six-day itinerary in East Africa that began in Nairobi and ended with a cruise through the Indian Ocean to Odessa. Open Society Archive, Budapest (hereafter HU OSA), Records of Radio Free Europe/Radio Liberty Research Institute (hereafter RFE RL RI), Soviet Red Archives, 1953–1994, Old Code Subject Files, 300-80-1, Container 1049; Alexei Popov, "Ekzotik-turi dlia geroev sotstruda: turisty iz Krimskoi oblasti v Azii, Afrike i Latinskoi Amerike," *Istoricheskoe nasledie Kryma*, no. 24 (Simferopol, 2009), 141–46. Still, most travel was to socialist countries, specifically Eastern Europe. *Turist* 8 (1970): 31; *Turist* 6 (1977): 33.

[7] Popov, "Sovetskie turisty za rubezhom."

[8] RGASPI, f. m- 5, op. 1, d. 217, ll. 2–3.

[9] Interview with Sergei Genrikhovich Arkavin (4 August 2009) courtesy of Alexei Golubev, Archive of the Oral History Centre, Petrozavodsk State University.

[10] Interview with Irina Ivanovna Kuropteva (9 July 2009), courtesy of Alexei Golubev, Archive of the Oral History Centre, Petrozavodsk State University.

Problem behavior also remained much the same. A passenger on a 1978 cruise to Greece, Egypt, and Turkey was sent home after drinking so much that he fell and hurt himself. A traveler to Czechoslovakia in 1977 was censured for having sexual relations with a Czech local.[11] A Finnish hotel offered an "Italian" striptease to eager Soviet visitors in 1984 (one of whom later defended the show as "quite cultured . . . something between dance and sport.")[12] Tourists to Bulgaria in 1986 were condemned for aggressively bargaining with shopkeepers.[13] Shopping continued to be a major attraction for international travelers, indeed increasingly so. Archival sources detail violations of Soviet customs law; tourists were caught bringing home too many bottles of alcohol, as well as multiple copies of items intended for resale: lipstick, fingernail polish, and sunglasses. Jeans and name brands such as Chanel were especially valued. Because tourists received so little hard currency to travel with, they often brought along items for barter or sale: vodka, caviar, camera equipment, watches, *matroshka* dolls, and, less extravagantly, pencils and school notebooks to barter with in India.[14] A few hundred well-spent rubles in Finland could be worth a few thousand rubles in resale at home.[15] By the mid-1970s, according to Hedrick Smith, "private commerce [was] well established as one of the perquisites of official travel abroad."[16] One group of communist "bigshots" voyaging via Soviet cruise vessel in the Mediterranean in the summer of 1974 were absolutely uninterested in touring. Upon landing at Naples, "the few Western tourists on the ship would all trip off to Pompeii to see the sights, but the Russians would go off in the opposite direction. . . . They would produce great bundles of American money—ten-dollar bills, twenty-dollar bills, 100-dollar bills. Lots of money. Obviously the kind of money that only special people get. And they would head off for the *cambio*, exchange the dollars for lire and head off in a great horde on a shopping spree . . . The Westerners would tour and the Russians would shop." "Travel abroad—especially to the West," Smith concluded in 1974, "has become the status symbol par excellence of the Soviet privileged class, the surest mark of political reliability."[17] The social divisiveness of travel was not exclusive to the USSR, of course. In nineteenth-century Russia, as in England during the era of

[11] Alexei Popov, "Tenevye storony zarubzhnogo (Byezdnogo) turizma v Sovetskom Soiuze 1960–1980-e gg." *Kultura narodov Prichernomoria* no. 152 (Simferopol 2009): 151–55.

[12] Interview with Gol'denberg.

[13] Popov, "Tenevye storony."

[14] Interviews with Belkovskii, Arkavin, and Kuropteva; Popov, "Tenevye storony."

[15] Interview with Sergei Kurochkin (3 September 2009), courtesy of Alexei Golubev, Archive of the Oral History Centre, Petrozavodsk State University.

[16] Smith, *The Russians*, 622–23. By the late 1980s, Soviet embassies abroad encouraged Soviet tourists to enrich Soviet, not foreign, coffers by providing travelers with a small shop on Embassy grounds where they could purchase inexpensive electronic goods. With thanks to David Priestland for this information.

[17] Smith, *The Russians*, 622. On the "acquisitive socialism" of the Brezhnev era, see James Millar, "The Little Deal: Brezhnev's Contribution to Acquisitive Socialism," *Slavic Review* 44, no. 4 (1985): 694–706.

the Grand Tour, tourism contributed to a social fissure between upper class, mostly male, travelers and a new, more democratized group of middle-class and female travelers.[18] In the Soviet Union, however, the social divide was a different one, partially one of class (white-collar workers versus manual workers), but even more one of political privilege and personal connection. Inequities, such as those between exiters and non-exiters, resembled inequities of distribution and access in other areas of Soviet life. Soviet citizens experienced endemic shortages of desirable goods which contributed to a system in which *blat* (personal connections) mattered more than money.[19]

This was not, presumably, what Khrushchev had in mind with his promise to reform communism and provide a plausible and more equitable alternative to capitalism. The distinctive post-Stalinist culture of Sovietism rejected the oppressive excesses of Stalinism, openly engaged with and even emulated modernizing aspects of the capitalist West, and yet defended the superiority of a modern Soviet state newly willing and able to attend to the needs of its population without exploitation. Sovietism was a promise which inspired optimism, and not only in the 1950s. Irina Kuropteva enjoyed her 1986 trip to Finland, but found Finland boring in comparison to the Soviet Union, in which people lived more interesting and cheerful lives. Her trip, she asserted, did not alter her views on Soviet reality.[20] For others, the promise eventually turned sour, although just when and how, and for whom, is still to be researched. Some were disheartened early on by the unstable mixture of optimistic openings, profound anxieties, and authoritarian prescriptions characteristic of Khrushchev, particularly perhaps by the cultural reversals of 1963 when Khrushchev declared: "The Thaw is over."[21] For still others, perhaps the majority, it took much longer. A contributing factor was the democratizing of knowledge and experience about the rest of the world, information which aggravated the impact of shortages at home and the inequities they made visible. Stalin had avoided direct comparisons between Soviet socialism and capitalist reality, arguing that "an entirely new world was being built" in the USSR, a new world "that could not be compared with any proceeding system."[22] Khrushchev, in contrast, set up a comparison with the West with his promise to "catch up and surpass America," a promise that went unfulfilled. By the mid-1970s, the optimism of the early 1960s appears to have sunk under

---

[18] Susan Layton, "The Divisive Modern Russian Tourist Abroad: Representations of Self and Other in the Early Reform Era," *Slavic Review* 68, no. 4 (Winter 2009), 853.

[19] Alena V. Ledeneva, *Russia's Economy of Favours: Blat, Networking and Informal Exchange* (Cambridge, 1998).

[20] Interview with Kuropteva.

[21] Vladislav Zubok, *Zhivago's Children: The Last Russian Intelligentsia* (Cambridge, 2009), chps 6 and 9; Benjamin Tromly, "Soviet Patriotism and its Discontents among Higher Education Students in Khrushchev-Era Russia and Ukraine," *Nationalities Papers*, 37, no. 3 (May 2009): 299–326; Jeremi Suri, "The Rise and Fall of an International Counterculture, 1960–1975," *American Historical Review* 114, no. 1 (February 2009): 50–54.

[22] Zdeněk Mlynář as cited in Zubok, *Zhivago's Children*, 116.

the weight of Brezhnev-era stagnation and consumer disappointment with long-promised goods and services, a deficit now judged in open and explicit comparison with offerings visible elsewhere.[23] If in 1961, the possibility of travel abroad was illustrative of a reforming Soviet Union, by the 1970s travel was, according to Vladislav Zubok, the desperate, addictive pleasure of an intellectual elite unhappy at home: "The trips gave the temporary effect of euphoria, liberation, and excitement at the discovery of the wealth of world culture, while offering an escape from the squalor, humiliation, and fear of everyday Soviet life."[24]

Soviet tourism was political, but as this book has demonstrated it was not only that. Tourism is evidence of ways in which Soviet citizens internalized Soviet norms and supported Soviet goals, but also of ways in which they eluded official efforts to regulate their experiences and their understandings in pursuit of individual agendas. Many tourists willingly accepted, even actively promoted, Soviet narratives of superiority. The tourist experience, no matter how carefully supervised, was unpredictable, however. The act of crossing a supposedly fixed border, be it the Soviet frontier or the Iron Curtain, had the potential to challenge previous understandings, to contribute to the "making and remaking of identities," political but also personal.[25] If tourism was olive branch and propaganda tool, it was also an opportunity for personal encounter, private life, and pleasure. These more private experiences did not lead inevitably to anti-Soviet opinions or actions—it was possible to be changed by travel abroad and happily return home—but they did offer possibilities for personal as well as political alternatives.

All This is Your World has described the Soviet Union as part of the wider world. The USSR was not an empire unto itself, but a state, and increasingly a populace, in contact with the rest of the world. Some of this contact was conflictual—Hungary, Cuba—but there were also new opportunities for peaceful encounter and exchange. The classic emblem of aggressive internationalism under Stalin was that of the hammer and sickle superimposed on the world. Under Khrushchev, the new motif, as displayed on postal stamps, was of a Soviet jet airliner flying across the globe. Communist victory would come not via coercion (or not only that) but via soft power, persuasion, and cultural internationalism. How effective this was depends on what we see as the goal. Akira Iriye argues that the many educational and cultural exchanges developed in the post-1945 period, of which tourism was one, broadened the very meaning of international relations by creating a new and unprecedented "sense of transnational

---

[23] On this issue, see the discussion in chapters 5 and 9 in Stephen Lowell, *The Shadow of War: Russia and the USSR, 1941 to the present* (West Sussex, 2010).

[24] Zubok, *Zhivago's Children*, 328; Interview with Belkovskii.

[25] James Clifford, *Routes: Travel and Translation in the Late Twentieth Century* (Cambridge, 1997), 7.

experience" on a "massive scale."[26] The "emerging global community" was not necessarily homogeneous, however. Indeed, Soviet tourism was a site for negotiating difference in a newly globalizing world. English students were not, by and large, converted to communism by virtue of encounters with Soviet tourists. Nor, in the 1950s, were most Soviet travelers persuaded that the West was best. Both tourist and local were more willing, however, to consider the possibility of peaceful coexistence.

[26] Akira Iriye, *Global Community: The Role of International Organizations in the Making of the Contemporary World* (Berkeley, 2002), 84.

Bibliography

PRIMARY SOURCES

ARCHIVAL SOURCES

Estonia

Eesti Filmiahiiv (EFA)
Eesti Riigiarhiivi (ERA)
  f. R-2002 Estonian Soviet for Tourism and Excursions
  f. R-2288 Intourist
  f. R-4958 Estonian Youth Tourism
Eesti Riigiarhiivi Filiasali (ERAF)
  f. 1 Central Committee of the Communist Party of Estonia
  f. 31 Komsomol
Tallinna Linnaarhiiv (Tallinn City Archive)

Hungary

Open Society Archive (HU OSA)

Russia

Gosudarstvennyi arkhiv Rossiiskoi Federatsii (GARF)
  f. 9228, USSR Ministry of Health Directorate for Sanatoria
  f. 9493 Central Trade Union Spa Directorate
  f. 9520 Central Soviet for Tourism and Excursions
  f. 9576 Union of Soviet Friendship Societies and Cultural Connections with Foreign
    Countries
  f. 9559 All-Union Soviet of Trade Union Voluntary Sports Societies
  f. 9612 Intourist
Rossiiskii gosudarstvennyi arkhiv noveeishei istorii (RGANI)
  f. 5 General Department of the Central Committee of the CPSU
    op. 17 Department of Science and Higher Education
    op. 30 Materials on Cultural, Scientific, Technical, and Economic Cooperation
      between the USSR and other Countries
    op. 33 Department of Propaganda and Agitation
    op. 36 Department of Culture
Rossiiskii gosudarstvennyi arkhiv sotsial'no-politicheskoi istorii (RGASPI)
  f. m-1 Central Committee of the Komsomol
    op. 30 International Department
    op. 47 Department of Sport and Defence Activities

f. m-5 Bureau of International Youth Tourism (Sputnik)

United Kingdom

Society for Cultural Relations with the USSR (SCR Archive)
The National Archives

United States

National Archives and Records Administration, Washington, D.C. (NARA)
*Larry Zim World's Fair Collection, Archives Center, National Museum of American
   History, Smithsonian Institution*

NEWSPAPERS AND PERIODICALS

Current Digest of the Soviet Press
Harper's Magazine
Izvestiia
Komomolskaia pravda
Krokodil
Life
Newsweek
New Yorker, The
New York Times
Novyi mir
Ogonek
Sovetskaia Estoniia
Pravda
Time
Times, The
Trud
Turist
Vokrug sveta

FILMS

Brilliantovaia ruka [The Diamond Arm]. Director: Leonid Gaidar, 1968
Disko ja tuumasõda [Disco and Atomic War]. Director: Jaak Kilmi. Estonia, 2009
Estonian Alpinists around the World. Estonia, 1970
Hotel Tallina. Estonia, 1964
Ia shagaiu po Moskve [I walk around Moscow]. Director: Georgii Daneliia. USSR, 1963
Inostranka [A Foreign Woman]. Directors: Aleksandr Seryj and Konstantin Zhuk. USSR,
   1965

Inostrantsy Kinofel'eton. Part of Sovershenno ser'ez Komediinyi al'manakh 1 [Completely Serious. Comedy Almanac 1]. Director: Eduard Zmoiro. USSR, 1961

Iul'skii dozhd' [July Rain]. Director: Marlen Khutsiev. USSR, 1967

Moi mladshii brat [My Younger Brother]. Director: Alexander Zarkhi. USSR, 1962

O Manute Siberiano [The Siberian Mammoth]. Director: Vicente Ferraz. Brazil, 2005

Russkii suvenir [Russian Souvenir]. Director: Grigorii Aleksandrov. USSR, 1960

Sametki o putesheshvie v Svettsiiu. Estonia, 1960

Soy Cuba [I Am Cuba]. Director: Mikhail Kalatozov. USSR, 1964

Tallinna mosaiik [The Mosaic of Tallinn] Director: Andrei Dobrovolski. Estonia, 1967

Vsesouiznyi Marshrut # 0043. Estonia, 1963

Vernye druzia [True Friends]. Director: M. Kalatozov. USSR, 1954

Zapasnoi Igrok [The Reserve]. Director: Semen Timoshenko. USSR, 1954

TRAVEL ACCOUNTS, GUIDEBOOKS, LITERARY WORKS, MEMOIRS, DOCUMENT COLLECTIONS

Aksakoff, Sergei. *Years of Childhood*, trans. J.D. Duff. London, 1916.

Aksenov, Vasilii. *It's Time. My Friend. It's Time*, trans. Olive Stevens. London, 1969.

—— *A Ticket to the Stars.* New York, 1963.

Antonov, Sergei. *Alyona*, trans. Helen Altschuler. Moscow, 1960.

Arkhangel'skaia, O. *Kak organizovat' turistskoe puteshestvie.* Moscow, 1947.

Bukovsky, Vladimir. *To Build a Castle: My Life as a Dissenter*, trans. Michael Scammel. London, 1978.

Clark, Katerina and Evgeney Dobrenko. *Soviet Culture and Power: A History in Documents, 1917–1953.* New Haven, 2007.

Dobkovich, V.V. *Turizm v SSSR.* Leningrad, 1954.

Face to Face with America. Moscow, 1960.

Fedenko. I.I. *Volga—velikaia russkaia reka.* Moscow-Leningrad, 1946.

Feifer, George. *Russia Close-up.* London, 1973.

Galbraith, John Kenneth. *Journey to Poland and Yugoslavia.* Cambridge, MA, 1958.

Gens, Iulii. *Staryi Tallinn.* Tallinn, 1947.

German, Mikhail. *Slozhnoe proshedshee: Passé composé* (St. Petersburg, 2000).

Gibney, Frank. *An Informal Guide to Poland.* New York, 1958.

Gordy, Michel. *Visa to Moscow*, trans. Katherine Woods. London, 1953.

Grushin, B.A. *Chetyre zhizni Rossii v zerkale obshchestvennogo mneniia. Epokha Khrushcheva.* Moscow, 2001.

Gutnova, Evgeniia Vladimirovna. *Perezhitoe.* Moscow, 2001.

Haskell, Arnold L. *Heroes and Roses: A View of Bulgaria.* London, 1966.

Henderson, Larry Wills. *A Journey to Samarkand.* Toronto, 1960.

Hingley, Ronald, *Under Soviet Skin: An Untourist's Report*, London, 1961.

Kapuściński, Ryszard. "The Open World: A legendary travel writer's first trip abroad." *The New Yorker* (5 February 2007).

Karol, K.S. *Visa for Poland.* London, 1959.

Kelly, Marie Noële. *Mirror to Russia.* London, 1952.

Kennan, George. *Memoirs, 1925–1950.* New York, 1967.

Khrushchev, Nikita S. *Khrushchev Remembers: The Last Testament*, trans. and ed. Strobe Talbott. Boston, 1974.

———. "Report of the Central Committee of the 22nd Congress of the Communist Party of the Soviet Union." In *Documents of the 22nd Congress of the CPSU*. vol 1. http://www.archive.org/details/DocumentsOfThe22ndCongressOfTheCpsuVolIi, 120.

Khrushchev. Sergei. ed. *Memoirs of Nikita Khrushchev: Statesman [1953–1964]*. vol. 3. University Park, 2007.

Konchalovskii, Andrei. *Nizkie istiny*. Moscow, 1998.

Kotel'nikov, B.B. ed. *Sputnik turista*. 2nd ed. Moscow-Leningrad, 1941.

Kozlov, Aleksei. *Kozel na sakes*. Moscow, 1998.

Kruiznoe puteshestvie vokrug Evropy na teplokhode "Estoniia." Intourist brochure, 1961.

Kul'turnoe stroitel'stvo: Statisticheskii sbornik. Moscow, 1956.

Kuleshov, N. and A. Pozdnev. *Vysotnye zdaniia Moskvy*. Moscow, 1954.

Kurashova, V., L.G. Gol'dfailia, and G.N. Pospelovoi. ed. *Kurorty SSSR*. Moscow, 1962.

Kuznetsov, Anatolii. *The Journey*, trans. William E. Butler. New York, 1984.

Levine, Irving R. *Main Street. U.S.S.R.* New York, 1959.

Loginov, Anatolii. *Nasha Moskva*. Moscow, 1947.

MacKintosh, May. *Rumania*. London, 1963.

Mass, Vladimir and Mikhail Chervinsky. "Around and About. (A Guide For Tourists Wishing To Write Travelers' Diaries)." In *The Year of Protest: An Anthology of Soviet Literary Materials*, ed. and trans. Hugh McLean and Walter Vickery. New York, 1961.

Metelitsa, V.I. *Stranitsy zhizni*. Moscow, 2001.

Mikhailov, Nikolai. *Discovering the Soviet Union*. Moscow, 1965.

Miller, Wright. *Russians as People*. London, 1960.

Moskva poslevoennaia, 1945–1947. Arkhivnye dokumenty i materialy. Moscow, 2000.

Nekrasov, Victor. *Both Sides of the Ocean: A Russian Travel Writer's Travels in Italy and the United States*, trans. Elias Kulukunis. New York, 1964.

Newman, Bernard. *Behind the Berlin Wall*. London, 1964.

Newman, Bernard. *Berlin and Back*. London, 1954.

Pevcheskii prazdnik Sovetskoi Estonii 1950g. Tallinn, 1951.

Programma Kommunisticheskoi partii Sovetskogo Soiuza priniata XXII s"ezdom KPSS. Moscow, 1962.

Savitskii, Iu. *Moskva: Istoriko-Arkhitekturnyi Ocherk*. Moscow, 1947.

Shalinian, Mirietta. *Puteshestvie po Sovetskoi Armenii*. Moscow, 1951.

Smith, Hedrick. *The Russians*. New York, 1976.

Smith, Walter Bedell. *Moscow Mission 1946–1949*. London, 1950.

Solzhenitsyn, Alexander. *Invisible Allies*. Washington. D.C, 1997.

Sovetskaia zhizn, 1945–1953: Dokumentov sovetskoi historii. Moscow, 2003.

Spravochnik: Ob usloviiakh i marshrutakh puteshestvii sovetskikh turistov za granitsu. Moscow, 1960.

Steinbeck, John. *A Russian Journal*. New York, 1949.

Sytin, V. *Po staroi i novoi Moskve: istoricheskie raiony, glavnye ulitsy i ploshad velikogo goroda*. Moscow-Leningrad, 1947.

Tallin, Tallinn, 1965.

The Cities of the USSR. Moscow, 1966.

Turistskaia poezdka v Germanskuiu Demokraticheskuiu Respubliku. Moscow, 1959.

Turistskie marshruty po SSSR. Moscow, 1956, 1958.

Wassermann, Charles. *Europe's Forgotten Territories.* Copenhagen, 1960.

SECONDARY SOURCES

Books and Articles

Adler, Judith. "Travel as Performed Art." *The American Journal of Sociology* 94. no. 6 (May 1989): 1366–391.

Aksiutin, Iurii. *Khrushchevskaia 'ottepel' i obshchestvennye nastroeniia v SSSR v 1953–1964 gg.* Moscow, 2004.

Azar, V.I. *Otdykh trudiashchikhsia SSSR.* Moscow, 1972.

Balina, Marina. "A Prescribed Journey: Russian Travel Literature from the 1960s to the 1990s." *Slavic and East European Journal* 38. no. 2 (1994): 261–70.

Baranowski, Shelley and Ellen Furlough. "Introduction." In *Being Elsewhere: Tourism. Consumer Culture. and Identity in Modern Europe and North America.* ed. Shelley Baranowski and Ellen Furlough. Ann Arbor, 2001.

Baranowski. Shelley. "Strength through Joy: Tourism and National Integration in the Third Reich." In *Being Elsewhere: Tourism, Consumer Culture, and Identity in Modern Europe and North America,* ed. Shelley Baranowski and Ellen Furlough. Ann Arbor, 2001.

Bardasarian, V.E. et al. *Sovetskoe zazerkal'e: inostannyi turizm v SSSR v 1930–1980 gg* Moscow, 2007.

Bennett, Todd. "Culture, Power and *Mission to Moscow*. Film and Society in American Relations during World War II." *Journal of American History* 88 (September 2001): 489–518.

Bergson, Abram. *The Real National Income of Soviet Russia Since 1928.* Cambridge. MA, 1961.

Berkowitz, Michael. "A 'New Deal' for Leisure: Making Mass Tourism during the Great Depression." In *Being Elsewhere: Tourism. Consumer Culture. and Identity in Modern Europe and North America,* ed. Shelley Baranowski and Ellen Furlough. Ann Arbor, 2001.

Bittner, Stephen V. *The Many Lives of Khrushchev's Thaw: Experience and Memory in Moscow's Arbat.* Ithaca, 2008.

Boym, Svetlana. *Common Places: Mythologies of Everyday Life in Russia.* Harvard, 1994.

Brandenberger, David. *National Bolshevism: Stalinist Mass Culture and the Formation of Modern Russian National Identity, 1931–1956.* Cambridge, MA, 2002.

Brent, Jonathan. *Inside the Stalin Archives.* New York, 2008.

Brooks, Jeffrey. "Official Xenophobia and Popular Cosmopolitanism in Early Soviet Russia." *American Historical Review* 97. no. 5 (December 1992): 1431–448.

———. "The Press and its Messages: Images of America in the 1920s and 1930s." In *Russia in the Era of NEP: Explorations in Soviet Society and Culture,* ed. Sheila Fitzpatrick, Alexander Rabinowitch, and Richard Stites. Bloomington, 1991.

———. *Thank you. Comrade Stalin! Soviet Public Culture from Revolution to Cold War.* Princeton, 2000.

Brown, Archie. "Gorbachev, Lenin, and the Break with Leninism." *Demokratizatsiya.* 15. no. 2 (Spring 2007): 230–44.

Bushnell, John. "The 'New Soviet Man' Turns Pessimist." In *The Soviet Union since Stalin*, ed. Stephen F. Cohen, Alexander Rabinowitch and Robert Sharlet. Bloomington, 1980.

Buzard, James. *The Beaten Track: European Tourism, Literature, and the Ways to Culture. 1800–1918.* Oxford, 1993.

Caute, David. *The Dancer Defects: The Struggle for Cultural Supremacy during the Cold War.* Oxford, 2003.

Chandler, Andrea. *Institutions of Isolation: Border Controls in the Soviet Union and its Successor States, 1917–1993.* Montreal and Kingston, 1998.

Chapman, Janet G. *Real Wages in Soviet Russia since 1928.* Cambridge. MA, 1963.

Cherry, Deborah. "Algeria in and Out of the Frame: Visuality and Cultural Tourism in the Nineteenth Century." In *Visual Culture and Tourism*, ed. David Crouch and Nina Lübbren. Oxford, 2003.

Clark, Katerina. *The Soviet Novel: History as Ritual.* 3rd ed. Bloomington, 1981, 2000.

Clifford, James. *Routes: Travel and Translation in the Late Twentieth Century.* Cambridge, 1997.

Coleman, S. and M. Crang, ed. *Tourism: Between Place and Performance.* New York, 2002.

Corten, Irina H. *Vocabulary of Soviet Society and Culture: A Selected Guide to Russian Words. Idioms and Expressions of the Post-Stalin Era, 1953–1991.* Durham and London, 1992.

Crouch, David and Nina Lübben. "Introduction." In *Visual Culture and Tourism*, ed. David Crouch and Nina Lübben. Oxford, 2003.

Crowley, David. *Warsaw.* London, 2003.

——. "Warsaw's Shops. Stalinism and the Thaw." In *Style and Socialism: Modernity and Material Culture in Post-War Eastern Europe*, ed. Susan E. Reid and David Crowley. Oxford, 2000.

David-Fox, Michael. "From Illusory 'Society' to Intellectual 'Public': VOKS. International Travel and Party-intelligentsia Relations in the Interwar Period." *Contemporary European History* 11. no. 1 (2002): 7–32.

——. "Stalinist Westernizer? Aleksandr Arosev's Literary and Political Depictions of Europe." *Slavic Review* 62. no. 4 (2003): 733–59.

——. "The Fellow Travelers Revisited: The 'Cultured West' through Soviet Eyes." *The Journal of Modern History* 75 (June 2003): 300–35.

Davis, Sarah. "Soviet Perceptions of the Allies during the Great Patriotic War." In *Russia and the Wider World in Historical Perspective*, ed. Cathryn Brennan and Murray Frame. London and New York, 2000.

Denby, David. "Big Pictures: Hollywood looks for a Future." *The New Yorker* 8 (January 2006).

Dening, Greg. "The theatricality of observing and being observed: Eighteenth-century Europe discovers the ? century 'pacific'." In *Implicit Understandings: Observing, Reporting, and Reflecting on the Encounters between Europeans and Other Peoples in the Early Modern Era*, ed. Stewart Schwartz. Cambridge, 1994.

Desmond, Jane C. *Staging Tourism: Bodies on Display from Waikiki to Sea World.* Chicago, 1999.

Dickenson, Sara. *Breaking Ground: Travel and National Culture in Russia from Peter I to the Era of Pushkin.* Amsterdam, 2006.

Dobrynin, Sergei. "The Silver Curtain: Representations of the West in the Soviet Cold War Films." *History Compass* 7. no. 3 (April 2009) available at http://www3.interscience.wiley.com/cgi-bin/fulltext/122314400/HTMLSTART.

Dobson, Miriam. *Khrushchev's Cold Summer: Gulag Returnees, Crime, and the Fate of Reform after Stalin.* Ithaca, 2009.

Dockrill, Saki and Günter Bischof. "Geneva: The Fleeting Opportunity for Détente." In *Cold War Respite: The Geneva Summit of 1955,* ed. Günter Bischof and Saki Dockrill. Baton Rouge, 2000.

Dolzhenko, G.P. *Istoriia turizma v dorevoliutsionnoi Rossii i SSSR.* Rostov, 1988.

Drace-Francis, Alex. "Towards a Natural History of East European Travel Writing." In *Under Eastern Eyes: A Comparative Introduction to East European Travel Writing on Europe,* ed. Wendy Bracewell and Alex Drace-Francis. Budapest, 2008.

Dubinsky, Karen. "'Everybody Likes Canadians: Canadians, Americans, and the Post-World War II Travel Boom." In *Being Elsewhere: Tourism, Consumer Culture, and Identity in Modern Europe and North America,* ed. Shelley Baranowski and Ellen Furlough. Ann Arbor, 2001.

Duncan James and Derek Gregory, ed. *Writes of Passage: Reading Travel Writing.* London and New York, 1999.

Dunham, Vera S. *In Stalin's Time: Middle-Class Values in Soviet Fiction.* Cambridge, 1976.

Dvornichenko V.V. *Razvitie turizma v SSSR (1917–1983 gg).* Moscow, 1985.

Edele, Mark. "Strange Young Men in Stalin's Moscow" The Birth and Life of the Stiliagi, 1945–1953." *Jahrbücher für Geschichte Osteuropas* 50 (2002): 37–61.

Edelman, Robert. *Serious Fun: A History of Spectator Sports in the USSR.* New York, 1993.

Edensor, Tim. "Staging Tourism: tourists as performers." *Annals of Tourism Research* 27. no. 2 (April 2000). doi:10.1016/S0160-7383(99)00082-1

———. *National Identity. Popular Culture and Everyday Life.* Oxford, 2002.

Ellerbee, Linda. "No Shit! There I Was . . . " In *A Woman's Path: Women's Best Spiritual Travel Writing,* ed. Lucy McCauley, Amy G. Carlson, and Jennifer Leo. San Francisco, 2000.

Ely, Christopher. "The Origins of Russian Scenery: Volga River Tourism and Russian Landscape Aesthetics." *Slavic Review* 62. no. 4 (Winter 2003): 666–82.

Endy, Christopher. *Cold War Holidays: American Tourism in France.* Chapel Hill, 2004.

English, Robert D. *Russia and the Idea of the West: Gorbachev, Intellectuals, and the End of the Cold War.* New York, 2000.

Field, Deborah. *Private Life and Communist Morality in Khrushchev's Russia.* New York, 2007.

Filtzer, Donald. "From mobilized to free labour: De-Stalinization and the changing legal status of workers." In *The Dilemmas of De-Stalinization: Negotiating Cultural and Social Change in the Khrushchev Era,* ed. Polly Jones. London, 2005.

Filtzer, Donald. *Soviet Workers and De-Stalinization. The consolidation of the modern system of Soviet production relations, 1953–64.* London, 1993.

———. "The Standard of Living of Soviet Industrial Workers in the Immediate Postwar Period, 1945–1948." *Europe-Asia Studies* 51 (1999): 1013–38.

Fitzpatrick, Sheila. "Postwar Soviet Society: The "Return to Normalcy", 1945–1953." In *The Impact of World War 2 on the Soviet Union*, ed. Susan Linz. New Jersey, 1985.

———. "Social Parasites: How tramps, idle youth, and busy entrepreneurs impeded the Soviet march to communism." *Cahiers du Monde Russe* 47. nos. 1–2 (January-June 2006): 377–408.

Fürst, Juliane, ed. *Late Stalinist Russia: Society between reconstruction and reinvention.* London, 2006.

———. *Stalin's Last Generation: Soviet Post-War Youth and the Emergence of Mature Socialism.* Oxford, 2010.

———. "The arrival of spring? Changes and continuities in Soviet youth culture and policy between Stalin and Khrushchev." In *The Dilemmas of De-Stalinization: Negotiating cultural and social change in the Khrushchev Era*, ed. Polly Jones. London, 2006.

———. "The Importance of being stylish: Youth, culture, and identity in late Stalinism." In *Late Stalinist Russia: Society between reconstruction and reinvention*, ed. Juliane Fürst. London, 2006.

Ghosh, Amitav. "Foreword." In *Other Routes: 1500 Years of African and Asian Travel Writing*, ed. Tabish Khair, Martin Leer, Justin D. Edwards, and Hanna Ziadeh. Bloomington, 2005.

Gilburd, Elenory. "Books and Borders: Sergei Obratzov and Soviet Travels to London in the 1950s." In *Turizm: The Russian and East European Tourist under Capitalism and Socialism*, ed. Anne E. Gorsuch and Diane P. Koenker. Ithaca, 2006.

———. "Picasso in Thaw Culture." *Cahiers du Monde Russe* 47. nos. 1–2 (January-June 2006): 65–108.

Gorsuch, Anne E. *Youth in Revolutionary Russia: Enthusiasts, Bohemians, and Delinquents.* Bloomington, 2000.

Gorsuch, Anne E. and Diane P. Koenker, ed. *Turizm: The Russian and East European Tourist under Capitalism and Socialism.* Ithaca, 2006.

Graffy, Julian. "Film adaptations of Aksenov: The Young Prose and the Cinema of the Thaw." In *Russian and Soviet Film Adaptations of Literature, 1900–2001: Screening the Word*, ed. Stephen Hutchings and Anat Vertitski. London, 2004.

———. "Scant Sign of Thaw: Fear and Anxiety in the Representation of Foreigners in the Soviet Films of the Khrushchev Years." In *Russia and its Other(s) on Film: Screening Intercultural Dialogue*, ed. Stephen Hutchings. Houndmills, 2008.

Grandits, Hannes and Karin Taylor, ed. *Yugoslavia's Sunny Side: A History of Tourism in Socialism (1950s–1980s).* Budapest, 2010.

Grant, Bruce. *The Captive and the Gift: Cultural Histories of Sovereignty in Russia and the Caucasus.* Ithaca, 2009.

Grewal, Inderpal. *Home and Harem: Nation, Gender, Empire and the Cultures of Travel.* Durham, 1996.

Gronow, Jukka. *Caviar with Champagne: Common Luxury and the Ideals of the Good Life in Stalin's Russia.* Oxford, 2003.

Gundle, Stephen. "Hollywood Glamour and Mass Consumption in Postwar Italy." In *Histories of Leisure*, ed. Rudy Koshar. Oxford, 2002.

Hagenloh, Paul M. "'Socially Harmful Elements' and the Great Terror." In *Stalinism: New Directions*, ed. Sheila Fitzpatrick. London and New York, 2000.

Hall, Colin Michael. *Tourism and Politics: Policy, Power, and Place.* Chichester, 1994.

Hallas, Karin. ed, *20th Century Architecture in Tallinn: architectural guide.* Tallinn, 2000.

Hansen, Philip. *Advertising and Socialism.* London, 1974.

Harris, Steven E. "In Search of 'Ordinary' Russia: Everyday Life in the NEP, the Thaw, and the Communal Apartment." *Kritika: Explorations in Russian and Eurasian History* 6. no. 3 (Summer 2005): 583–614.

Haynes, John. "Reconstruction or Reproduction? Mothers and the Great Soviet Family in Cinema after Stalin." In *Women in the Khrushchev Era*, ed. Melanie Ilič, Susan E. Reid, and Lynne Attwood. London, 2004.

Hessler, Julie. "A Postwar Perestroika? Towards a History of Private Enterprise in the USSR." *Slavic Review* 57. no. 3 (Fall 1998): 516–42.

——. "Cultured Trade: The Stalinist Turn towards Consumerism." In *Stalinism: New Directions*, ed. Sheila Fitzpatrick. London and New York, 2000.

Hixson, Walter L. *Parting the Curtain: Propaganda, Culture, and the Cold War, 1945–1961.* New York, 1997, 1998.

Hopf, Ted. *Social Construction of International Politics: Identities and Foreign Policies. Moscow, 1955 & 1999.* Ithaca, 2002.

Humphrey, Caroline. *The Unmaking of Soviet Life: Everyday Economies after Socialism.* Ithaca, 2002.

Hunter, Holland. "Successful Spatial Management." In *The Impact of World War 2 on the Soviet Union*, ed. Susan Linz. New Jersey, 1985.

Hutchings, Stephen. "Introduction." In *Russia and its Other(s) on Film: Screening Intercultural Dialogue.* ed. Stephen Hutchings. Houndmills, 2008.

Ilic, Melanie and Jeremy Smith, ed. *Soviet State and Society under Nikita Khrushchev.* London, 2009.

Iriye, Akira. *Cultural Internationalism and World Order.* Baltimore, 1997.

——. *Global Community: The Role of International Organizations in the Making of the Contemporary World.* Berkeley, 2002.

Isakov, Sergei. *Russkie pisateli i Estoniia.* Tallinn, 1985.

Jobs, Richard Ivan. "Youth Movements: Travel, Protest, and Europe in 1968." *American Historical Review* 114. no. 2 (April 2009): 376–404.

Johnson, Priscilla and Leopold Labedz. ed. *Khrushchev and the Arts: The Politics of Soviet Culture, 1962–1964.* Cambridge, Mass., 1965.

Jones, Polly, ed. *The Dilemmas of De-Stalinization. Negotiating Cultural and Social Change in the Khrushchev Era.* London, 2006.

Kaiser, Robert and Elena Nikiforova. "The performativity of scale: the social construction of scale effects in Narva, Estonia" *Environment and Planning D: Society and Space* 26. no. 3 (2008): 537–62.

Keep, John. *A History of the Soviet Union, 1945–1991.* Oxford, 1994, 2002.

Kelly, Catriona. "'The Little Citizens of a Big Country': Childhood and International Relations in the Soviet Union." *Trondheim Studies on East European Cultures and Societies.* no. 8 (March 2002).

———. *Refining Russia: Advice Literature, Polite Culture, and Gender from Catherine to Yeltsin.* Oxford, 2001.

Kelly, Catriona and Vadim Volkov. "Directed Desires." In *Constructing Russian Culture in the Age of Revolution. 1881–1940*, ed. Catriona Kelly and David Shepherd. Oxford, 1998.

Kessler, Gijs. "The Passport System and State Control over Population Flows in the Soviet Union, 1932–1940." *Cahiers du Monde Russe* 42. nos. 2/3/4/(April-December 2001): 477–504.

Kharkhordin, Oleg. *The Collective and the Individual in Russia: A Study of Practices.* Berkeley, 1999.

Koenker, Diane P. "Historical Tourism: Revolution as a Tourist Attraction." presented at the conference "Historical Memory and Society in the Russian Empire and Soviet Union (1860–1939)." St. Petersburg, June 2007.

———. "The Proletarian Tourist in the 1930s: Between Mass Excursion and Mass Escape." In *Turizm: The Russian and East European Tourist under Capitalism and Socialism*, ed. Anne E. Gorsuch and Diane P. Koenker. Ithaca, 2006.

———. "Travel to Work. Travel to Play: On Russian Tourism, Travel, and Leisure." *Slavic Review* 62. no. 4 (2003): 657–65.

———. "Whose Right to Rest? Contesting the Family Vacation in the Postwar Soviet Union." *Comparative Studies in Society and History* 51 (2009): 401–25.

Koivunen, Pia. "The 1957 Moscow Youth Festival: Propagating a new, peaceful image of the Soviet Union" In *Soviet State and Society under Nikita Khrushchev*, ed. Melanie Ilic and Jeremy Smith. London, 2009.

Koshar, Rudy. "Seeing, Traveling, and Consuming." In *Histories of leisure*, ed. Rudy Koshar. Oxford, 2002.

———. *German Travel Cultures.* Oxford, 2000.

Kotkin, Stephen. "Mongol Commonwealth? Exchange and Governance across the Post-Mongol Space." *Kritika: Explorations in Russian and Eurasian History* 8, no. 3 (Summer 2007): 487–531.

Kovalov, Oleg. "Zvezda nad step'iu. Amerika v zerkale sovetskogo kino." *Iskusstvo kino* 10 (2003) available at http://www.kinoart.ru/magazine/10-2003/review/Kovalov0310.

Kriuchkov, A.A. *Istoriia mezhdunarodnogo i otechestvennogo turizma.* Moscow, 1999.

Kropotkine, Anne. "Les ambiguités du Dégel: Que faire du patrimoine culturel?" *Cahiers du Monde Russe* 47. nos. 1–2 (January/June 2006): 269–302.

Kvatal'nov, A. and V. K. Fedorchenko. *Orbity 'sputnika:' iz istorii molodezhnogo turizma.* Kiev, 1987.

L'Heureux. Marie Alice. "Representing Ideology. Designing Memory." In *The Sovietization of the Baltic States, 1940–1956*, ed. Olaf Mertelsmann. Tartu, 2003.

Laakkonen, Simo and Karina Vasilevska. "From a fishing resort to a leading Soviet health resort: Reminiscences of the social and environmental history of Jurmala, Latvia." unpublished paper, 2008

Laanemets, Mari and Andres Kurg, ed. *Tallinna juht. A User's Guide to Tallinn*, Tallinn, 2002.

Layton, Susan. "Russian Military Tourism: The Crisis of the Crimean War Period." In *Turizm: The Russian and East European Tourist under Capitalism and Socialism*, ed. Anne E. Gorsuch and Diane P. Koenker. Ithaca, 2006.

——. "The Divisive Modern Russian Tourist Abroad: Representations of Self and Other in the Early Reform Era." *Slavic Review* 68. no. 4 (Winter 2009): 848–71.

Lebina, N. *Entsiklopedia banal'nostei. Sovetskaia povsednevnost': Kontury, simvoly, znaki.* St. Petersburg, 2006.

Ledeneva, Alena V. *Russia's Economy of Favours: Blat, Networking and Informal Exchange.* Cambridge, 1998.

Leder, Mary M. *My Life in Stalinist Russia: An American Woman Looks Back.* Bloomington, 2001.

Light, Margot. *The Soviet Theory of International Relations.* New York, 1988.

Lion, Jill A. "Long Distance Passenger Travel in the Soviet Union." Paper prepared for the Research Program on Problems of International Communication and Security. MIT. October 1967.

Lloyd, David W. *Battlefield Tourism: Pilgrimage and the Commemoration of the Great War in Britain, Australia, and Canada, 1919–1939.* Oxford, 1998.

Löfgren, Orvar. "Know Your Country: A Comparative Perspective on Tourism and Nation Building in Sweden." In *Being Elsewhere: Tourism, Consumer Culture, and Identity in Modern Europe and North America*, ed. Shelley Baranowski and Ellen Furlough. Ann Arbor, 2001.

——. *On Holiday: A History of Vacationing.* Berkeley, 2002.

Loginov, L.M. and Iu. V. Rukhlov. *Istoriia razvitiia turistsko-ekskursionnogo dela.* Moscow, 1989.

Lowell, Stephen. *The Shadow of War: Russia and the USSR, 1941 to the present.* West Sussex, 2010.

MacCannell, Dean. *The Tourist: A New History of the Leisure Class* (Berkeley, 1976, 1999).

Magnúsdóttir, Rósa "'Be Careful in America. Premier Khrushchev!' Soviet perceptions of peaceful coexistence with the United States in 1959." *Cahiers du Monde Russe.* 47. nos. 1–2 (January–June 2006): 109–30

Matthews, Mervyn. *Privilege in the Soviet Union: A Study of Elite Life-Styles under Communism.* London, 1978.

——. *The Passport Society: Controlling Movement in Russia and the USSR.* Boulder, 1993.

McCannon, John. *Red Arctic: Polar Exploration and the Myth of the North in the Soviet Union, 1932–1939.* New York, 1998.

McReynolds, Louise. "The Prerevolutionary Russian Tourist: Commercialization in the Nineteenth Century." In *Turizm: The Russian and Soviet Tourist under Capitalism and Socialism*, ed. Anne E. Gorsuch and Diane P. Koenker. Ithaca, 2006.

——. *Russia at Play: Leisure Activities at the End of the Tsarist Era.* Ithaca, 2003.

Millar, James. "The Little Deal: Brezhnev's Contribution to Acquisitive Socialism." *Slavic Review* 44. no. 4 (1985): 694–706.

Misiunas, Romauld J. and Rein Taagepera. *The Baltic States: Years of Dependence, 1940–1990.* London: 1993 (revised edition).

Moranda, Scott. "East German Nature Tourism, 1945–1961: In Search of a Common Destination." In *Turizm: The Russian and East European Tourist under Capitalism and Socialism*, ed. Anne E. Gorsuch and Diane P. Koenker. Ithaca, 2006.

Muawska-Muthesius, Katarzyna. "The Cold War Traveller's Gaze: Jan Lenica's 1954 Sketchbook of London," In *Under Eastern Eyes: A Comparative Introduction to East European Travel Writing on Europe*, ed. Wendy Bracewell and Alex Drace-Francis. Budapest, 2008.

Näripea, Eva. "Medieval Socialist Realism: Representations of Tallinn Old Town in Soviet Estonian Feature Films, 1969–1972." In *Koht ja Paik. Place and Location: Studies in Environmental Aesthetics and Semiotics* IV (2004): 121–43.

———. "Turistlik eskapism ja sümfoonilised variatsioonid: Tallinna vanalinn vaatefilmides 1960–1970. aastail." *Kunstiteaduslikke Uurimusi* 2–3 (14) (2003): 69–91.

Nettleton, Nordica. "Driving Towards Communist Consumerism: AvtoVAZ." *Cahiers du Monde Russe*. 47. nos.1–2 (January–June 2006): 131–49.

Noack, Christian. "Coping with the Tourist: Planned and 'Wild' Mass Tourism on the Soviet Black Sea Coast." In *Turizm: The Russian and East European Tourist under Capitalism and Socialism*, ed. Anne E. Gorsuch and Diane P. Koenker. Ithaca, 2006.

Nyíri, Pál. *Scenic Spots: Chinese Tourism, the State, and Cultural Authority*. Seattle, 1996.

O'Connor, Kevin. *The History of the Baltic States*. Westport. CT, 2003.

Paperno, Irina. "Personal Accounts of the Soviet Experience." *Kritika: Explorations in Russian and Eurasian History* 3. no. 4 (Fall 2002): 577–610.

Patterson, Patrick Hyder. "Dangerous Liaisons: Soviet-Bloc Tourists and the Yugoslav Good Life in the 1960s & 1970s." In *The Business of Tourism: Place. Faith and History*, ed. Philip Scranton and Janet F. Davidson. Philadelphia, 2006.

Pesmen, Dale. *Russia and Soul: An Exploration*. Ithaca, 2000.

Péteri, György. "The Occident Within—or the Drive for Exceptionalism." *Kritika: Explorations in Russian and Eurasian History* 9. no. 4 (Fall 2008): 929–37.

Petrov, Peter. "The Freeze of Historicity in Thaw Cinema." In *KinoKultura*. 8 (April 2005) accessible at http://www.kinokultura.com/articles.apr05-petrov.html.

Poiger, Uta G. *Jazz, Rock, and Rebels. Cold War Politics and American Culture in a Divided Germany*. Berkeley, 2000.

Popov, Aleksei. "Ekzotik-turi dlia geroev sotstruda: turisty iz Krimskoi oblasti v Azii, Afrike i Latinskoi Amerike." *Istoricheskoe nasledie Kryma*. no. 24 (Simferopol, 2009).

———. "Sovetskie turisty za rubezhom: ideologiia, kommunikatsiia, emotsii (po otchetam rukoroditelei turistskikh grupp." *Istorichna panorama: nayk. statei*. vol 7 (Chernovci, 2009).

———. "Tenevye storony zarubezhnogo (Vyezdnogo) turizma v Sovetskom Soiuze (1960–1980-e gg." *Kultura narodov Prichernomoria* no. 152 (Simferopol 2009).

Pratt, Mary Louise. *Imperial Eyes: Travel Writing and Transculturation*. London and New York, 1992.

Prokhorov, Alexander. "Inherited Discourse: Stalinist Tropes in Thaw Culture." Ph.D. dissertation. University of Pittsburgh, 2002.

Qualls, Karl D. "'Where Each Stone Is History': Travel Guides in Sevastopol after World War II." In *Turizm: The Russian and East European Tourist under Capitalism and Socialism*, ed. Anne E. Gorsuch and Diane P. Koenker. Ithaca, 2006.

Ragamey, Amandine. *Prolétaires de tous pays, excusez-moi! Dérision et politique dans le monde soviétique.* Paris, 2007.

Raleigh, Donald J. ed. and trans. *Russia's Sputnik Generation: Soviet Baby Boomers Talk about Their Lives.* Bloomington, 2006.

Ramanauskiaté, Egidijam "Lithuanian Youth Culture versus Soviet Culture." In *The Baltic Countries under Occupation: Soviet and Nazi Rule, 1939–1991*, ed. Anu Mai Kõll. Stockholm, 2003.

Raun, Toiva, U. *Estonia and the Estonians.* Stanford, 1987.

Reid, Susan E. "Cold War in the Kitchen: Gender and De-Stalinization of Consumer Taste in the Soviet Union under Khrushchev." *Slavic Review* 61. no. 2 (Summer 2002): 211–52.

———. "In the Name of the People: The Manège Affair Revisited." *Kritika: Explorations in Russian and Eurasian History* 6. no. 4 (Fall 2005): 673–716.

———. "Khrushchev Modern: Agency and Modernization in the Soviet home." *Cahiers du Monde Russe* 47. nos. 1–2 (January-June 2006): 227–60.

———. "The Pioneer Palace in the Lenin Hills. Moscow, 1962." In *Picturing Russia: Explorations in Visual Culture*, ed. V. Kivelson and J. Neuberger. New Haven, 2008.

———. "Who Will Beat Whom? Soviet Popular Reception of the American National Exhibition in Moscow, 1959." *Kritika: Explorations in Russian and Eurasian History* 9. no. 4 (Fall 2008): 855–904.

Susan E. Reid and David Crowley. "Style and Socialism: Modernity and Material Culture in Post-War Eastern Europe." In *Style and Socialism: Modernity and Material Culture in Post-War Eastern Europe*, ed. Susan E. Reid and David Crowley. Oxford, 2000.

———. *Style and Socialism: Modernity and Material Culture in Post-War Eastern Europe.* Oxford, 2000.

Richmond, Yale. *Cultural Exchange and the Cold War: Raising the Iron Curtain.* University Park. PA, 2003.

Ricoeur, Paul. *Freud and Philosophy: An Essay on Interpretation.* New Haven, 1970.

Roberts, Mary Louise. "Gender, Consumption, and Commodity Culture." *American Historical Review* 103. no. 3 (June 1998): 817–44.

Roth-Ey, Kristen. "'Loose Girls' on the Loose?: Sex. Propaganda and the 1957 Youth Festival." In *Women in the Khrushchev Era*, ed. Melanie Ilič, Susan E. Reid, and Lynne Attwood. London, 2004.

Rotkirch, Anna. "Traveling Maidens and Men with Parallel Lives –Journeys as Private Space During Late Socialism." In *Beyond the Limits: The Concept of Space in Russian History and Culture*, ed. Jeremy Smith. Studia Historica 62. Helsinki, 1999.

Ruppert, Peter. "Tracing Utopia, Film, Spectatorship and Desire." *Utopian Studies* 7, no. 2 (1996): 139–54.

Rydell, Robert W. *All the World's a Fair: Visions of Empire at American International Expositions. 1876–1916.* Chicago, 1984.

Salmon, Shawn Connolly. "To the Land of the Future: A History of Intourist and Travel to the Soviet Union 1929–1991." PhD dissertation. University of California. Berkeley, 2008.

———. "Marketing Socialism: Inturist in the Late 1950s and Early 1960s." In *Turizm: The Russian and East European Tourist under Capitalism and Socialism*, ed. Anne E. Gorsuch and Diane P. Koenker. Ithaca, 2006.

Sandomirskaia, I.I. "Novaia zhizn' na marshe. Stalinskii turizm kak 'praktika puti'." *Obshestvennye nauki i sovremennost'* 4 (1994).

Siegelbaum, Lewis H. *Cars for Comrades: The Life of the Soviet Automobile.* Ithaca, 2008.

Siverson, Randolph M., Alexander J. Groth, and Marc Blumberg. "Soviet Tourism and Détente." *Studies in Comparative Communism* 13. no. 4 (Winter 1980): 356–68.

Smirnov, Dimitrii. "Sovietization, Terror and Repression in the Baltic States in the 1940s and 1950s: The Perspective of Contemporary Russian Society." In *The Sovietization of the Baltic States, 1940–1956,* ed Olaf Mertelsmann. Tartu, 2003.

Solomon, Susan Gross. "Circulation of Knowledge and the Russian Locale" in "Special Issue: Circulation of Knowledge and the Human Sciences in Russia." *Kritika: Explorations in Russian and Eurasian History* 9. no. 1 (Winter 2008): 9–26.

Sovetskoe zazerkal'e: inostrannyi turizm v SSSR v 1930–1980-e gody. Moscow, 2007.

Steward, Jill. "Tourism in Late Imperial Austria: The Development of Tourist Cultures and Their Associated Images of Place." In *Being Elsewhere: Tourism. Consumer Culture. and Identity in Modern Europe and North America,* ed. Shelley Baranowski and Ellen Furlough. Ann Arbor, 2001.

Stewart, Susan. *On Longing: Narratives of the Miniature, the Gigantic, the Souvenir, the Collection.* Durham, 1993.

Strain, Ellen. *Public Places. Private Journeys: Ethnography, Entertainment, and the Tourist Gaze.* New Brunswick, 2003.

Suri, Jeremi. "The Rise and Fall of an International Counterculture, 1960–1975." *American Historical Review* 114. no. 1 (February 2009): 45–68.

Svede, Mark Allen. "All You Need is Lovebeads: Latvia's Hippies Undress for Success." In *Style and Socialism: Modernity and Material Culture in Post-War Eastern Europe,* ed. Susan E. Reid and David Crowley. London, 2000.

Taubman, William. *Khrushchev: The Man and his Era.* New York, 2003.

Taylor, Neil. *Estonia: The Bradt Travel Guide.* Bucks, 2005.

Taylor, Richard. "'But Eastward, Look, the Land is Brighter': Toward a Topography of Utopia in the Stalinist Musical." In *The Landscape of Stalinism: The Art and Ideology of Soviet Space.* ed. Evgeny Dobrenko and Eric Naiman. Seattle: 2003.

Tchoukarine, Igor. "Politiques et représentations d'une mise en tourisme: le tourisme international en Yougoslavie de 1945 à la fin des années 1960." PhD dissertation. École des hautes études en sciences sociales, Paris, 2010.

Todorova, Maria. *Imagining the Balkans.* New York, 1997.

Tromly, Benjamin. "Soviet Patriotism and its Discontents among Higher Education Students in Khrushchev-Era Russia and Ukraine." *Nationalities Papers.* 37. no. 3 (May 2009): 299–326.

Trud v SSSR: Statisticheskii sbornik. Moscow, 1988.

Urbain, Jean-Didier. *Sur la plage: Moeurs et coutumes balnéaires.* Paris, 1994.

Urry, John. *Consuming Places.* New York, 1995.

———. *The Tourist Gaze. Leisure and Travel in Contemporary Societies.* London, 1990, 2002.

Usyskin, Grigorii. *Ocherki istorii rossiiskogo turizma.* Moscow-Saint Petersburg, 2000.

Vardys, Stanley. "The Role of the Baltic Republics in Soviet Society." In *The Influence of East Europe and the Soviet West on the USSR*, ed. Roman Szporluk. New York, 1975.

Vail, Petr and Aleksandr Genis. *60-e. Mir Sovetskogo cheloveka*. Moscow, 1998.

van der Post, Laurens. *Journey into Russia*. London, 1964.

Varga-Harris, Christine. "Forging citizenship on the home front: reviving the socialist contract and constructing Soviet identity during the thaw." In *The Dilemmas of De-Stalinization: Negotiating Cultural and Social Change in the Khrushchev Era*, ed. Polly Jones. London, 2005.

Verdery, Katherine. *The Transition from Socialism: Anthropology and Eastern Europe*. Cambridge, 1992.

von Geldern, James. "The centre and the periphery: cultural and social geography in the mass culture of the 1930s" In *New Directions in Soviet History*. ed, Stephen White. Cambridge, 1992.

Watanabe, Aiko. "Cultural drives by the periphery: Britain's experiences," accessible at http://www.history.ac.uk/ihr/Focus/cold/articles/watanabe.html

Werth, Alexander. *Russia under Khrushchev*. Westport, 1961.

Widdis, Emma. *Visions of a New Land: Soviet Film from the Revolution to the Second World War*. New Haven and London, 2003.

Wolff,. Larry. *Inventing Eastern Europe: The Map of Civilization on the Mind of the Enlightenment*. Stanford, 1996.

Woll, Josephine. *Real Images: Soviet Cinema and the Thaw*. London, 2000.

——. *The Cranes are Flying*. London, 2003.

Wood, Elizabeth. *Performing Justice: Agitation Trials in Early Soviet Russia*. Ithaca, 2005.

Youngblood, Denise. "Americanitis: The *Amerikanshchina* in Soviet Cinema." *Journal of Popular Film and Television* 19. no. 4 (Winter 1992):148–57.

Yurchak, Andrei. *Everything Was Forever, Until It Was No More: The Last Soviet Generation*. Princeton, 2006.

Zakharova, Larissa. "Fabriquer le bon goût: La Maison des modèles de Leningrad à l'époque de Hruščev." *Cahiers du Monde Russe* 47. nos. 1–2 (January–June 2006): 195–225.

Zezina, M.R. "S tochki zreniia istorii kinozala." in *Istoriia strany. Istoriia kino*, ed. S.S. Sekirinskogo. Moscow, 2004.

Zubkova, Elena. *Russia after the War: Hopes, Illusion, and Disappointments, 1945–1957*, trans. Hugh Ragsdale. New York, 1998.

Zubok, Vladislav M. "Soviet Policy Aims at the Geneva Conference, 1955." In *Cold War Respite: The Geneva Summit of 1955*, ed. Günter Bischof and Saki Dockrill. Baton Rouge, 2000.

——. *Zhivago's Children: The Last Russian Intelligentsia*. Cambridge, 2009.

Index

CPSIA information can be obtained
at www.ICGtesting.com
Printed in the USA
LVOW13*0848120717

541010LV00009B/220/P